W9-AIX-706

Sleeping
with Custer
and the
7th Cavalry

Sleeping with Custer and the 7th Cavalry

An Embedded Reporter in Iraq

Walter C. Rodgers

outhern Illinois University Press · *Carbondale*

Copyright © 2005 by Walter C. Rodgers
All rights reserved
Printed in the United States of America
08 07 06 05   4 3 2 1

Library of Congress Cataloging-in-Publication Data
Rodgers, Walter C., 1940–
Sleeping with Custer and the 7th Cavalry : an
embedded reporter in Iraq / Walter C. Rodgers.
    p. cm.
  1. Iraq War, 2003. 2. United States. Army. Cavalry, 7th.
I. Title.
DS79.76.R64 2005
956.7044'342—dc22   2005010035
ISBN 0-8093-2672-8 (cloth : alk. paper)

*To the fine soldiers of the U.S. Army's 7th Cavalry
and to another fine soldier, Eleanor*

Contents

Illustrations

IX

Illustrations

Acknowledgments

Perhaps the most emotionally moving discovery of the entire Iraqi war experience was the countless expressions of fervent support I received from people I never met or knew. Hundreds of Americans wrote or e-mailed me during and after the war, and their messages were ever the same: "We are praying for you." It spoke to the goodness and decency of the American people, which we all too often lose sight of in our rush to label people as fundamentalists, born-agains, evangelicals, or Roman Catholics. "We are praying for you and your crew every day," they wrote. Each of us who took this hell-bent-for-leather cavalry chase from Kuwait to Baghdad will always be in their debt. To them, I say, "Thank you" and recall a line from Alfred Lord Tennyson's "Idylls of the King:" "More things are wrought by prayer than this world dreams of."

During World War II, when I was a boy, my father taught me some of the lyrics of a soldier's song, "Praise the Lord, and pass the ammunition." I will ever remember those soldiers of the 7th Cavalry who passed the ammunition and who were unstinting in their help and counsel during the preparation of this essay. As in war, so afterwards, certain soldiers were always there for me to help reconstruct the battles and supply insights and facts I overlooked, among them Lt. Col. Terry Ferrell, the 7th Cavalry's commander. During the war, he kindly included me and my crew in so many of his frontline briefings with his junior officers that it seemed as if we were members of the squadron who could be trusted never to compromise the security of his soldiers with irresponsible or premature reporting. In my own case, I suspect they were deferring to the only person in the unit with gray hair.

Apache Troop's commanding officer, Capt. Clay Lyle, will always be a friend. He has been most generous and encouraging with his recollections of his unit's engagements in March and April of 2003, and his notes often remain the best record of the 7th Cavalry's combat engagements. Any mistakes made in this book reflect my own inattention to detail, for Clay is a fine combat officer, as good as they come, and nothing slipped through the cracks in his unit, which may account for how he brought everyone through without the need to award a single Purple Heart despite our ride through the valley of the shadow of death.

Acknowledgments

I confess a special affection for the noncommissioned officers of Apache Troop, the sergeants, who are the best of their breed. Patiently and repeatedly, they took my telephone calls and e-mails after the war and explained the engagements the unit had fought from the perspective of their tank turrets with incoming shells and machine-gun fire raining down on them. Sgts. Paul Wheatley and Matthew Chase presented me the human side of war from the perspective of the best of American soldiers. Sgt. Todd Woodhall was about as close to a cuddly sergeant as any unit had. He was a fine soldier, a humanitarian, a wonderful, earthy, witty observer of the human species.

Capt. Rick Cote, an army reservist and civil affairs officer, was the good ole boy of the unit, and his special insights into the engagements and the campaign as someone who was an outsider as opposed to regular army are most appreciated.

This book could not have been written at all, however, without the help of my own crew. Jeff Barwise was our good-ole-boy engineer (our field-broadcast engineer) whose photographs of the campaign were so generously shared with my publisher. Jeff's digital record of the combat offered the best time line I had in preparing this manuscript, and inevitably, I deferred to his recollections because his memory is invaluable and unfailing. Charlie Miller, my free-lance cameraman during the war, generously took my telephone calls after the war wherever he was on assignment in the world. His laconic recollections added spare Scottish wit to these writings. Paul Jordan, our CNN-assigned security guard from the AKE Security Company, even when twelve time zones away, shared his insights and memories of the combat from his unique perspective behind the steering wheel of Old Betsy, the CNN Humvee. In combat, Paul was always a good sounding board for questions such as, "What should we do next?" And if I am ever wounded, I want him taking care of me as my combat medic.

There are people not at the front line to whom I am no less indebted, especially Maj. Mike Birmingham, an army public affairs officer who more than anyone else was responsible for this fine assignment I received. How he selected me for the 7th Cavalry's embedded journalist bears repeating. I had spent December 2002 on maneuvers with the 3rd Infantry Division in Kuwait and had done two video essays about tanks and how they would be used in the coming war with Iraq. The major had seen the essays and made it clear to the CNN bureau chief in Kuwait City, Steve Cassidy, that he wanted me embedded with the army. In Mike's words, "Rodgers said things about tanks I had always felt but never been able to express." Later, Birmingham would write, "There were many things that were considered for your embed

Acknowledgments

assignment—some of which might be divulged after massive amounts of single-batch bourbon—but one of the most important was your sense of history." It now seems funny how a seemingly insignificant story comparing tanks to mythical dragons can win favor with those who are in a position to give one a career-capping assignment.

There are so many people at CNN I need to thank but most of all the kids in the stacks in Atlanta, the faceless, tireless, good people who worked so hard to get our stuff on the air and who were indispensable in helping me tell this story, among them Eileen Hsieh and Igor Krotov. Several CNN anchors were quick to recognize the risks we embedded journalists were taking and went out of their way to help us tell our stories, among them a long-time friend and former ABC News colleague Aaron Brown, along with Anderson Cooper, Bill Hemmer, Wolf Blitzer, and another former colleague from ABC News Paula Zahn. They are pros.

My friend Pierre Bairin was indispensable in teaching me how to call up from CNN computers transcripts of my broadcasts. My editor Rick Stetter, a Vietnam War veteran, was unflagging in his encouragement of my writing. He above all believed in this story and me long before I did.

As this story unfolded during the war and afterward in the writing, I incurred special debts, the nature of which will remain private and personal. Without either of these people, this story would not have been told. They know the extent of my indebtedness. One of them is my friend Christiane West Little, a soldier's widow. The second is my wife Eleanor who is ever my commanding officer. She has continually offered her wisdom, love, and advice, and I am, of course, grateful beyond words.

Whatever errors occur are solely mine. I especially regret any omissions in the telling of this story. There are far more heroes than I have been able to compress into this volume. Lastly and humbly, I am deeply grateful to all of General Custer's soldiers for the ride of my life. I will never forget them.

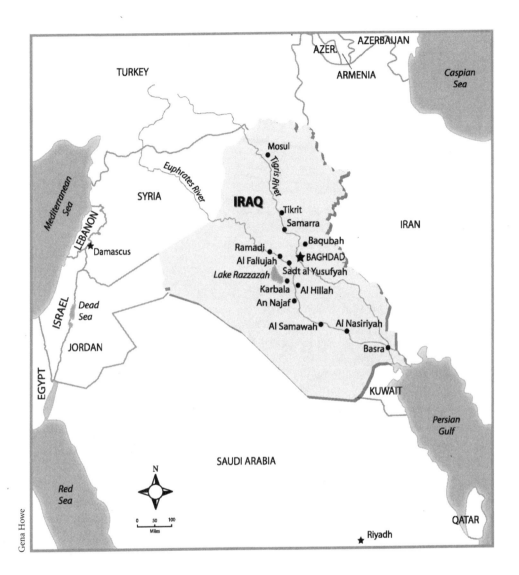

Sleeping
with Custer
and the
7th Cavalry

Introduction

The stranger walked up and introduced himself, "Hi, I'm David Bloom from NBC."

I had lived outside the United States for the last twenty years and worked for CNN about the last ten, so I had no idea who he was or that he was being groomed by rival NBC to be its next-generation evening news anchor. Intuitively, I suppose I knew, however. He oozed from every pore the confidence and poise of a network television anchorman. Bloom was straight out of central casting: tall and handsome with a head of hair to rival Bill Clinton's. Ineffably courteous, he was the young star paying court to a graying foreign correspondent. In a word, Bloom was gracious. I envied his hair, his genes, his pipe, his bank account, and his future. Professionally I had gone as far as I was going to go, and the world lay at young Mr. Bloom's feet. He had come to Kuwait to cover George W. Bush's war to depose Iraq's President Saddam Hussein, and he had come to earn his stripes, which every anchor must do on the way up the ladder. In the generation before Bloom, a reporter during the Cold War did a tour of duty in Moscow or at the White House. For this young man and his peers, there had to be a war.

We shook hands and exchanged pleasantries at a resort hotel in Kuwait about ten days before the war was launched on 19 March 2003. He told me he was very keen on being assigned to the U.S. Army's 3rd Infantry Division. It was no secret they would be the hammer that would pulverize those units of Saddam's army that chose to stand and fight. I had trained with the 3rd ID the previous December on the Udari range in Kuwait, and they were a fine outfit. I, too, hoped to be assigned to them, but I also believed an NBC anchorman-in-the-making would have priority and get the premier assignment.

Suddenly, and with none of his previous self-effacement, Bloom announced to me: "I am going to own this war."

"Oh?" I replied, somewhat nonplussed. For a moment, I felt as if I were witnessing a skit in which I was Woody Allen chatting with John Wayne.

Across the room was my cameraman, Charlie Miller, one of the more laconic Scots one would ever meet. Reflecting on Bloom's pronouncements or trying to flee from them, I walked over to Charlie and said, "Charlie, all we want to do is survive this damned war. No heroics. We just want to survive."

He grinned, his large ears accentuating the broad smile, and replied, "I'd already decided that."

Unlike other long assignments, this time I'd allowed myself no plans for a postwar getaway with my wife, Eleanor. None of us journalists and soldiers knew if we would survive the war, of course, especially with the perceived threat out there that Saddam would order the use of chemical or biological weapons. In Sarajevo in the 1990s, the greatest threat to a journalist was Serb snipers. But, if one did not get whacked by snipers or the errant mortar or artillery round, the R and R for a couple of days in Rome afterward became a kind of tranquilizer and nearly made the previous danger worthwhile. The combat highs going into Afghanistan, especially with the Soviets on the other side, were unparalleled. I was on the ceiling with an adrenalin high for four days after returning to our home in Moscow. Even a good stone-throwing day in Hebron on the West Bank, when I was caught between Israeli sharpshooters and Palestinian boys, was a high if one of those Palestinian rocks didn't crack the head open or if the those same kids with the slingshots and glass marbles didn't put out one's eye.

But this war was different before the first bomb was dropped. The hype over Saddam's chemical and biological weapons ate away at the minds of every U.S. soldier in the desert. I had spoken with scores of men, from grunts to senior officers, and they each worried about it. It was almost the only thing they feared, because they knew the tanks they had could stand off most weapons and demolish any armor the Iraqis possessed. The American soldier was totally confident he would survive any conventional combat engagement, but in the back of that soldier's mind was a real fear of the unknown. Would Saddam unleash the horrors of the much-discussed unconventional weapons in his arsenal? Each soldier and journalist was trained in varying degrees on how to use gas masks and chemical-weapons suits, but none of us knew how effective our protective gear would be.

I had taken more than the usual precautions before shipping out to the Iraqi theater, saying good-bye to friends and family on e-mail and leaving little around of an incriminating or ambiguous nature at work in the event I did not come back. I recall extinguishing the daydreams I usually engage in about going off on a good spring birding trip with my wife. There would be no trip to South Stack, the Royal Society for the Protection of Birds Preserve, this spring to see the puffins, razorbills, and murres come in from the sea to breed on the Welsh cliffs.

Introduction

On the surface, when Eleanor and I said good-bye, there was little different than any other farewell. Unsaid, however, was that this was a different farewell. The Pentagon had already indicated that anyone who died in a chemical or biological attack would not have his remains sent home but would be cremated in the Iraqi desert. That did not bother me so much as the regret I would not be able to have my wedding ring returned to my wife. There is little sentimental about another journalist vaporizing in a big desert bonfire. Generally, people believe we are crazy to do what we do anyway. But I wanted my wife to have my ring, and that was out of the question if we died in a VX gas or anthrax attack. That spring, not only did we not know when we would come home again, we knew some of us would not return at all. For some Iraqis, Americans, and Brits, there would be no spring.

All this ran through my mind on the first day of what reporters referred to as Embed U., the army's processing center for journalists about to be integrated into individual combat units for the coming assault on Iraq. The campus was the Hilton Hotel compound south of Kuwait City. It could have been any junior college campus in south Florida except the faculty appeared to be uniformed ROTC officers and the rest of us ill-disciplined recruits at a boot camp seriously short on sergeants. Those in army uniforms were left asking themselves, "What the hell are we going to do with five hundred journalists?"

Although journalists had gone to war with armies before, the new technology for filing stories and for broadcasting made this a unique experiment that would work so well that the army, it is the opinion of many, would never risk it again. We journalists were about to report the location and progress of military units in the field faster than unit commanders could get back to their commanding officers. Generals in the Pentagon and Kuwait would soon be watching CNN and other news organizations on their TV screens and having a pretty good idea where their troops were before their subordinates could call in progress reports.

Embedding was the brainchild of Deputy Secretary of Defense Victoria "Torie" Clark, a tall woman with short blonde hair and an intelligent face, who proposed the idea of embedding to the White House. Later, Clark sat in on a White House staff meeting with representatives from other agencies. Those present were given to believe the president would have a drop-by, one of those staged impromptu moments when the Commander in Chief would stick his head in the door and tell everyone what a great job they were doing and how grateful he was to have them on his team.

Word of the Pentagon's embed program proposal had bounced about the Bush White House all the previous autumn. So, when Bush saw Clark sitting at the large mahogany table, he grinned and announced that he thought embedding was the silliest idea he had heard of in a very long time. Then he disappeared, no doubt leaving Clark feeling a bit of the fool. The president was not alone in high-level opposition to integrating reporters and television crews into combat units. Vice President Dick Cheney had opposed the idea as well. Only the Secretary of Defense Donald Rumsfeld backed his deputy's idea but with reservations.

There are few human groups less disciplined or organized than journalists. Most are in the profession because they are a feckless lot who, for the most part, could not otherwise fit into the corporate world. In the eyes of the president and vice president, embedding journalists into combat units was akin to drafting a battalion of Falstaffs and sending it to the front. And a battalion of Falstaffs is what the army had milling about that morning at Embed U. on the eve of the Second Gulf War. None of us knew what we were doing in that lecture hall that morning. We all just waited marching orders.

I continued to watch NBC's David Bloom work the briefing room and try to connect with any senior officer who could guarantee him a prime combat unit for an assignment. Most reporters were "working the room," schmoozing with mid-level officers like Maj. Mike Birmingham. Ultimately, he decided the postings although few of us recognized his absolute authority at the time. If I had, I might have been jockeying for position, too. The secrecy surrounding which journalists got which assignments was akin to the Manhattan Project. I am not sure why the army was so secretive about which reporters were assigned where, but it seemed a wise policy not to tell us before we were deposited in the desert. "Tell us nothing, and isolate us quickly" seemed the army's strategy, a tactic that was at least as brilliant as the overall plan for taking Iraq.

The army rarely tells its lowest-ranking grunt what it has in store for him, and reporters who didn't wear the uniform certainly deserved even less consideration. Still, the stars from the New York Times, NBC, Fox, ABC, and CBS were sucking up to the officer corps, seeking to guarantee themselves a front-line assignment. Every reporter's worst nightmare was that he or she would be assigned to the motor pool or some place else in the rear. The army had already warned us that some would get that kind of assignment, which would mean our next posting after the war would be rewrites on the obituary page, or for me, the overnight shift in Atlanta. Getting shot at remains the best career ticket upward for greater professional success. In this day and age, covering combat has increasingly become almost the only nonstop elevator to better assignments and audience recognition, and it is the latter that translates into a correspondent's currency. More than a few correspondents assume they have to do it. After the war, the CBS Washington bureau chief, Janet Leissner, said at a seminar in Chicago she had to actively discourage her younger reporters from feeling they had to try to get themselves killed in Iraq to be sure of promotion at CBS News. She lamented that no one believed her.

By now, Bloom had all but lassoed Major Birmingham and was furtively whispering in his ear. For all his good looks, charm, and youth, Bloom was unaware that the army had already promised CNN, CBS, Fox, and ABC the same thing Bloom was lobbying so heavily to secure for NBC. The secret to hitting a reportorial home run for a TV journalist in this war was getting army permission to take along the network's own satellite truck or Humvee, giving the reporter the ability to broadcast live from the battlefield. In fairness, NBC's engineers came up with what was far and away the superior vehicle technologically, but the rest of us also had more modest live capability, and each of us had had our earlier whisper sessions with the major. I genuinely believed the army was playing no discernable favorites at this point. I was wrong, discovering later that I was to have the best embed assignment of all with the 3rd Squadron of the U.S. Army's 7th Cavalry. But that would be somewhere over the horizon closer to the Euphrates River.

Regrettably, it was the last time I saw David Bloom alive. He died somewhere on the road to Baghdad of deep-vein thrombosis, an affliction more than a few of us came to fear as we sat cramped in Humvees and tanks rolling across the desert, sometimes for seventy hours straight. The tragedy with Bloom was that an army doctor had told him to abandon the campaign. He did not need to die, and he certainly did not need the combat ribbon to become the next Tom Brokaw. Lynn Cheney, the wife of the vice president, later told me at a private dinner that both an army doctor and Brokaw urged Bloom to heed the medical warning signals, and he did not. In retrospect, I am reminded of John Donne's observation, "Any man's death diminishes me." I don't think that is true, but our profession was diminished by the loss of young Mr. Bloom and more than a few other fine journalists who died in the war. It is sad; David never got to hit his reportorial grand slam. He really thought he needed it. In truth, none of us needed it.

More painful for me personally was the death of my friend and colleague from the *Boston Globe*, Elizabeth Nueffer, killed in an automobile accident at Samarra, Iraq, a few days after the war ended. We had served in Berlin and Sarajevo together and were good pals, both of us old New England Yankee Congregational stock. The news of her death hit me harder than any other of the war. On the ride to Baghdad, I could look with indifference upon row after row of Iraqi soldiers' corpses. Elizabeth felt professionally she had to be there, and I regret she'll not be around to give me a big hug farewell when I am sent to the next pesthole.

Right up until the moment U.S. troops crossed the line of departure, Rumsfeld actively vetoed network-television transmission trucks and vehicles from traveling with forward combat units. Gradually, however, it became like the Pentagon's policy toward gay soldiers. "Don't ask, don't tell" crept into the equation. The U.S. Army already knew the British were going to allow the BBC to roll off to war with the British army. So, while publicly declaring no satellite-transmission TV trucks would be on the battlefield, the 3rd Infantry Division commanders were determined this was going to be one war in which the historically slick British public-relations machine was not going to dominate.

Poor Rummy. His generals outflanked him. The American TV networks in Kuwait City had for weeks been quietly assured by army officers on the ground, "Get your trucks ready. You are going with us. But," they added reproachfully, "if word of this gets back to Rumsfeld, it's all off." The networks had had the vehicles ready months in advance. The marines were surreptitiously doing the same thing with their embeds. CBS bought a new Humvee for its people, shipping it into theater. NBC had a truck that could have broadcast from the moon. CNN bought at least three reconditioned vehicles. In the end, however, after the exorbitant cost of refitting them in Kuwait, I suspect we could have purchased a brand new vehicle for the price King Hummer, a used car salesman in Kuwait, was charging for the used vehicles we ended up buying. King Hummer was as duplicitous an Arab trader as ever plied the deserts. In Kuwait City, he bought up used army vehicles that had been run into the ground and then sold them to journalists, charging nearly as much for reconditioning as a new Humvee would have cost. One of the CNN Humvees bearing my colleague Martin Savidge had to be towed all the way from the Kuwaiti border to Baghdad, over three hundred miles, behind a Marine armored vehicle. Besides being undisciplined, journalists have notoriously bad heads for business. If you don't think so, try to sell them a used car on the eve of a war—or simply audit their expense accounts.

Embed U. was offering only a few courses: Basic Principles of Gulf War II, Practical Survival of Saddam's Unconventional Weapons Arsenal 101, and Advanced Shots in the Arms and Ass (Laboratory Examination of How Not to Die by Anthrax and Smallpox). Matriculation was as disorganized as everything else at Embed U. though it was through no fault of the army.

Introduction

The rationale for war, which sold millions of others and me, was Bush's conviction that Saddam had weapons of mass destruction. The summer before the war, I was interviewing a senior Israeli general in Tel Aviv on the saber-rattling coming out of Washington in August of 2002. Having served as CNN's senior Middle East correspondent and Jerusalem bureau chief from 1995 to 2000, I knew that the Israeli lobby in Washington, the American-Israel Political Action Committee, AIPAC, had put the removal of Saddam at the top of its legislative agenda even during the Clinton administration.

Giora Eiland, then director of strategic planning for Israeli military intelligence, offered his overview and rationale for the coming war: "Walt, we can take a chemical or biological attack on Haifa. That will kill ten thousand, and we'll survive. We will destroy whoever the perpetrator is. But we cannot survive one nuclear bomb hitting Tel Aviv. That would be the effective end of the Jewish State." It was clear to me—and persuasive—that Saddam's Iraq could not be permitted to acquire a nuclear weapon.

In the run up to the war, it seemed to some that Bush, and later, the British Prime Minister Tony Blair, had both bought the Israeli rationale in its totality. From a rational perspective, intellectually the war became justified if one accepted the idea Saddam was pursuing a nuclear option although neither the Israeli nor the American intelligence communities believed the Iraqis were any closer than four to six years from acquiring a bomb.

Then or now, no American president nor British prime minister, especially men like Bush and Blair, both with deep religious beliefs, could allow the destruction of the Jewish state. Both believed Saddam erratic enough to pose a long-term threat to Israel, especially if the Iraqi leader developed an Arab bomb. Historically, U.S. foreign policy has become a conjoined twin with the survival of the Jewish state. And given the West's theological, cultural, and intellectual debt to the Jewish people, no American president could allow a nuclear-armed Saddam to exist.

If one accepted the premise that in 1991, Iraq was within eighteen months of acquiring a nuclear bomb, at the time of the first gulf war, and that Saddam had learned the appropriate lesson, to wit, never, never go to war with the United States unless you have a thermonuclear bomb, then the intellectual rationale for Gulf War II not only existed but was plausible and persuasive. The spanner in the works, of course, was that the Israelis' own presumed nuclear arsenal made them more than capable of defending themselves. At the time, however, no one mentioned that, because the Israeli factor in the march-to-war was never discussed publicly, and the Israelis were scrupulous about keeping their heads down and their mouths shut as Bush built his case for war. The rule was broken only once during the run-up to the war, by Rannan Gissan, Prime Minister Ariel Sharon's spokesman. For a brief period in August and September of 2002, Gissan spoke a little too enthusiastically about the coming war against Saddam. He raved rapturously how with Saddam out of the way, the United States and Israel could dominate the Middle East and how Israel's traditional Arab foes would have to respect the new Israeli-American division in the Middle East.

The remarks were impolitic, and subsequently, Foreign Minister Shimon Peres squashed Gissan like a bug. America's Israeli cheerleaders fell silent. The American president spoke only elliptically about the need to dispose of Saddam, who posed a threat to his "neighbors" meaning not just Israel but the Saudis and the Kuwaitis as well. As the tom-toms were beating, however, those were secondary concerns in the public mind. Saddam and his weapons of mass destruction were what were supposed to keep people quaking in their beds at nights and in the weeks before the outbreak of hostilities the Bush administration was laboring mightily to make citizens frightened of WMDs.

In retrospect, there may have been a casus belli, which should have been obvious to any Washington political reporter. Gulf War II had surely had an element of the son setting right the father's place in history. George Bush Senior won Gulf War I, but let Saddam get away. So, Saddam, who generally hated all foreigners, tried to blow up his nemesis when the elder Bush visited Kuwait. The son seemed at times out to avenge the father, and set history aright with Gulf War II. Saddam could not be allowed to thumb his nose at the Bushes. Simplistic? Perhaps, but all other theories justifying the war seem to have broken down. Even George W. Bush was forced to admit in September of 2003 that there was absolutely no connection between anyone in the Iraqi government, including Saddam, and the terror attacks on the United States in September of 2001. As of this writing, not only do Iraq's weapons of mass destruction pose no imminent threat to the United States or Britain, they have not been found. And it bears repeating: On more than one occasion, the Israelis have demonstrated they are capable of defending themselves from Iraq or any other hostile Arab state.

Also before the war, there existed an induced hysteria that Iraqi agents who were sleepers in the United States would launch terror attacks on Americans. In preparations for Gulf War II, American news organizations spent hundreds of thousands of dollars on courses, training their employees on how to recognize and survive the dangers of a chemical or biological attack on the battlefield. It was in no small way reminiscent of the movies we used to get in school in the late 1940s and early 1950s on how at school to survive a Soviet nuclear strike. All students, upon seeing a blinding flash of light, were to make their way to the interior corridor of the school and cover their heads to shield themselves from flying glass, even if the nearest plausible target of a Soviet attack was four hundred miles away.

Those of us based in London before Gulf II would traipse off to the Ministry of Defense's Nuclear, Biological, and Chemical Center to get lectures from a portly fellow named Ian Day who, by God, told you by God, he was going to teach you how to survive on the unconventional weapons battlefield. He had you fitted for gas masks, euphemistically called respirators, and aluminum-fabric chemical-weapons suits that made the wearer look like a shiny, foil-wrapped Thanksgiving turkey about to go into the oven. Then there were gloves and galoshes and scare lectures about how many millions would die in a gas attack on London or southern England. Everyone would die except those fortunate few who were taking this course, who recognized phosphene gas and knew it smelled like newly mown hay. There were drills teaching skills on how to dive into a chemical-weapons suits. In combat, in the field, it didn't work that way.

It was my impression then and remains now that CNN spent more preparing its personnel to survive a chemical and biological warfare environment than any other network. Still, that training fell considerably short of the weeks and months of training U.S. and British soldiers and marines received in preparation for the battlefield. The exigencies of news coverage where a correspondent may be covering the British royal family one week and be sent off to war the next simply do not permit the luxury of weeks of training and specialization needed to recognize and defend oneself against every possible situation on the battlefield. Everyone does what he or she can and prays for the best. That was and remains, I suspect, the corporate approach to this and virtually every other hazardous environment into which we are sent.

Fortunately for us, the army also threw in an additional refresher course at Embed U. the morning before we shipped out. In one sense, it was at least as good as what some private security firms offered because no one tried to dazzle us with the multiplicity of horrible gases, poisons, and biological weapons we might face that could kill us. The army course was taught by soldiers whose sole purpose was to keep themselves and us alive. They were less interested in dazzling us with all the dozens of various ways Saddam's chemical-weapons doctors could kill us. The army didn't practice overkill. It gave us the basic elements of what it took to survive, Staying Alive 101.

Introduction

What little I remembered from all this was that if a person started drooling at the mouth, couldn't breathe and easily vomited and went into convulsions, there was a pretty good chance that person had been hit by a nerve agent. In such an event, you haul out a needle the size of a volleyball pump and shoved it into the buttocks. A problem, however, was that it was not unheard of for one of these needles to jab someone accidentally, someone who had not been gassed, and who then would have atropine poisoning. Even knowing the risk of getting accidentally jabbed, though, I still used that part of my first-aid kit for a pillow at night. Little makes sense in a war.

Blister agent was my favorite Saddam weapon. The army handed out powder puffs with Fuller's Earth to blot off the garlic-, geranium-, or fish-smelling liquid. I had worked too many summers as a lifeguard not to be able to smell chlorine gas when and if it came. Ricin was another one of my favorite weapons. Hell, my mother warned me about that as a kid when she made me weed her castor-bean plants. "Don't eat the castor beans, they are poison," she admonished me. Like I would get anywhere near the things. The plant secreted a sweet sap that was addictive to wasps. I would have been stung to death before I ever could have retrieved one castor bean. The army taught us, "High doses of ricin by inhalation result in pulmonary damage, and you die." All of these warnings merely cultivated a healthy mental crop of fatalism. As we would discover, little of the training was of any value whatsoever on the battlefield before us.

Ian, our prewar instructor in Britain, also walked us through the horrors of biowarfare. Perhaps because of the earlier anthrax scare in the United States, the biowarfare prospects were easier to confront. There were rumors Saddam had dusted the Iraqi border north of Kuwait so that the predominantly American and British Coalition forces would have to roll their tanks through deserts seeded with anthrax spores. No big deal. Everyone who had spent the previous year in Afghanistan knew the cure for that was ciprofloxacin pills. Indeed, they acquired a reputation for curing everything from anthrax to the clap. It was in everybody's kit.

In retrospect, Iraq turned out to be the epitome of modernity compared to what many of us endured in Afghanistan in the opening phases of "the War on Terror." In the mid-1980s, when the Soviets began to take us into Afghanistan to see their war against militant Islam, some of the romantics among us thought we had been transported via a time warp into the world of Rudyard Kipling just west of the Northwest Frontier provinces. Upon returning from my first trip into that forbidden land, my Russian secretary coyly asked me what it was like there. Exuberantly, I told her it was "beautiful, magnificent, exotic, straight out of the nineteenth century." Under her breath I heard her say, "You mean the fourteenth century, don't you?" I always knew she was well connected to the Soviet establishment. Many of my colleagues in Moscow called her "the colonel," implying heavy ties to the KGB. Her reference to Afghanistan belonging to the world of the fourteenth century came as no surprise. All of us who covered that war knew the mujahideen beheaded captured Russian soldiers and used the heads as balls to play a kind of polo on ponies.

Denial, however, proved to be the best remedy for all the bioweapons the Iraqis allegedly had in their arsenal, and I simply suppressed any worry about biotoxins. Logic also breaks down in war, and I was naïvely amused by the thought of Saddam using bubonic plague against an American or British army. Following that naïve reasoning, I figured I was immune because I was descended from a long line of English ancestors who would have been exposed to the plague in the thirteenth and fourteenth centuries. The rule of thumb is that if someone in your lineage had contracted the plague and survived, you carried the same immunity gene.

The army's attempts to frighten us into getting smallpox shots were more intimidating. Some colonel gathered a number of us together in a lecture hall and showed us a collection of slides of dying smallpox victims. Now, if an army doctor, a full colonel, got a bunch of schoolteachers or computer programmers or airline pilots in a lecture hall and told them they needed smallpox vaccinations and showed them the gory slides, he might have achieved one hundred percent inoculation. Unfortunately for his batting average, this doctor was working with journalists.

After the second day of classes at Embed U., we were ordered to grab our backpacks and other kit, plus boxes of TV gear, and board some sorry-looking school buses that reminded me of what the Soviets used in Afghanistan in 1986 and 1987. Years of covering combat in Lebanon, the West Bank, the Balkans, Armenia, Azerbaijan, Soviet Afghanistan, and now Iraq gave me to believe my own survival skills would stand me in much better stead than some army colonel beckoning me with a needle dripping with smallpox scum. "Bet on yourself," I told myself. "Bet on your own street smarts, and throw in a healthy dose of common sense if you want to stay alive in war zones."

And so the U.S. Army turned loose its vaccinated and unvaccinated embedded journalists on the poor Iraqis. Embedding was a brilliant idea because it denied the Iraqis a propaganda edge. At no point in the war could Saddam accuse the Coalition forces of massacring thousands of Iraqi civilians, because independent journalists from a number of countries, including Russia, were traveling with U.S. forces.

Yet now, less than six months later, I feel the eddies of time swirling about me and carrying away what happened in the spring of 2003. I have a compelling need to validate what I experienced, especially as I begin to wonder what really happened and more so now as things seem to be going so wrong in Iraq. I find myself doubting the reality or at least the severity of the ambushes, the ferocity of the firefights, and the aching discomforts of the campaign. Five months after the war, a colonel in the 101st Airborne Division ran into me in northwestern Iraq and convinced me that what I am about to write was very real. His unit had followed the U.S. Army's 7th Cavalry on its thrust to Baghdad. "You guys really had the worst of it," he said. "I really admire you guys." Yet the most surprising reaction I got was from old soldiers who followed the campaign on their televisions, and it is even more telling. To the man, they all blurt out, "I sure am jealous. I wish I could have been there with you guys." And so I feel I have a duty to all the fine soldiers I rode with for the better part of the campaign to add this perspective to the historical record.

1

Marrying the Cavalry

Far I hear the bugle blow
to call me where I would not go.
—A. E. Housman, "A Shropshire Lad"

With the help of a dust storm, the desert night swallowed us up. The flat horizon of the Kuwaiti desert disappeared in darkness, and the only reference we had to the world about us was a dull, dim light somewhere above us in the bus that was rolling northward toward unnamed army encampments and beyond those the Iraqi border. Grown men with promising careers, name recognition, and enviable salaries were reduced to mere shadows on their way to link up with U.S. Army units bound for Baghdad. It was difficult to discern the identity of anyone on the bus that night. Everyone existed as but a shadow, and perhaps it was just as well. By war's end, four of the journalists sitting ahead of me in that dim light would be dead. Indeed, more journalists died in a year in Iraq than in the entire span of the Vietnam War.

The conversations in hushed tones were stilted and nervous. None of the journalists knew where he or she was going or to which assigned unit. The army was clever about that; no chance until it was just too late to write your Congressman if you didn't like your assignment. The army has centuries of experience in dealing with malcontents. I had wanted to be assigned to the U.S. Army's 3rd Infantry Division. My assessment of the coming war led me to believe the 3rd ID would see the most combat. It was where I wanted to be.

It was not that I saw myself as brave so much as resigned to what was required of me. If journalists are going to go to war as combat correspondents, they have to position themselves for the best part of the story, the best pictures, and the best narrative to report it. Reporters have to see, feel, taste, and smell the battle, the cordite from exploding shells. They have to be able to describe the terror when the ground shakes as tanks or the 155 mm Paladin self-propelled guns let fly. The one thing we feared more than gas was that somewhere ahead of us, beyond the horizon, we would hear the far-off rumbling and roar of a company of sixty-nine-ton M1A1 Abrams tanks firing at an even more distant foe, and we would have to report it from six or ten miles behind their 120 mm guns blasting a door through the Iraqi front. For a print reporter, it would mean reporting on a battle you never saw. For television, it would be professional death, total failure. Pictures are the mother's milk of television. Ten miles back from the war there would have been no war to report.

Somewhere forward on the darkened bus, a voice began to call out, "All right, listen up! BBC, Gavin Hewitt: 3rd Infantry Division." The roll call continued. It seemed every news organization on the bus but CNN was getting the 3rd ID. Charlie Miller, my free-lance cameraman, and I sat surrounded by boxes of TV gear. It would be several weeks yet and miles beyond the horizon before either of us realized we had been given the premier combat assignment of the war. We were about to win the lottery, but we didn't know it yet.

Then the same voice somewhere forward in the dark added, as if by way of footnote, "CNN to the 7th Cavalry." At first, I thought it a bad joke. The 7th Cavalry was Lt. Col. George Armstrong Custer's unit, wiped out by the Sioux and Northern Cheyenne at the Little Bighorn in eastern Montana in the summer of 1876.

One of the anonymous shadows half a dozen rows forward was overheard to say, "The 7th Cavalry! Man, those guys have balls of steel." At that moment, mine felt more like Jell-o. I had no idea what modern cavalry did, but obviously someone ahead of me did, and I began to become a little concerned about what I had bought into. Having toured the Little Bighorn battlefield years before, where Custer and the 7th Cavalry were slaughtered, and many of them scalped, I felt more than a twinge of anxiety. Was this an omen? I am not superstitious and don't believe in omens. But the question was now on the table.

What I remembered of the Custer Battlefield National Monument battlefield site was a sagebrush-covered slope looking down onto a grove of cottonwood trees. They would have been in full leaf that June of 1876. Sitting Bull and Crazy Horse had no difficulty concealing upwards of three thousand mounted warriors in that copse that hedged both banks of the Little Bighorn River. Custer's 250 cavalrymen had to be surprised when over ten times their number of Sioux and Cheyenne braves emerged shrieking in two pincer columns to flank and ambush them. Aboard that dark Kuwaiti bus,

I mused over the kinds of surprises the Iraqis had in store for us. At Embed U.'s Strategy and Tactics 101, I had learned what every army officer knew by heart: "The enemy always has a vote on the battlefield."

Somewhere an hour or two later, after my colleagues had been deposited at their unit-assignment stations, we were also left in the desert. It takes a TV crew longer to off-load its equipment boxes than it does an infantry soldier with a duffle bag. So, after the hauling, the blinding by flashlights, and general confusion, when our transport left, whatever was left of our geographic orientation disappeared into the desert night with the bus. I gazed upward for Polaris, the North Star, through a haze of blowing dust. Disorientation seemed part of the military's training strategy for embedded journalists, and why not? It had worked wonders for generations of draftees and new recruits. Blindfolding us would perhaps have been more desirable from the army's viewpoint, but, after all, we were still civilians.

When sometime later, after standing alone in the desert night without food or shelter, a Humvee came and collected us and took us to a darkened tent encampment, we knew the army owned our asses completely. We had no idea where we were and could only reply "Yes, sir," when even the lowest-ranking private offered a suggestion. After another ride in uncharted desert, with no lights, we stopped, and someone in uniform pointed toward a tent and said, "You'll find a couple of cots there. Be ready to go at 0530."

I don't remember whether I took the time to unfold my sleeping bag or whether I just collapsed and fell asleep among a chorus of farting, snoring soldiers. The tent was dark and malodorous. What little sleep there was, was soon interrupted by the two other members of our CNN crew joining us, neither of whom I had met before. They, too, were now stumbling about in the dark and foul canvas tent made barely habitable by a plywood floor laid over the desert sands. Both of our newfound colleagues had slipped through Secretary of Defense Donald Rumsfeld's media-blackout curtains, with the complicity of the army itself, which was determined the war was going to be "an army show, by God, and the secretary of defense could stuff it if he thinks the army brass is going to roll over and let the air force or the British get all the glory!"

The two new crew members—Jeff Barwise, our satellite engineer, and Paul Jordan, our private security guard and driver—had driven up in Old Betsy, our reconditioned Humvee. With the help of jumper cables for the battery, Betsy would take us all the way to the Iraqi capital in the next four weeks, a distance of close to four hundred miles. Betsy was stuffed with banks of electronic equipment that gave us the capacity to roll with the 7th

Cavalry's tanks and Bradley fighting vehicles and transmit a decent live TV signal of the conflict. Although the Bradleys carried ten men and were armed with a 25 mm cannon, a light machine gun, and missiles, there was next to no room for the four grown men in the CNN Humvee. We were secondary to the electronics and were supposed to snake our bodies around and among the electronic components. It would be the most physically discomforting ride any of us would ever experience, short of spending four weeks in a lifeboat in open ocean. It was miserable.

At dawn, we climbed into Betsy and were led farther into the Kuwaiti desert to an unnamed encampment where the 7th Cavalry was based. Stretched across the horizon in every direction was a large circular array of tents and men that reminded me of Bedouin encampments I had seen throughout the deserts of Jordan, Israel, Yemen, Kuwait, and Iraq, except this was an infinitely larger assembly. Instead of camels there were tanks and Bradleys, self-propelled Paladin gun carriages, and Kiowa helicopters. The dust clouds here were kicked up not by herds of goats and sheep but by Humvees. None of the elements that make a colorful Bedouin encampment so romantic to Europeans and Americans was present. The 7th Cavalry's arrayed tents were functional khaki and were not pitched to catch the warming morning sun as any Bedouin tent would have been.

We were introduced to the unit's senior officers, Lt. Col. Terry Ferrell, Col. Nicholas Snelson, Maj. Brad Gavle, and perhaps the best news source in the squadron, Sgt. Maj. Gabriel Berhane of Los Angeles, California. Berhane was barely five feet tall, Hispanic American, no-nonsense, and one of the few men in the unit who did not feed on rumors. He knew what was happening.

Colonel Ferrell was courteous but preoccupied and promised to give us a briefing, an outline of the war, but not now. He was as new to the embedding as we were, but if the embedding process could be said to have worked, no soldier in the army deserves more credit for its success than Colonel Ferrell. His orders were to lay it all out before us and adopt us into the unit, and he did that. As he briefed us on the plan of attack, I felt like an eagle floating on convection currents above the battlefield. I was being shown how the coming war was to unfold.

The only thing that ever came close was the briefing senior Israeli officers would give us before they took us into south Lebanon to cover their running war with Hezbollah guerrillas. That was a very different war because while the Americans in Iraq could point to lines and arrows and routes of attack, south Lebanon was very different for the Israelis. Instead of charts, they could point along the horizon to Lebanese villages where the Israelis seemed certain Hezbollah fighters slept by day and emerged to attack Israeli Defense Forces outposts by night. In the Israelis' wars with guerrillas, there were no real maps to share because there were no lines, or if there were, they shifted between daylight and darkness. By contrast, the U.S. Army had an offensive plan of attack. It shared that plan of attack with us, and as an embedded journalist, I was privy for the first time to more than just what lay before us on the horizon. I had a fantastic scoop and couldn't report it.

Before bidding us adieu, however, the colonel pointed to a sand berm that the army had bulldozed along the northern edge of the circular encampment and said, "That's Apache Troop out there by those Bradleys. They will lead the charge. That's where you will be." Implicit in that last phrase was "if you have the balls for it." Then he introduced Capt. Clay Lyle, who was in charge of Apache Troop.

Captain Lyle and I shook hands and took each other's measure. He was of medium height, square and stocky, "Texas," and a totally committed soldier. Killing Iraqi soldiers was part of his profession, and he would perform that task as methodically as a bricklayer lays bricks. He, too, was preoccupied and justifiably detached, although on more than one occasion in the heat of force-on-force battles, he would save our lives by positioning his own M1A1 Abrams tank to shield Old Betsy from machine-gun and small-arms fire. For the moment, however, he led us in his Humvee northward toward the sand berm that was punctuated with tanks and other armored vehicles every two hundred yards or so along a circular sweep. The wagons were drawn in a circle, the noncombatants on the inside.

We were driven to the Tactical Operations Center (TOC), an ugly armored vehicle festooned with radio aerials and a canvas awning shading the entrance. We were told to camp next to it. It was parked about four hundred yards back from the perimeter of the encampment. Beyond the perimeter were the Iraqis, not that far over the horizon. The TOC was a kind of inner sanctum that we were not to penetrate. At first, I imagined something top secret inside that we were not supposed to see, but generally what soldiers guard most assiduously is their pinups and creature comforts like cots or chairs. The one time I breached TOC's security barrier and stuck my head inside the awning, I noticed a small bulletin board on which was posted the following advisory: "Going to war without the French is like going deer hunting without your accordion." The American army's debt to Lafayette had been repaid in blood at the Argonne, the Somme, and the beaches of Normandy. In 2003, the American GIs held the Iraqis in somewhat less contempt than they held the French. The irony of course was that the French public's esteem for Americans at this time was as high as their contempt for the George W. Bush administration. Polls in France, even at the outset of this war, showed seventy-two percent of the French still held a favorable opinion of Americans. In similar polls in the United Kingdom at this time, only twenty-seven percent of the British public reported any particular admiration for America or Americans.

Setting up our own encampment gave us the first chance we had to look each other over. Except for Charlie with whom I had done a hitch in Afghanistan, none of us had ever met before we slept on adjoining cots that night. Jeff was responsible for making pictures fly through the air, although I knew when I picked Charlie as my cameraman I was building redundancy into the system because he had a degree in electrical engineering from a British university. Jeff was, like most of the television industry's technical wizards, taciturn, and he evinced no fear in the heat of the battles to come.

More difficult to get a fix on was Paul, a former Australian Special Air Services (SAS) soldier, retired and working for the private security company that CNN hired to accompany its people into war zones. He appeared more than a little disdainful of his charges although I had seen more combat than he had. Being Australian, he bonded quickly with Charlie because of his English accent, which presumably made Paul feel more comfortable than working with an older American correspondent. Paul's condescension toward Americans and the U.S. Army was never far below the surface, and it grew proportionately to the average American soldier's awe of his SAS credentials. Not infrequently did he repeat a statement he had apparently been taught in hand-to-hand combat training: "You have two choices: I can kill you instantly or leave you crippled from the neck down for the rest of your life."

Paul's presence occasionally reminded me of the gag about Australians being the most balanced people in the world because they have a chip on *both* shoulders. This tall, physically powerful Aussie always seemed to need to feel superior to someone, yet, psychologically, he was far more complex than his soldierly pedigree suggested and kinder than my initial impression led me to believe. There was, beneath the Crocodile Dundee exterior, a gentle streak in the man. I saw it when we chanced upon a wounded animal or when he nursed a wounded Iraqi soldier everyone else had left for dead. During our week or so in this staging camp, we often saw or heard buff-colored desert mice, resembling kangaroo rats, scurrying about at night. Often they would burrow under our sleeping bags for shelter. They were sweet, harmless creatures with abnormally large black eyes for enhanced night vision and long white tails for balance. When a U.S. soldier stomped one to death for sport, I saw the look in Paul's eyes and heard him mutter "stupid bastard." Had he not been so disciplined, I suspect Paul would not have given this mouse killer the option of being crippled from the neck down but would have murdered him on the spot for his cruelty.

This same gentleness was also present in some of the crustiest American soldiers in our unit. At one point, I observed some extremely bored 7th Cavalry soldiers slip a noose around the neck of a three-foot-long iguana-like lizard and then hoot and holler as they walked it around their tanks as it if were a pet poodle. Their top sergeant, Todd Woodhall, discovered them and proceeded to carve each a new asshole for treating the lizard cruelly. Sheepishly, they freed the animal, which may have been safer as a tethered army mascot than it was free to roam the Arabian deserts, because these lizards are hunted down by Bedouins who consider them delicacies, roasting them on spits over open fires. But this Australian SAS soldier and a U.S. Army sergeant, both of whom would not hesitate to kill an enemy soldier, seemed incapable of countenancing cruelty to lesser animals.

The Arabian desert is like the sea in that it can be deceptively calm one minute and violently threatening the next. At sunset, our first night with the 7th, the wind dropped, and the remaining warmth of the desert seemed to kindle an almost lavender sunset. There was no sense of foreboding, however, or any other warning. I sat snuggled in my spanking-new camouflage bivy tent with the head up against the left front wheel of Old Betsy. Charlie, Jeff, and Paul had spread their sleeping bags on a tarpaulin beside the Humvee beneath the sky. And then the wind came.

I had seen sandstorms in Israel, Afghanistan, and Iraq, but nothing had prepared me for that night. We were not quite asleep when the wind came powerfully, suddenly, violently, and without warning. It was soon blowing at least fifty miles an hour.

Driven sand lashed the nylon shell of my tent with the same sound as blowing snow, except that it did not melt or evaporate. My blue enamel drinking cup flew off the hood of the Humvee. Foolishly, I had left my boots, my socks, and my gas mask outside the tent when I bedded down. The snapping of the tent kept me awake, and because I had rigged my new tent incorrectly, there was a hole the size of a pea through which blowing sand gusted around inside my cocoon. It was much worse for my colleagues, who had bedded down on a tarpaulin imagining their sleeping bags would afford all the protection they needed.

Charlie, who had been lying atop his bivy bag, dived for its depths, pulling the zipper over his nose. Still, as he recalls, "The smell of dust was everywhere inside the shell and sleeping bag." In truth, it filled your mouth, and rinsing it out was only a temporary solution because it left a mouthful of mud. We didn't dare get up to pee that night because we might not be able to find our Humvee again. There was a terrible buffeting from the wind all night long, and whatever was left outside either blew away or was buried. I know I have a lost sock somewhere in Saudi Arabia. Jeff had more difficulty because he is claustrophobic, and every time he poked his nose out of his sleeping bag, he gagged.

Iraqis call these storms *ajaja ramleah*, but as so often with Arabic, there are multiple names. In classical Arabic, these blows out of the north in March and April are known as *assifah ramleah*. They can also be called *shamal*, literally the north wind, and as that implies cold air, often bitter-cold air is coming in behind. For us, it was as if Boreas, the ancient Greek personification of the north wind, was determined to bury the 7th Cavalry with all its tanks and soldiers deep in the deserts of Arabia.

The next morning, I discovered even the desert lizards had gone to ground, leaving only their tails poking out. I remember touching one and seeing a flaccid twitch. Lizards, being reptiles, are cold-blooded, and when the temperature dropped to fifty degrees Fahrenheit as the wind died, the beasts were left lethargic and vulnerable.

I don't recall anything that was not coated with grit the next morning: boots, tea kettle, drinking cups, computers, cameras, canteens, jackets, hats, toothbrushes, short-wave radio, and toilet paper. The electronics and the entire inside of our Humvee were blanketed with a quarter- to half-inch of pumice-fine sand and dirt. During the night, soldiers straying beyond their armored vehicles got lost in our encampment and had to be retrieved from the desert after some wandered blindly beyond the perimeter. Search parties were sent out to find them and guide them home. If the presidential order had come to cross the line of departure that morning, no one would have been ready. It would require several days to clean the grit from pistols, rifles, and artillery pieces. On our short-wave radios, we could hear descriptions of the storm as the worst in anyone's memory although I doubt if anyone asked the indigenous Bedouins.

The soldiers of the 7th Cavalry had been warned that some journalists were going to be embedded with them. Although embedding was a concept that was invented and improvised on a daily basis, the general idea was that we would be going to war with them. They expected us and were as predictably wary as we reporters on a Washington assignment would be if we were told a lieutenant from the Pentagon would be following us around for a couple of weeks. I decided to use whatever time before the invasion order came to file a few features, stories designed to win the soldiers' trust. Additionally, features reporting would be a diversion for the soldiers and for us. The first thing I learned was the only thing any one of them cared about was getting the hell out of there and going home. Regrettably for all of us, the road home went through Baghdad; not knowing when that would be was the hardest thing any of us faced that March in the desert.

An army-in-waiting is ever swept by rumors, and so it was in mid-March of 2003. No one we were talking to knew anything credible, and the rumors ran the gamut: the mobilization was a farce; we would still be sitting waiting till summer when the temperatures topped 130 degrees Fahrenheit; the war was being called off. Some of the 7th Cavalry's soldiers told me they believed their ultimate destination that spring would be North Korea, ten thousand miles from Iraq. And there was the persistent rumor emanating from opposition to the war in the House of Commons that the British were pulling out of the "coalition of the willing." The best way to track down a rumor was to ask a soldier where he first heard it. If he replied, "Down by the latrine, sir," then I knew what credibility to give it. I also suspected that because I was a reporter, innocent young soldiers would frequently approach me and ask for the latest, assuming I had insider's information. Regrettably, I had little although in the week before the war I flirted with the idea of floating a rumor that the Russians were marching to reinforce the Iraqis. I did not because given the soldiers' near-total isolation, they were likely to have believed it. Idle armies thrive on rumors as surely as they exist on MREs or meals ready to eat.

For the men and women, waiting in the desert was boring beyond the average mortal's comprehension. The classic soldier's lament was "We never know what we are doing until we do it." Thus, mail from home was better than hot food or a shower. More than a few soldiers would pen letters home every day. Nineteen- and twenty-year-old men were reduced to staging beetle fights. The desert had a surfeit of them, too, big, fat carrion beetles, some the size of ping-pong balls. Bored soldiers would tie their pet beetles to strings and pit the insects against each other. The winning beetle lived to fight another day; losers became the first victims of one of the Arabian desert's lesser wars.

At night during this waiting period, the men would huddle around their vehicles and talk politics, as soldiers in the armies of any democracy inevitably do. Iraq's President Saddam Hussein was "the worst," except for the French. Few of the soldiers in the 7th Cavalry could have named the French president, but they knew whoever the French president was, he was a "real bastard." All of the soldiers were persuaded that Saddam had to be deposed. But when the GIs learned the Turks had closed their borders to passage of the U.S. 4th Infantry Division, putting more pressure on the 3rd ID, the Turks were right up there with the French and Saddam. In their view of the world, most U.S. soldiers in Iraq believed the British public stood solidly behind its Prime Minister Tony Blair. They were shocked when I cited one British poll on the eve of the war that more Brits believed Bush a greater threat to world peace than Saddam. Outsiders like me were not welcome at these discussions atop darkened tanks or inside the Bradleys. In the eyes of soldiers young enough to be my grandchildren, I had not been tried in battle, in their view at least, and until I was, I was not to be totally trusted. The soldiers' politics were probably irrelevant, although their political discussions seemed to keep them focused on what lay ahead. Political discourse among soldiers is probably a healthy component and certainly an inevitable one of an all-volunteer army in a democratic country.

By day, tank crews practiced bore sightings on their 120 mm guns. I found it difficult to believe that after firing just five rounds of ammunition, a tank's muzzle reference system had to be realigned. It seemed all the more implausible with the realization that in combat, the American M1A1 Abrams was expected to overcome a four-to-one enemy advantage in soldiers. If the tank crew had to pause after firing five rounds to resight the gun barrel after it heated up, how could the crew overcome such odds? I was told the heat changed the actual composition of the barrel.

Occasionally, I would wander up to a group of soldiers and inquire what their role would be in the days ahead. There seemed a rule of thumb that the less willing a soldier was to discuss what he did, the less relevant his role would be in the coming war. When a group of soldiers pretended their work was hush-hush or said that they had to get an officer's permission before they could talk with us, I came to correctly conclude their importance in combat was likely to be minimal. Civilian affairs and psychological warfare units—PSYOPS—were extraordinarily secretive about what they did, and what I discovered they did often made them not nearly as indispensable as they pretended to be.

The soldiers who would lead the fight, like Apache Troop commanding officer Captain Lyle, shared virtually everything with us. The CO even offered to take us for a ride in his tank just days before we crossed the line of departure. Actually, the "joy ride" became crucial to my reporting. I would soon be describing an armored armada rolling toward Baghdad, and I needed to have ridden in a tank so I could describe what the soldiers endured for close to seventy hours straight with no sleep. The captain offered to let me stand in the turret with him as we raced about the perimeter of our nameless camp, but I declined, asking instead to ride in the cramped gunner's seat. "Like riding in the bowels of a dragon," I wrote in my notebook. The engine, which burned the same JP8 fuel as the helicopters, whined and rumbled, and I was sure a dragon had swallowed me.

Tankers call the Abrams the Cadillac of the battlefield. Maybe in terms of relative price tags, but I found it singularly uncomfortable, with the 120 mm gun barrel over my left shoulder and some clouded cannon sights in front of me. As we bounced and bucked across the sand dunes, I was grateful to have my helmet on, or I would have had a cracked skull as my head ricocheted off steel overhead and on both sides. Above the loader (the soldier who aims the tank's cannon), the commander watches the flank and rear security. From my gunner's seat, it was exhilarating when that turret swung to fix on a target.

I have heard gunners talk in soft caressing words to their 120 mm guns. A tanker's euphemism for this sex object is "the most lethal survivable weapons system on earth, carrying seven days of basic load ammunition, food, water, and batteries."

Another downside is that in the desert there would be no ventilation in the belly of this Cadillac, and it would become stifling in the days ahead. With a commander having to stand sometimes days on end in the tank's turret, the most comfortable seat in the house was the driver's. He drove in a two-thirds reclining position; it was not unheard of for tank drivers to have to be yelled at to "Stay awake!" and not fall asleep at their periscopes.

When Colonel Ferrell finally sent word he was ready to brief us, I was totally unprepared for what was to follow. Another reporter and his photographer from the *Army Times* newspaper joined Charlie, Jeff, Paul, and me. It was then that I discovered we six were the only embeds attached to the 7th Cavalry. I still had not fully grasped what a plum assignment I had, but I had already figured out it was likely to be dangerous.

On easel tripods in the colonel's tent were maps that had so many lines resembling isobars, they could have been confused with meteorologists' charts. Quickly, however, it was clear that the senior commanding officer was letting us see the map of the battle to come, and it was mind-boggling. It was also only the beginning of what he was willing to share, because no one ever fully defined the operational parameters of embedding to the officer corps. "The First Marine Expeditionary Force is off to the northeast, and the 7th Cavalry is here on their flank," Colonel Ferrell said. He told us we would be crossing the line of departure at about midnight and racing northwest twelve to fourteen hours ahead of the main body of 3rd Infantry Division force.

Modern cavalry are no less scouts than Jeb Stuart's horse soldiers were for Robert E. Lee during the American Civil War. When we were told we would be operating way out ahead of the main army, I realized why we needed balls of steel. We were to be the tip of the tip of the spear.

Colonel Ferrell said, "The 7th is the eyes and ears of the mechanized division that will follow. We will probe the Iraqi positions, seek the best routes to Baghdad, and look for potential enemy locations where they can be located, identifying that or any other hazards along the way that would impede the Division's main body."

It sounded exciting and hazardous, but we had no idea yet just how exciting and how hazardous. This was still only a briefing.

We were told there would be sparse enemy forces, nothing bigger than reconnaissance elements at the outset. Colonel Ferrell assured us that the Kiowa helicopters would be out in front of the unit and married to the 7th's tanks, Bradleys, and mortars. He was giving us the whole order of battle days in advance of the attack. I doubt reporters have ever before been entrusted with this kind of information—knowing the exact position of every unit on the battlefield, the routes to the objectives, the code names for the objectives along the way. Yet, the responsibilities imposed upon me and some other well-placed embedded reporters were obvious. We were forbidden to report the order of battle, of course, according to the Pentagon's rules of embedding agreed to by CNN and other news organizations. I also had the sense that if I even hinted at what I knew to my office in Atlanta, I was endangering soldiers' lives, the success of the mission, and most persuasively, my own life. The best way to guarantee someone will keep a secret is to make divulging the secret life threatening. I never even hinted to CNN headquarters how much I knew.

As I sat in the colonel's tent, I kept pinching myself and saying to myself, "My God! What a story! And you can't file it." There would be many such moments to come. I knew where along the border the 7th Cavalry was crossing into Iraq, our route to our first objective at Al Samawah, and that our first objective there was to secure specific bridges crossing the Euphrates River for the 3rd Infantry's mechanized division that was behind us. I had this huge story, and I couldn't say a word. "Hey, World," I wanted to scream, "I know what's going to happen! I know we are out to find the Iraqis, and this is where we are going looking for them." The cavalry's standing operation order is grab the enemy by the nose, and don't let him go.

More prophetically than he could then imagine, Colonel Ferrell said, "It's going to be hard for the Iraqis not to just say, 'I've had it.'" At this point, U.S. forces were still expecting massive defections or surrender by the regular Iraqi army, especially in the south where the less than committed to Saddam Shiite Muslim Iraqis were dominant. The Coalition forces were in for a few surprises in the weeks ahead. But these surprises would be tactical, not strategic. The Iraqis' only wild card might be the use of gas or chemical or biological weapons, but the American side was boasting that even this would be "no showstopper." In his tent, the colonel was able to confidently say, "We will be bold and audacious . . . if a hostile force is there, and he is demonstrably hostile toward my soldiers, I will kill him."

I can't say I totally shared Colonel Ferrell's confidence, and judging by the attendance at the chaplain's last service before we moved out, it seemed my uncertainty was shared by many of the soldiers of the 7th Cavalry. Word was passed that the chaplain of the 7th, Capt. Steve Balog, would be holding services at the Tactical Operations Post, and I was curious about how many soldiers would attend. I expected only a handful. I was amazed to see more than a hundred of the 138 men from Apache Troop alone at the brief ecumenical service. Catholics clutched their rosaries. Protestants, especially the religiously devoted African Americans, clutched their Bibles.

"God is watching over you," the Protestant Episcopal priest assured the men. He commenced reading the Ninety-first Psalm, the comforting promise that "He that dwelleth in the secret place of the most High shall abide under the shadow of the Almighty." Sadly, the chaplain affectionately known to the men as "Chappy" read only about a third of that lovely Psalm of David. Standing on the periphery, I kept wishing he would tell me where that secret place of the most high was. At the time, I thought the chaplain may have assumed too much in letting everyone figure out the exact location, for these men were soon to go through a hell laced with hot lead. The men who came looking for spiritual coordinates had to settle for what seemed to me platitudes.

The chaplain then called up the name of another mighty Hebrew warrior, Joshua. Balog exhorted the men of Apache Troop, "Be strong and courageous," adding that God told Joshua, "Be not terrified." As the chaplain uttered those words, I looked at the gas mask firmly strapped to his leg. All of us had gas masks strapped to our legs then, fearing Saddam's chemical weapons at least as much as we feared the Lord God of Abraham, Isaac, Jacob, and the prophets. Gas masks were mandated for everyone going on

25

this ride. When Balog offered communion, the line of soldiers was again quite long. Grizzled sergeants opened their mouths, not to bellow this time but to have the communion wafers placed on their tongues, confirming yet another adage about there being no such things as atheists in fox holes.

When communion was over, I saw a shy, perhaps embarrassed, soldier sidle up to the chaplain and in a hushed whisper ask if perhaps he had a spare Bible. Balog turned to an assistant, asking him to fetch two boxes of scriptures that had been set aside. Faster than one could dive into a foxhole because of incoming, two cartons of Bibles were emptied by the soldiers. One soldier caught me chuckling. Turning to me, he grinned and said, "You have to be right with yourself."

The betting on when we would be off to the battlefield was never a contest. Berhane was omniscient. I know he worked for the squadron commander, but I always had the feeling that everyone else in the unit worked for Berhane. He knew everything, and when he said we would be on our way to the line of departure, I knew it was time to roll up my bivy tent and restuff the backpack. I should have known better than to bet him five dollars, me wagering Saddam would use chemical or biological weapons against Coalition forces. Berhane was never wrong.

What seemed a full moon was rising over the Kuwaiti desert even before the last light of day was extinguished. I looked at that moon for the longest time as soldiers scrambled to strike their tents, strap their gear to their tanks and other vehicles, and load the last ammunition and fuel. In retrospect, it seems foolish, but I recall wondering if that was the last full moon Saddam would ever see. Would he be sticking his head out of his bunker wherever he was to glimpse it? The United States had allowed Osama bin Laden to get away the previous year in Afghanistan, and I recall saying that "surely they wouldn't let this second one get away." I even read a boast by some high U.S. military official that Saddam was a good as dead. Those American boasts now seem so arrogant, considering the vast deserts of Iraq. Still, there I stood, also believing Saddam would not survive the American onslaught. We all thought so, I suspect. Glancing at the moon a last moment, the thought also went through my mind, "You know, Walt, this could also be the last full moon you ever see." It was a beautiful opalescent moon, and while at times the thought aggressively presented itself I might get killed, I never really believed it.

Moments later, I noticed a large number of soldiers had gathered around Captain Lyle's tank about forty yards away.

"Listen up! This is it," the captain said to the men.

I had Charlie shooting the remarks, which sadly never made air because there was a news blackout, and they would be dated by the time we could file again. Jeff was scrambling to pack the transmission cables and the satellite dish aboard Old Betsy. Paul was eavesdropping on the captain's locker-room talk, the Aussie ever judging the Americans who never seemed to measure up to his Australian standards.

"He's just fired six tactical ballistic missiles at our army," Captain Lyle said. "So it's him versus us. This is a dictator, a tyrant who gasses his own people and oppresses them. We are ready to liberate the people of Iraq."

I kept my mouth shut, but having worked the Muslim world for years, I felt my first twinges of skepticism. "Liberate them from what? To be what?" I asked myself. The Arabian desert had proved infertile soil for Western ideals from Christianity to democracy. The sands of Islam had centuries earlier swallowed up whatever outposts of Christianity had taken root there after the first millennium. I had heard the same talk about the need to nurture democracy in Russia a dozen years earlier after the collapse of the Bolshevik tyranny there. Perhaps it was years of accumulated reportorial cynicism, but I had come to the view that democracy was traditionally and historically the province of the English-speaking peoples. It was scarcely half a century since it had taken root in Germany, Spain, Greece, Italy, or Japan, and expecting the Iraqi desert to bloom with democratic values in time for President Bush's reelection bid strained credulity. A pillar of democratic societies is the separation of church and state, an idea that is stillborn in Muslim countries like Iraq. Besides, had not Russia proven resistant to Bill Clinton's and later Bush's democratic assumptions? Russians are still parading on the streets of Moscow with posters and pictures of Stalin. Iraq was Muslim, Islamic, authoritarian, and bloody. Even before we crossed the line of departure, it seemed to me America had about as much chance of democratizing Iraqi Arabs as Henry the Fifth had at anglicizing France after Agincourt.

"That's a conscription force up there," Captain Lyle continued, the implication being the Iraqi soldiers would surrender en masse or welcome the liberating American army or at least not stand and fight. "We are the greatest army this earth has ever seen. All they want is to see an American tank to surrender to. It's payback time. We are going to liberate those people and remove that tyrant."

I wanted to believe him. His men did.

2

Crossing the Line

And let slip the dogs of war.
—Antony in Shakespeare's *Julius Caesar*

I was sitting in the Humvee on the first night of the war, 19 March, thinking of Alexander the Great, 331 B.C. Mesopotamia then, Iraq today, another invasion, the same real estate. Alexander never bothered to coin media-grabbing names like Operation Iraqi Freedom, which more than a few people found a bit pompous. Alexander wanted the wealth of the Persian Empire, and he wanted his enemy Darius dead. The great Macedonian warrior invaded from the west and north. This American and British invasion force of 2003 was coming up from the south and east. They were only the most recent invaders. And, as an impatient American, I suspected even before we crossed into Iraq that an American army would not stay very long against the great sweep of the history in that region. Patience, a willingness to stick it out for long decades, is not the nature of the American beast, but it is innate to Arabs.

All around our Hummer, main battle tanks and Bradley fighting vehicles were growling about, clawing up the desert, making a column five, perhaps ten miles long. The 7th Cavalry was forming, becoming a moving steel spear pointing toward Iraq. Somewhere, miles behind us, the U.S. Army's 3rd Infantry Division had amassed many more M1A1 Abrams and Bradleys, more 155 mm self-propelled guns, and hundreds of support vehicles. The Pentagon's military planners used a template for the coming battle quite similar to the one first designed by the great Macedonian warrior 2,334 years earlier when he laid claim to this same part of the world.

Alexander's genius was his ability to balance and use infantry, cavalry, Cretan and Macedonian archers, and Agrianian javelin throwers. Now, the weaponry had been updated, but the tactics were similar. The U.S. Army's combination of arms that evening had its intellectual roots in Alexander's strategic thought. Kiowa helicopters scouted out in front of the armored column. The cavalry—the M1A1 Abrams main battle tanks and Bradley fighting vehicles—were the shock force. That was us that night. The archers raining arrows down on the Iraqis in the coming days and nights would be the superior air power of the Coalition forces. For Alexander, the goal had been the defeat of Darius, the great Persian leader who occupied Mesopotamia. For the Americans, Darius had become Saddam Hussein.

Archaeological excavations have uncovered human settlements in Iraq dating back ten thousand years. As we ground our way through the sands on a northwesterly course toward Iraq, it occurred to me that no one could possibly have recounted all the waves of invaders who had ploughed through this sand. Off the top of my head, I could remember the Assyrians, the Medes, the Scythians, the Persians, Alexander and his Greeks, the Romans, and the Arabs. In the twentieth century, it was the British who failed in Iraq, and now it was the Americans' turn to try, although failure was the farthest thing from our minds that night. The possibility of failure should have occurred to all of us. The same stars had also winked at the arrogance of earlier invaders. Had not Alexander the Great proclaimed himself the lord of Asia? It seemed to some that hubris had also infected President George W. Bush and would increasingly plague him. Indeed, in a series of interviews granted around his second inauguration, the American president appeared to have second thoughts and said he regretted some of the language he had earlier used in the "war on terror." Among others, he said he regretted saying in the context of the war were "bring it on" and the phrase "dead or alive" in the context of the pursuit of Islamist militants and Saddam. However well these frontier Americanisms may have played in the United States, they would ultimately play poorly in much of the rest of the world especially in Europe and the Islamic world.

The day before the actual launch across the line of departure, Apache Troop had been ordered to creep closer to that line and the Iraqi border for the 7th's night launch. We spent the day on hold in the desert. It was the classic hurry-up-and-wait, an affliction shared by TV journalism and armies. Except for one volley of Iraqi missiles off in the distance, reminding me how ill-equipped I was to go to war, it was an uneventful day although not without a comic element.

Scud has become a term loosely applied to any short- or medium-range ballistic missile. More precisely, they are those ugly green rockets the Russians used to roll through Red Square, celebrating the Great October Socialist Revolution Day. The missiles gained international renown when Saddam fired them at Saudi Arabia and Israel, with varying degrees of effectiveness, during the First Gulf War in 1991. Most of the time, however, now as then, when armed with conventional warheads, Scuds are not very accurate. The Soviets originally designed them to deliver nuclear warheads, for which accuracy is not that important.

This Iraqi Scud volley wasn't even close. U.S. Patriot antiballistic missile batteries took out five Scuds with distant booms. A sixth Scud seemed to hit closer to us, judging by the sound, exploding harmlessly off in the desert several miles distant.

It was so far away it was hardly worthy of notice or news. But for reasons never clear, Capt. Clay Lyle started yelling at his soldiers to seek the comparative security of the tanks and other tracked vehicles. He was hopping mad because some soldiers were not taking the alert seriously. Then someone else, another soldier, began yelling loudly, "Gas! Gas! Gas!" the standard alert of the release of chemical and biological weapons. Another soldier was yelling, "MOPP four, MOPP four," meaning we were to don full protective suits (MOPP stands for mission oriented protective posture suit). Some vehicles began sounding horns, another battlefield warning of an unconventional weapons attack. Old Betsy's horn didn't work.

"Oh shit," was my initial reaction, not so much out of concern for my life as sheer annoyance of having to put on the chemical-weapons suit. Because we had not yet crossed the line of departure into Iraq, none of us, including many soldiers, had donned the MOPP suits, the army's designation for the protective chemical-weapons trousers and jackets.

It is estimated that in an actual chemical-weapons attack, a person has about nine seconds to get a gas mask on before dying an agonizing death. The sun was beating down on us that day, and we were perspiring wickedly such that we stood just as good a chance of dying of heat prostration as sarin nerve gas. I ran to the Humvee: three seconds. Grabbed my chemical-weapons bag, which I had shed: eight seconds. By the time I pulled the gas mask properly over my head, it was probably fifteen seconds, and I was dead. Next, I pulled the jacket out of my ruck sack. Then came the trousers. They were difficult to pull over my boots and pants. Those trousers really wanted me dead. They wouldn't slide over my boots. My watch now showed that at least thirty seconds had elapsed. Swearing vigorously, I was annoyed to see that Paul, Charlie, and Jeff were all fully dressed and surviving safely inside the Humvee while I was still wrestling with my suspenders and rubber gloves.

Once clad in our chemical-weapons suits, we just sat there although Jeff was concerned about his satellite dish, which was still in an erect position on the Humvee's roof. If we had been ordered to move out now, we would have crippled our ability to transmit later when the shooting began. So, risking life, limb, and lungs and hampered by his gas mask and MOPP suit, Jeff climbed aboard the roof of our vehicle and disassembled the satellite gear. Paul, Charlie, and I only sat there, sucking filtered air in and out of our gas masks' canisters. It was hot. I had a canteen full of water, but it was a nuisance to drink through the straw in the gas mask. So we sat there, roasting, while poor Jeff recalls "sweating like a pig," working in his chemical-protection suit on the roof of the Hummer. My only consolation was that as slow as I was in getting into my protective MOPP suit, I could see there were a dozen much younger soldiers who took even longer to get into their gear. Laughing to myself, I said, "At least they are deader than you are." When the all-clear was sounded twenty minutes later, one of those young soldiers confessed to being "damned scared." My gut feeling, however, that no chemical weapon had been fired was borne out. The launched Scuds were only marginal as news events in this war, but the chemical-weapons scare had a modicum of reporting value.

By the time we received orders later that evening to cross the LD, our threat condition had dropped to MOPP 2. The expansive Iraqi desert with dispersed troop units was a poor theater for use of chemical or biological weapons, so Lt. Col. Terry Ferrell decided to stand down to a lower threat level: off with the gas mask, chemical-weapons galoshes, and gloves. In that cold desert night and in many such nights to come, those insulated MOPP suit trousers and jackets were welcome.

Sitting in the back of a Humvee that night in the dark on a dusty track and plowing through drifts of sand and dust, there wasn't much compelling to think about or report. The moon had not risen, and I couldn't see very much except a greenish-black night sky. Imagining myself in a different historical context, in an earlier campaign in ancient times, lent some relevance to the physical discomfort we were beginning to suffer. There would be no sleep that night, and unless one is at the head of an armored column leading the charge, going to war is pretty banal at that point. War is about dust and noise and confusion as much as anything else. Our Humvee was simply another link in a long train of vehicles, a cog. If we had fallen by the wayside, another vehicle would have moved up and filled the gap.

Earlier, we had negotiated a scheme with the army by which we would actually be extracted from the armored column and taken ahead to get TV video of the 7th Cavalry breaching the berm, the great bulldozed sand wall that formed the border between Kuwait and Iraq. Television feeds on pictures, and what better picture could we get than American tanks pouring through the breach into Iraq? It was, in retrospect, a foolish plan. If we had stopped long enough to transmit whatever video we shot in the dark, we would have been left far behind. If we waited until we first stopped, seventy hours into the campaign, to feed that video of tanks crossing into Iraq, it would have been more dated than a carton of last summer's milk.

So, our dilemma remained. Television news is extremely competitive. The pressure to be first is sometimes excruciating. It became apparent that despite a promise of help in getting launch-of-the-war pictures, the army had a different set of priorities that night, one that did not include posing for a class photo along the Iraqi border. And it was absurd even then to think we could somehow jump to the head of the armored column marching off to war without getting shot, run over by a tank, or, worse, left behind. We recognized the folly of the idea before we ever tried to execute it, and CNN was better served for it. If we had dropped out for those pictures, we never could have rejoined Apache Troop, and although they promised us we would be able to catch up later, we knew if we got those pictures, we would miss the war.

We were farther away from the Iraqi border than I had previously imagined, and our column stopped for several hours in the middle of nowhere before we ever left Kuwait. Feeling totally isolated in a dark desert, I began to fret about just being along for the ride while other embedded correspondents would have been filing action video of storming the breach into Iraq. Yet, I had nothing to report.

Getting out of the Humvee, we stood in the not unpleasantly cold desert night. Word was passed down the line that the delay was a consequence of the army's engineers clearing a passage through the sand berm and having encountered some annoying Iraqi resistance. Among other things we heard passed down the line was that there were some Iraqi trucks that had to be cleared away, and there was still a military engagement under way. But because of the rules laid out by the Pentagon, we were forbidden to report any of it. Still with little happening where we were, I deemed it prudent to check in by satellite phone with headquarters in Atlanta just to inquire what was happening elsewhere. I discovered Atlanta was under competitive pressure to get some pictures on the air during this opening phase of the war. Unbeknownst to those of us bored and shivering in the increasingly frigid desert night, ABC News and Fox were miles behind where we were and had been broadcasting video of some rear-echelon army artillery units firing over the border into Iraq. I suspect it was quite a sound-and-light show. To stay competitive, I was asked by the news desk to "File something, file anything" to put our coverage on the map. I tried to explain that not only had we not left Kuwait yet, we were standing stock-still, and except for the low-growling engines, it was quiet as the grave on our front. I hadn't heard a shot fired, and frankly, at that point, I did not know if there was a war going on or not. Still television news, like war itself, becomes a messy process at times.

I was again urged, "Give us something, give us anything."

"Where is old Martin Savidge and the Marine unit he's assigned to?" I asked.

"He is under radio silence and can't even call in," I was told. "You're all we have."

At that point, that was more responsibility than I wanted. It was my impression we had an army of embeds of our own in theater, and in truth, I had next to nothing to report on what was, at the moment from my vantage point, phony war.

"Who is beating us?" I asked our news desk.

"Fox and ABC," I was told.

Having grown up at ABC News, I asked down the satellite line, "What's ABC got?"

"Ted Koppel's got pictures of bang-bang," a television euphemism for guns of any sort firing. "Koppel's got artillery firing, big 155 mm guns. It's all over ABC."

I paused for a few seconds after suddenly recalling that some officer had made me a similar offer earlier in the day, and I'd turned it down. The army had proposed that if we wanted pictures of those same big guns firing in the rear, we would have to dis-embed and fall back fifteen miles or so. I reasoned this would have netted a minute of repetitive video of 155 mm Paladin self-propelled guns banging away, signaling the start of the American ground offensive. Worse, however, going back would have been the beginning and the end of my war, and I was determined not to be left out. I was convinced we would never find our unit if we detached, and we would have been stuck with the slower-moving 3rd Infantry, which was awash with other correspondents. By now, I felt certain that we were in the right place at the right time, and there was no way short of getting shot that we were going to pull out or dis-embed.

At best, this artillery barrage was akin to covering a scheduled news event such as a press conference back in Washington, and at worst, it smacked of staging. Of course, Atlanta and millions of television viewers could not have known that at the time.

Still, at the time, I had to make a command decision, which in retrospect now seems so obviously correct, but at the time, it was perhaps a risky judgment call. The problem was that if we fell back into the night, the artillery shelling might have concluded, and we could well have gotten lost in the desert. So, we decided we were going to stay with the 7th Cavalry until the war was over, or our wheels fell off. It was Baghdad or bust for Charlie, Paul, Jeff, and me.

Yet, there remained the problem of giving CNN something from our front to put down a network footprint. We couldn't turn on any lights for a live broadcast of our armored column when we were trying to sneak up on the Iraqis. The moon was not in evidence so there was no natural light available, and anything we tried to transmit would come out a dark-green, amorphous blob by the time it was downlinked from the satellite to Atlanta.

Charlie had a small PD150, nicknamed a "weenie camera," which he set up for a broadcast to demonstrate our predicament, and I was more than a little surprised that a show producer decided to put us on the air at that moment. I began my live transmission with what I recollect to have been a necklace of banalities strung together. We could not reveal where we were or why we had stopped or even the minor skirmish that had earlier transpired ahead of us at the border. I was, as they say, sucking air until the Iraqis came to my rescue midway through my live transmission. They fired a ballistic missile that WHOOOOOOOOOSHED right over our heads and exploded harmlessly but with a helluva loud boom in the desert off to my right. Captain Lyle declared it a Scud although the Iraqis also had numerous other Soviet-vintage ballistic missiles of relative short range that were quite legal under the post–Gulf War restrictions. In retrospect, many U.S. officials believe the first Bush administration erred in allowing Saddam any ballistic missiles, especially when the U.S. was poised for another invasion.

Despite all the training, it never occurred to me at the time that the rocket might have had an unconventional warhead with nerve gas. All I knew was that it missed the cavalry's column and landed harmlessly off in the dark. I don't recall a flash of light that might have accompanied a high-explosive warhead, but thankfully, there was a loud boom. That was reassuring because chemical and biological weapons explode with a dull thud or popping sound.

The camera never picked up video of the missile, but the microphone transmitted the sound through the videophone beautifully, including my startled "What the hell was that?" broadcast around the world. "I think we'd better get out of here," I said on air, abruptly concluding my first live shot of the war. That was also Captain Lyle's reaction. He ordered Apache Troop to "move out," and we scurried back into our Hummer as the column began to roll onward again. The Iraqis knew where we were and had almost found our range. We had come under fire, and Atlanta's perception of our enterprise changed rapidly, and the change now seemed no less dramatic than St. Paul's conversion, only this time on the road to Baghdad. I was professionally redeemed.

Our network now had a startled correspondent of its own who had been seriously shot at. The entire episode had been transmitted and recorded on a piece of very grainy, green video and broadcast round the world. Some Iraqi missile man with terrible aim probably should have received a cash award for his dramatic special effects of his rocket launch in our direction.

Apache Troop's convoy now began moving more quickly. If our pulses did not quicken, we were at least a heck of a sight more alert, having had a ballistic missile fired at us. After that event, however, crossing the berm became a nonevent. A big hole was bulldozed through the sand wall just as a snowplow would slice through a snowdrift. Because we were in a wheeled vehicle, our passage required somewhat more effort than the tracked vehicles, tanks, Bradleys, mortar carriages, and the self-propelled guns. In the serpentine-stone darkness, the only evidence we'd crossed into Iraq was deeper sand and some dark and abandoned United Nations' outposts whose occupants had decided discretion and flight were the better part of duty.

We traveled without headlights. Even use of normal flashlights was strictly forbidden. We all carried the mini-Maglites with dark-red light filters to reduce visibility to snipers. Soldiers I knew, like Maj. Mike Birmingham, wouldn't even use the light-filtered flashlights without additional protection. They didn't feel totally secure from snipers until they pulled ponchos over their heads to read maps at night. In this environment, that seemed excessive. Any Iraqi with an ounce of brains wasn't going to take on an armored column with an AK-47, which is not a sniper's rifle anyway. We never saw good snipers' rifles like the Soviet Draganov until we got into the Sunni triangle after the declared end of the conflict. Later in the war and closer to Baghdad, some Iraqi soldiers did undertake stupid and suicidal attacks, and the soldiers I was with were more than happy to hasten their ascendancy to an Islamic paradise.

It was always a given that the initial strike into Iraq would come after dark, because it was assumed the American army with its superior technology, infrared scopes, and night-vision goggles would, as the military jargon went, "own the night." Officers boasted that American tanks operating at night would roll over the Iraqis before they even saw what hit them. There had been last-minute news stories just before the war that the Syrians had smuggled night-vision equipment to the Iraqis, but our experience was that the Iraqis generally had a hard time hitting anything by day or night. In our vehicle, only Paul, our driver, had night-vision goggles. They retailed for about twenty-five hundred dollars a pair, so the rest of us just rode blindly into the night, oblivious of threats, as later events would confirm. The plastic windows on the side door of the used Hummer were scarred and clouded, so in the back seat, Jeff and I were really blind.

Our first few miles into Iraq we got lost. It was no big deal, but as one of the officers attached to our unit later recalled, we went off paralleling some pipeline instead of taking the correct road. In our vehicle, we didn't know anything was wrong until the lead elements of the 7th Cavalry's column passed us going back in the other direction. The screw-up was camouflaged under the cover of darkness.

Five or six hours nonstop in the back of the Hummer cruising at only twenty to thirty miles an hour are excruciatingly painful. Because Paul had sandbagged the floor in case we ran over land mines or unexploded ordnance, my knees were propped under my chin. Jeff was in the other side of the back of the Hummer, so cramped that he lost all sensation in three toes of his left foot. It took him six months before he recovered feeling. The distance between the soles of my boots and my rear was fewer than six inches. I knew exactly how the Soviet cosmonaut Yuri Gagarin must have felt in 1961 when the Russians shot him off in a cramped, spherical space capsule, in a fetal position, with no legroom. Gagarin, the first man in space, had to be one of the bravest men in history. I lay claim only to being the most cramped and uncomfortable to the point of being in considerable physical pain that night.

Dawn is more welcoming in war zones than anywhere else on the planet. You know you've survived the night. I recall waiting one night for a sunrise in Afghanistan with the Soviets. Some of the Afghan tribesmen allied to the Soviets were wrapped in coarse, woolen blankets, sleeping around the dying embers of a wood fire. I had shivered then in the biting desert cold and shivered again most of that first night of the Second Gulf War.

Off to the east, my side of the Hummer, dawn also brought the appearance of what we were told at the time was one of those Iraqi reconnaissance patrols, about which we had been warned. We heard some shooting, and I figured it had to be an act of suicidal bravado on the part of the Iraqis. We were told there were a couple of white pickup trucks with machine guns mounted behind spotted in the direction of where the sun was rising. All of this took place over the horizon. We did not see it. A couple of main battle tanks peeled out of the column and hightailed it across the desert. In Kuwait, on maneuvers in December, I had been driving a four-by-four across open desert, racing beside these M1A1 tanks and had clocked them at fifty-five miles an hour. Soldiers boast they do at least seventy miles an hour.

When the U.S. tanks tracked down the Iraqi pickup trucks, the battle we had all anticipated simply did not happen. Not long afterwards and after firing a couple of rounds, the U.S. tanks returned to the advancing column that had not stopped for the engagement. It wasn't until months after the war that I was told the only thing that was "killed" that morning was a couple of dead pickup trucks rusting since the First Gulf War, twelve years earlier.

In less than ten hours, the 7th Cavalry had, we believed at the time, been fired at by a battery of Iraqi ballistic missiles, targeted by another lone Scud, and bested and obliterated an Iraqi reconnaissance patrol. Now we were rolling faster and faster on a northwesterly course through Iraq's Muthanna province. It was perfect tank country: an ancient seabed now a sparse prairie with tufts of tender grass nourished by winter rains. The landscape was so flat that I concluded we could now safely commence broadcasting on the move. Charlie and Jeff set up the videophone and handed me a microphone. Charlie plugged in a camera and pointed it out the window. Jeff turned on a handset telephone and told it what satellite to find, what carrier to use, Stratos, British Telecom, Comsat, Telinor, or whatever, after which the capsat dish, the bubble on the roof of the Hummer, searched and locked on. A little dish inside that bubble had motors that locked on the satellite, and as far as I knew, we simply telephoned Atlanta and told them we could broadcast if they wanted. Nothing about us in the landscape would betray our location other than that we were in the middle of South Nowhere, Iraq. A more technically sophisticated enemy than the Iraqis could have locked in on our radiation and targeted us with a homing missile.

It was a splendid picture we transmitted, an open desert in spring, nothing as far as the eye could see in any direction but an armada of tanks and Bradleys. We were riding like surfers on an intimidating wave of steel, rolling along and swelling, moving ever forward in the direction of Al Samawah on the Euphrates River somewhere well over the horizon. It was exciting. We sensed we were making television history covering war in real time. We were embedded in an invasion force that was prepared to shoot and kill anything that got in its way. I felt it in my gut and said so in my broadcast as we spread across the desert. I was riding on a cavalry charge, and it was a hoot, a total hoot. Dozens of times since that broadcast, active-duty soldiers, old soldiers and old men have approached me all over the United States and whispered, "I really envied you. God, what I would have given to have been there." They meant it, too.

Several vehicles ahead of us, atop the troop commander's M1A1 Abrams main battle tank, Captain Lyle was trying to get a fix on something with his binoculars. There was something out there, squat on the horizon. "Hot damn!" Captain Lyle said. He thought he had an Iraqi Scud missile launcher in his glasses. What a kill this was going to make. Regrettably, while the U.S. military spends vast sums on night-vision goggles, the diurnal binoculars they give their soldiers are generally far inferior even to what Soviet tank commanders were issued. I still have a pair of Russian 12 x 40 *binokuls* I bought when I was based in Moscow, and they were pretty good—far-reaching to peer at a hostile NATO target. On Operation Iraqi Freedom, however, even my 10 x 40 Swift Plovers were superior to what Captain Lyle was using to fight a war and find that suspected Iraqi missile launcher. I wished Captain Lyle had my bird-watching binoculars in his turret at that moment. He was about to turn his 120 mm laser-guided tank cannon on that Iraqi target and claim a prize kill.

I am never quite sure how close he got to blowing away the "Scud launcher" before he discovered it was only an Iraqi Bedouin's tent. Out across the horizon, to someone who never had been in this desert, it may well have appeared to be a Scud launcher. But to any journalist worth his salt in the Middle East, there could be no question this was a nomad's tent. Inside would have been the women. Under Islamic strictures, they would naturally have remained hidden and especially with a foreign army approaching.

About the tent outside were huddled herds of sheep and goats, eager to begin feeding on the fresh grass. Yet, like the Bedouins, the animals were too intimidated by the steel monsters bearing down on them to seek out spring pastures.

Actually, Captain Lyle's instincts were only somewhat in error. U.S. intelligence sources generally believed the Bedouins of Iraq and Kuwait were prime sources of information for Saddam. Although known for their desert hospitality, Bedouins are also xenophobic. Their kinship with fellow Arab Muslims was much stronger than with any American dream of sowing democracy in the barren deserts of Iraq. As for freedom, it doesn't get much freer than a nomad of the desert, at least if you are an Arab man.

Just before the war, U.S. diplomats in Kuwait told me the Bedouins in that country were clearly wary of the American presence. Perhaps, I thought, they just didn't like sixty-nine-ton tanks tearing up their grazing lands. Either way, the Bedouin tribesmen stared inscrutably at the armored vehicles reaching out far across the horizon, probably grateful we wouldn't be stopping for tea. As the day moved on, we would come across dozens of these Bedouin encampments below the Euphrates in southern Iraq, usually just a twenty- to thirty-yard-long, single, horizontal tent made out of brownish-black wool, staked down and anchored against the persistent desert winds.

We had expended considerable fuel and were due for a ROM, refueling on the move. At the rate we were traveling, we would soon outrun our re- fueling trucks, which were big, lumbering, five-thousand-gallon tankers. The armored column would have to stop. When they do, they are most vulnerable to enemy attack. Fortunately, at that moment, there were no Ira- qis about to threaten the refueling armored column.

One of the more clever aspects of the modern army is the uniformity of fuel usage. The tanks with their diesel engines, the helicopters, the Humvees, the Bradleys, every vehicle burns the same fuel, JP8. I guess it's no big deal for the average soldier, but I thought it fascinating. Another innovation, which was really slick, was the refueling process itself. A high-powered hose blasts fuel into the tank in a matter of seconds. Our Humvee tank could fill in ten seconds. Tanks, with their five-hundred-gallon fuel tanks, took maybe two minutes. It was an extraordinarily well-engineered system to juice up the vehicles and send them on their way. Regrettably, it was so fast there was little time to stretch one's legs or catch a nap on the ground, which is where some of us were destined to sleep for the next couple of weeks.

There were no further encounters with Iraqis that day, and we became increasingly numbed by the journey and ubiquitous fatigue. By sunset, Paul had been behind the wheel for close to twenty-four hours. Except for be- ing spelled by Jeff for four hours to get a nap, Paul still faced another thirty- two hours of driving. The agony of being cramped up continued. It was painful. Finally, more out of desperation than inspiration, I said to hell with it and opened the back door of the Humvee and kicked my legs out to stretch them, imitating a flutter-kicking motion as we rolled along through the desert, night, day, and now night again. I discovered if I kept my heels a few inches above the sand, I could actually get some circulation moving through my body. Occasionally, a hummock of sand caught my heels, which was jarring but not nearly as painful as the constriction and lack of circulation in my legs. It was days later when I heard that David Bloom, six inches taller than Jeff or I, had died trying to endure these same conditions. Riding with the back door of the Humvee open and kicking my legs like a backstroker may have saved me Bloom's fate.

By nightfall, the sun had disappeared behind an ominous cloudbank. Soon, rain began to fall as we followed the tracked vehicle in front of us. Part of the time we were rolling across a hardtop road built years earlier. Much of the night, however, we were driving up a rock-strewn *wadi*, a dry riverbed, which the U.S. soldiers preferred to call "a moonscape." Under the overcast sky, it was indeed gray pumice, littered with boulders. The rain brought yet another misery, mud. I am not sure what I thought would happen, but the proper mixture of rain with dust the consistency of pumice results in a glue ten inches thick and coating the world. Tread vehicles like tanks and bulldozers clawed their way through it. Humvees groaned and strained. And human beings as often as not slipped and fell into it.

Mud is a bosom companion of most military campaigns. In Sarajevo in the Bosnian Muslim lines, we slogged through trenches a foot deep in mud and snow. Splashing noisily was particularly awful because the Serb trenches were so close to the Bosnian Muslims. The Serbs would simply lob hand grenades across a thirty-yard stretch between the lines. For soldiers, working in mud goes with the job, but trying to get sensitive electronic TV gear to work in those conditions was a totally new challenge created by the embedding process.

When the network's secondhand Humvees were reconfigured to have huge blocks of electronic equipment rammed into them, no one ever checked ours to see if it was waterproof. Where once a machine-gun turret was mounted on the roof and then removed, CNN engineers mounted a plastic dome to shield rotating gears to position the satellite. The gears stayed dry, but the seals of the old turret were never checked for waterproofing. A desert cloudburst poured into the Hummer, and Jeff desperately scrounged for plastic trash bags to protect the electronics console and the videophone.

In a selfish way, I found the rain inside the Humvee welcome. A leaking Jerry can (a spare gas can) filled with JP8 fuel on our roof rack had been sloshing huge waves of highly flammable fuel down the roof and in through my window. I had become a human Molotov cocktail, and the rain served to dilute and thus lower my degree of flammability.

One of the questions most frequently asked after the war was, "Don't you think the embeds got too personally close to the army?" In the first seventy hours of the war, the soldiers were too busy to know we were even there, and they were totally unaware that from the inside of our Hummer, we had been broadcasting their daylight assault on Iraq the entire day. When we told the soldiers what we were doing, they were dumbfounded and scratched their heads. And they asked, "Why didn't you tell us?" Even the officers in the unit had no idea we were on the air. It was too early in the campaign to get feedback from the generals in Kuwait or from the Pentagon although both were watching.

The first two days the 7th Cavalry moved like a ghost troop through southern Iraq. Apache Company was scouting its way through largely uninhabited and uncharted barren land. In Baghdad, the Information Minister, Mohammed Saeed al-Sahaf, was denying the U.S. had ever crossed into Iraq from Kuwait. Several days later, I was asked on camera by an anchorperson in Atlanta about al-Sahaf's denial. Clearly irritated by my earlier physical discomfort, I curtly dismissed the anchor's question, saying, "I'll stake my credibility against the information minister's any day of the week." The Iraqis became irate, but hourly, we were moving close to Baghdad.

In the combat units of the Cavalry, there are no women except for those flying the Kiowa helicopters. It's difficult to explain why without sounding sexist. It's not so much a matter of space. The navy straps men and women in the cramped cockpits of two-seat F-14 fighters. But without putting too fine a point on it, try baring your buns, squatting down to urinate or defecate in the desert with eight hundred men watching. I used to think that if I just held my bowels until nightfall, I would gain a modicum of privacy to squat. Then I realized most of the soldiers have night-vision goggles, turning the night into day. Squatting with a large audience is an acquired talent, and each of the vehicles, including ours, carried a shovel for burying our scat. The army does not stop for those who have to relieve themselves, women or men.

Some of the soldiers were inventive when it came to the toilet. We could see a plastic chair strapped to tanks with a potty hole sawed into it. Other soldiers used the heavy, MRE (meals ready to eat) boxes with potty holes cut into them. Jeff later observed, "I don't think anyone in Atlanta ever had any idea what it's like to shit in a hole in the desert for five weeks." It was, however, just what we did, like feral cats.

That same night, my colleague Anderson Cooper, a CNN anchor in Atlanta, and I did a running narrative of the 7th Cavalry's progress. Knowing how long we had been rolling without sleep, he asked, "When do the troops, when do the members of the 7th Cavalry sleep? I mean, this has been going on all night long and many hours before the evening began?" It's gratifying when one's colleagues in business suits in New York or Atlanta understand what correspondents in the field endure.

My answer to him was, "You don't sleep. You really don't sleep out here. Of course, you're on an adrenaline high, you know that you're traveling toward the jaws of what could be a major military battle as the 7th Cavalry and the 3rd Infantry Division move toward Baghdad." The only nap I saw any of the solders get was during the refueling as other tanks lined up ahead of them. They would simply close their eyes and fall asleep, the preferred sleeping quarter being the after-carriage of the tank, back of the turret, on the engine itself, which gave them some warmth. Having no tank, I found an inviting sand dune and flopped down. My MOPP suit and body armor kept me warm, and in seconds, I was unconscious for about five minutes, that is, until Paul awakened me with "We're moving again."

Our pace slowed to twenty or twenty-five miles an hour when we hit soft sand. When we found a hardtop road, the tanks picked up the pace, moving at thirty to forty miles an hour. The worst part of that desert push was the moonscape, the *wadis*. Treaded vehicles had no difficulty grinding their way through, but the boulders bouncing beneath our Humvee felt like they would knock the bottom off. The 7th's main battle tanks would climb up steep grades to ridges and pause at the apex, checking the other side for Iraqis before rocking forward and grinding onward.

The going to this point had been a cakewalk. No one believed it would last. In addition to Saddam's purported chemical weapons, the other wild card in the deck was the possibility the regime in Baghdad would simply implode. Assassination? Flight into exile? A Republican Guard revolt? If any of those occurred, the American generals' entire battle plan, the maps, the grids, the arrows crossing and crisscrossing, all would be tossed out like the ubiquitous plastic trash bags that blow about the deserts of Arabia. Under those circumstances, the 7th Cavalry's orders, according to its SCO, Colonel Ferrell, were to race to Baghdad as quickly as we could get there, taking advantage of the confusion and shock to secure the Iraqi capital.

Meanwhile, most of us were riding blind, simply following the vehicle in front of us, following the lines of the arrows on grid maps drawn by someone far from where we were.

All the 7th Cavalry's graph lines and arrows pointed to the city of Al Samawah on the Euphrates River. It was the Fertile Crescent, a subject of my fourth-grade geography lessons.

3

The Bridge at Al Samawah

The best laid schemes o' mice an' men
Gang aft agley.
—Robert Burns, "To a Mouse, on Turning
Her Up in Her Nest with a Plough"

The 7th Cavalry's mission at the town of Al Samawah was a quick thrust through the city and seizure of a bridgehead, followed by a dash across the Euphrates River. The Iraqis were not expected to fight or make a last stand until the U.S. forces approached Baghdad. I could see the American plans beginning to unravel on the outskirts of the city with the mother of all traffic jams. Overnight, our Humvee had become separated from the tip of the spear, the fighting elements of Apache Troop, and we found ourselves somewhere back along the shaft toward the butt. We were now following Capt. Rick Cote's Humvee, which seemed like a Mercedes Benz compared to our jalopy. Captain Cote was a reserve army civilian affairs officer who would be stuck in Baghdad long after the 7th Cavalry went home. In civilian life, he was a lieutenant in the Myrtle Beach, South Carolina, Fire Department. His charm was a certain laconic detachment. What he cared about most was the crinkled photograph of his wife and two daughters, taped to the glove compartment of his Hummer. He was not going to see them for another eighteen months.

Along the road among the stalled vehicles, it was evident how far to the rear of the column we had slipped. A clutch of four bedraggled Iraqi prisoners of war, all dressed in black, was squatting in the dirt off on the shoulder. There was a pickup truck with a 7.62 mm machine gun mounted on the back, which obviously belonged to them. Additionally, there were two white, Japanese-made pickup trucks. One had a New York Fire Department bumper sticker propped up inside the windshield. At first, it seemed the Iraqis had a sense of humor, but as we passed closer, we could see U.S. Special Forces soldiers in civilian clothes guarding them. The Iraqis had their hands bound with plastic cords. They wore black, pajama-like combat fatigues, suggesting they belonged to Saddam Hussein's Fedayeen, who were to acquire a reputation as fanatical suicide fighters.

The road, chockablock with vehicles, actually worked to our advantage. It gave Paul a chance to maneuver Old Betsy forward, between and around the fuel-tank trucks, the auxiliary tracked vehicles, and the other Humvees. We had to get back up to the front of the column. The back of the column was miles to the rear of the tanks and Bradleys, which were beginning to take fire from Iraqi forces up the road. Several days into the ground war, the officers of the 7th Cavalry were still far too busy to concern themselves with our keeping up with them. It was as if we were not there. Soldiers are not babysitters, and in their eyes, our mettle had not yet been tested under fire. It is not that the officers and soldiers were scornful so much as indifferent. First, we had to learn to keep up with the tip of the spear. And, despite constant post-war criticism that journalists were "too close" to the soldiers with whom they were embedded, my impression at this point was that the army still saw us as strays. If we could keep up, OK, and if we fell behind, we were not worthy of playing in the game.

From what we could determine as we slithered forward among the support vehicles, the advanced units in the column seemed to be taking modest fire from a residential area shaded by trees down the road, one of the entrances to Al Samawah. Suddenly, there was a huge explosion, and a dramatic column of blackish-gray smoke and fire rose into the air. We had seen the Cavalry's mechanized mortar units, taking positions in the fields on our flanks, but the hit could just as easily have come from one of the 7th's Kiowa helicopters or other armored vehicles. Someone scored a direct hit, however, and it was a direct hit on an Iraqi fuel dump in a grove of trees ahead, and it blew thousands of gallons of fuel sky high. We struggled to get the videophone to transmit live pictures, but there was a problem with the transmission, and extraordinary live coverage was denied.

Paul had by now maneuvered us much closer to the shooting and had drawn up pretty close to Captain Lyle's M1A1 Abrams tank again. The army was beginning to realize it had more than token resistance ahead. It had been laboring under the hope that in southern Iraq, it would be facing disgruntled, regular army units, Shiite Muslims who hated Saddam. There was even an expectation they would surrender en masse, and all the officers in the 7th Cavalry had instructions on how to deal with surrendering Iraqis. Saddam also considered the probability that his troops in the south upon encountering invading Americans might surrender. The U.S. Army's intelligence units were now discovering that to prevent defections, the Iraqi leader had sent about a thousand members of his ruling Ba'ath Party south along with his crack Republican Guard and Fedayeen officers to put steel into the spines of his conscript army troops. *Fedayeen* loosely translates from the Arabic as "faithful unto death." They were fanatic fighters and would be savage in their guerrilla attacks on U.S. forces in the months after the war ended.

U.S. Air Force enlisted men were attached to the 7th Cavalry to coordinate close air support with bombing and strafing. One of these forward air observers approached our camera position and said, "Hey, we're calling in an F-16 air strike on that Iraqi emplacement up ahead in that grove of trees. Perhaps you want to keep that camera rolling. You'll get some good pictures." I told Charlie, who was shooting something else, what I had been told. If an air strike was about to take place, we wanted pictures to broadcast.

We waited as the Iraqis put up sporadic resistance, shooting in the general direction of the groups of armored vehicles, with no effect. Behind us, a Black Hawk helicopter landed in a cloud of dust in the general position of where we had passed those Iraqi prisoners of war. Word was passed along the line that the Medivac helicopter had been called up to remove a badly wounded Iraqi, shot when the special forces captured three others. A day later, one of the officers in the unit reported the badly shot-up Iraqi didn't make it. It was pointed out to me the effort the army went to save that Iraqi POW's life. It was hearsay that I could not independently confirm. It would have been nice if it was true, but later in the war, I concluded medical assistance to wounded Iraqis became more a function of how busy soldiers were than of any altruism. Soldiers under fire are usually too busy staying alive to concern themselves too much with dying enemies.

Twenty minutes later, I found Lt. Col. Terry Ferrell and asked him whatever came of the air strike that had been called in.

"Oh, we had to scrub that," he replied. "The forward intelligence observers saw the Iraqis moving women, children, and old men into their positions as human shields."

Intel also had reports that some of the men in Al Samawah had been taken from their homes by the Iraqi army, given guns, and told to fight while their families were collected as human shields. Like the colonel and other officers of the 7th Cavalry, we were dependent on the unseen observers who had gone forward to determine why Al Samawah was not the walkover we anticipated.

I heard on my short-wave radio that other Coalition units were also encountering stiff resistance: the British in the east over toward Basra and the marines on our southeastern flank at Al Nasiriyah. The hot knife that was supposed to slice through warm butter had encountered increasing resistance. The Iraqis had thrown up a defense line along the Euphrates River. BBC short-wave–radio newscasts made it sound like a rout of Coalition forces. On more than a few occasions, I heard U.S. soldiers complain that BBC radio broadcasts sounded as if the BBC was openly cheering for the defeat of the Americans. We had only just arrived in Al Samawah. We couldn't even report where we were. But with great gravitas and authority, BBC was reporting the Americans thwarted. Scant mention was ever made of frustrated British units. The BBC is nothing if not patriotic.

The slowing of the Coalition's advance may have been a reality on other fronts. In our case, however, it was yet too soon to draw that conclusion. However, there was a twenty-four-hour reassessment of the situation by the officers of the 7th Cavalry to consider whether to charge through the town and seize the planned bridge for a crossing of the Euphrates or to seek an alternate crossing.

The officers had drawn their vehicles into a tight formation on the west side of the road. It was now apparent that the Iraqis had marshaled a force that was determined to put up a fight in an urban area. That meant, potentially, major civilian casualties, and as the campaign subsequently unfolded, I noticed a disinclination on the part of Colonel Ferrell to fight in or even pass through Iraqi cities and towns. Not yet having learned of the colonel's reluctance, however, I had begun to worry if we were going to be ordered to launch a cavalry charge into Samawah, with snipers pouring down fire on us from the roofs of buildings. If that occurred, Charlie, Jeff, Paul, and I would be dead meat in an unarmored Humvee.

It would have been bloody, shooting our way through the city to the bridge to get across, especially when the size and resistance of the opposition were greater than intelligence had originally calculated. It was a ride I was not keen to take although embeds like myself had no veto. Still, cavalry units lacked dismounts, infantry soldiers who are necessary to clear buildings, so the chiefs went back to their maps to consider options. Not much earlier Captain Lyle had warned his men, "These are Goddamned ruthless people, and I don't want anyone left behind. At this point, we are all sticking close to each other." Too close, as it turned out.

Kiowa helicopters were called in to try to take out the Ba'ath Party officials and their headquarters where the Americans believed the Republican Guard and Fedayeen were directing the resistance. These quick, wasp-like choppers had been flitting in the skies about us ever since we had paused about midday. At speeds of close to a hundred miles an hour, they flew little more than thirty or forty feet above the ground because it makes it much harder for the Iraqis to shoot them down. On one of these runs, one Kiowa let fly with a Hellfire missile, which roared across the landscape, finding a target. Whether anyone was in the building in downtown Al Samawah I do not know. However, the resistance did continue even after the building had collapsed. The U.S. believed the structure served as an Iraqi intelligence headquarters, making it a legitimate military target. There was one helluva illumination of the sky when the Hellfire hit its target. The Iraqi forces, however, continued to be laid out in a broad front on the south side of Al Samawah, and our forward progress would stall for about twenty-four hours as the commanders considered alternate routes. We were not as far north at this point as the SCO, Colonel Ferrell, had believed we would be. It was a tactical hiccough, strategically meaningless but frustrating to soldiers who were in a hurry to get to Baghdad.

During this period, all of us badly needed rest, and the warm March sun was therapeutic. The soldiers let down the rear ramps of their Bradleys, climbed out of their tanks, and stood down. They broke out their MREs, and they ate. I stripped to my gray athletic t-shirt. Soldiers who had been wearing protective chemical-weapons garb now stripped to their khaki t-shirts and sprawled on the ground. It was fortunate that scorpions tend to be nocturnal. Colonel Ferrell stood down a little as well. His officers and he chatted about their progress so far and what to do next. We set up for a live interview with the colonel on CNN, which was unique in throwing a battlefield commander on live television in the middle of an engagement.

The original estimates of only 150 to 200 resistance fighters were now upgraded to 400 to 500, many of them hard-core Fedayeen. All along the towns of the Euphrates River, the Iraqis were putting up a fight. The U.S. Marines were encountering tough going in Al Nasiriyah. They were seriously stalled and would be so for days. Our situation was less serious, but still, a decision had to be made. Would we charge down the road to where the fire was coming from, or would we search for another Euphrates River crossing? In the meantime, it was decided to stand down and give the men some desperately needed rest on both sides of the road while officers considered the second-best bridge for the 7th Cavalry to seize.

There now seemed to be dozens and dozens of Bradleys and tanks assembled in the fields below the elevated, graded roadbed. I climbed the grade to get a better assessment of what was on the other side. Over there were even more vehicles from units other than the 7th Cavalry. It was a gathering of the forces, waiting to cross the river and resume the push to Baghdad.

Everyone was relaxing, some snoozing. The forward sentries were beginning to allow Iraqi pedestrians, not cars, to exit the town and hike down the road. Men only. There was a cursory screening, and, according to Captain Cote, the civilian affairs officer, none of those who left town was allowed to return. Most of the Iraqis meandered down the road in the direction from which we had come four hours earlier. They were now aliens in their own land. A few waved at us. Beyond that, there wasn't much communication with the natives. Apache Troop had only one civilian translator.

The handful of Iraqis leaving Al Samawah passed down the road while most of us slept with one eye open, savoring a few minutes of quiet, free of incarceration in our vehicles. The tranquility was short lived. Three very loud explosions slammed down just across the road from where I was lying in the dirt. I ran directly toward the explosions, dashing back up the embankment to the top of the road. It is as instinctive in TV as it is foolhardy.

Everyone from the unit who had been resting on the other side was wildly scrambling to get out of there. They piled into their armored vehicles, Humvees, and trucks and tore out. In the field, which moments earlier had been filled with soldiers and vehicles, a tight pattern of three plumes of steel-gray smoke was rising from the ground about forty yards from where I was crouching. It was a stupid thing I did, running toward falling artillery shells. A halfway professional army would have kept firing more mortar rounds, moving their sights in a second volley to our side of the road. I lay on my belly on the shoulder of the road, dialing up my Thuraya satellite phone to describe the surprise shelling the 7th had taken at Al Samawah. It appeared now that one of those Iraqis using the road a short while earlier had been an Iraqi forward artillery observer. He had called in the mortars in a perfect pattern in the middle of the unit across the road.

Later, Captain Lyle would tongue-lash his civilian affairs officer for letting those Iraqis pass through the U.S. lines. Captain Cote defended himself saying no Iraqi who passed through earlier was allowed to return. It seemed a pretty lame defense, and Captain Lyle was livid.

Getting through to Atlanta on the first try, I demanded to be put on the air straightaway. Atlanta producers took me immediately. Traditionally, CNN has been at its best in war coverage. I began reporting the hasty scramble of all those units to get the hell out of there. The scene was amazing. In a matter of less than thirty seconds after the mortars fell, the units on both sides of the road were all gone. Paul, Charlie, Jeff, and I were left behind. I had a broadcast, and it took precedence over retreat and regroup. I later learned that a sergeant in the other unit across the road where the mortars fell was wounded and later Medivaced out after his unit withdrew to the rear. I also noticed that for some reason, a lone soldier on foot had been left behind, and a fourth mortar fell near him. Short of some track star, I don't believe I ever saw a grown man run so fast. You laugh at the stupidest thing in wars. That poor, terrified bastard was running like hell through a fairly tall wheat field with his M-16 over his head, leaving behind another one of those gray plumes of smoke that marked where yet another mortar had just hit. And I stood there laughing uproariously as the fleeing soldier got away. Most everyone else escaped or fled as well, and when I looked about, Paul, Charlie, Jeff, Old Betsy, and I were the only things standing between the regrouping 7th Cavalry and the Iraqi forces ahead of us in Al Samawah. We had been left behind again. If for some reason the Iraqis counterattacked, we would be very much alone in that field. We joined the retreat. It was ignominious and comical in retrospect. But most of these soldiers had never been in combat before. It was an irony of that war that everyone in our CNN crew had been shot at on more than a few occasions before this war. Getting shot at was what we did for a living. Jeff had been in Somalia. Charlie and I had done Afghanistan together. We both had plenty of combat ribbons. Charlie had also been a captain in the British army. I had been shot at in Lebanon, the old Soviet Union, the Balkans, and the West Bank. Paul got his first whiff of grapeshot with the Australian SAS in Rwanda in 1995 and like most SAS types was not allowed to tell anyone about what he really did in the war, Rwanda or anywhere else. If I had to go into battle anywhere, however, I would want Paul on my hip.

As I have said, some critics thought embeds were too close to the army; I can tell you that at that moment, I wished we had been. We were abandoned, between the lines, and alone, and no one came looking for us. We could see some units of Apache Troop go forward to assume an attack position closer to the perimeter of Al Samawah, a mile or so off to our right of what had been our line of advancement. Paul drove us, alone, forward a little in the direction of Apache Troop's armored units. It was a gutsy thing to do. These tanks and Bradleys were engaging Iraqis holed up in the town, and the closer we approached, the more imprudent it seemed to come up directly behind and attempt to rejoin them while they were shooting at the Iraqis. Captain Lyle's soldiers were engaged in combat, and we were just looking for anything familiar to which we could reattach ourselves. Just then Captain Cote's Humvee came trundling up from the rear. He had been hung out to dry like we were when everyone else got the heck out of there. After consultation with Cote and given the fact the only weapons among us were the M-16s in the captain's Hummer, we all decided to pull back a little. That meant crossing some railroad tracks and backtracking down the road out of Al Samawah to the assembly point where we had initially been shelled. It was now dusk, and while a sense of order was being restored, there was still enough confusion to leave us jittery, especially when we found ourselves back where the mortars had fallen earlier. The Iraqis had our range, and it was time to find another place to assemble before it became completely dark.

Around us in the gathering dusk were other vehicles whose commanders were trying to figure out where to hunker down next. Along with Captain Cote and his men, we drove off to attach ourselves to the other units. At this point, looking toward Al Samawah, we felt as if any of the mud homes we saw could have been housing Iraqi fighters. And there was sporadic fire coming our way. When it did, the soldiers about us dived into their protective vehicles. I crawled into a shallow ditch and began broadcasting on my belly using my satellite phone. I could hear the popping of weapons in the distance, but nothing had found my range. I described the confusion that had followed after the earlier mortar attack. It was now nearly dark so the hostile fire tapered off. Perhaps they deemed it wise to go to ground because the 7th Cavalry called in a punishing air strike that lit up the sky over Al Samawah. It was a splendid fireworks display at sunset: F-16s dropped blockbusting bombs on Iraqi emplacements suspected of shelling and shooting at us earlier. The show-stealer was another aircraft, the A-10 Warthog with its 30 mm Gatling gun. It has a distinctive signature. It burps loudly; moments later when the 30 mm shells hit, they explode with phosphorescent brilliance, incinerating anything around their target. The Iraqis in the city were firing shoulder-fired SAMS, surface-to-air missiles, at the incoming U.S. aircraft. We could see the air force jets commencing their bombing run from a high altitude, but concerned about those shoulder-fired missiles the Iraqis had, the air force pilots never actually made what one would call a low bombing run, and the F-16s climbed again very quickly after releasing their ordnance. After they delivered their destructive payloads, the night about Al Samawah became eerily quiet as did the patch of desert where we waited with some other vehicles and soldiers we did not recognize.

It was a dark night. We were too close to the Iraqi positions to dare turn on any flashlights, even with the red filters. Any of the homes four hundred yards away could have been infiltrated under the cover of night by snipers or other Iraqis eager to fire rocket-propelled grenades at us, as indeed they would do in the coming days and weeks. The Iraqis could also have sent out patrols to probe the still-disorganized Apache Troop. It was so dark we could not see Bradleys or other Humvees fifty yards away. Night-vision goggles helped, but even with those, objects beyond a hundred yards were blurred. We stayed pretty close to our vehicles. In the darkness, there was always the risk of being shot by one's own soldiers who were still confused and jumpy. There was nothing to do but go to sleep.

Those who have never been in combat may find this difficult to fathom, but it is easy to go to sleep in a war zone, even with guns and rockets booming about. You just throw a mental switch in your head and tell yourself there's nothing you can do about it, and then you shut your eyes. Snoring disturbing my sleep is worse than shooting. My colleague Christiane Amanpour and I had discussed this in an earlier war zone, Sarajevo in 1995. We were surprised to discover both of us slept better in war zones than anywhere else. It was her opinion that a person just collapsed out of "physical and mental exhaustion, because you have been enduring endless hours in fear and danger." Throughout this latest war in Iraq, I found myself sleeping either on the ground or on the hood of the Humvee. When the war was over, some of us discovered a normal hotel bed was damned uncomfortable and took some adjustment. Jeff told me he was half tempted to sleep on his hotel balcony just so he could go to sleep again under the stars.

Many of the lessons we learned with the 7th Cavalry were uncomfortable. Some were quite painful. One of those lessons was that the army gets more done by 0900 than most people accomplish all day. Usually, we found ourselves awake at about 4:30 A.M. and moving out within the hour.

When this dawn came, we were still alive and feeling pretty good, especially after Paul brewed some tea. Not long after dawn, Captain Lyle's tank came looking for us. Perhaps he was becoming attached to his charges after all, or perhaps he was just returning a favor. I had loaned my Thuraya satellite phone to him so he could call his wife a couple of times to let her know he was OK. It was a courtesy extended all the time by foreign correspondents to the military units to which they were assigned. Was it calculating? Not really, it was just the decent thing to do.

Captain Lyle—I never called him Clay until well after the war—told us he was going out on an early-morning scouting party to try to locate a Euphrates River crossing other than the one that had been denied us up to that point. Another scouting party with the Cavalry? Why not? We were now re-embedded right behind the company commander's tank, and it was there we stayed pretty much throughout to the end of the war. Every shared deprivation and discomfort, every bullet aimed in our direction increasingly earned us the acceptance of those soldiers about us. I do recall somewhere in this bonding process one soldier asking in disbelief, "You didn't volunteer for this, did you?" When we grinned and said yes we did, he just shook his head as if to say, "You are crazy." Of course, because ours is now a volunteer army, he had done the same thing himself. Another alpha-male personality.

Enjoying danger and taking risks seem characteristic of some aggressive, male personality types. Years earlier, as a young reporter with the White House press corps, I recalled President Gerald Ford's secret-service agents had a reputation for being physically rough on journalists in situations when the president "worked the crowd." They seemed to enjoy roughing those of us who tried to get close enough to hear the presidential exchanges with the crowd. Once they even scheduled a flag-football game with the White House press corps in Vail, Colorado, in the summer of 1976 after the Republican convention in Kansas City, Missouri, to rough us up a little. As I recall, I was the only journalist dumb enough to play, so they fleshed out the press team with White House staff including, fortuitously, the president's physician, Dr. William Lukash. Several of Ford's secret-service agents had played in the National Football League, and they were monsters even without pads. In the third quarter, Dr. Lukash took a rest as quarterback, and I took over the ball. One agent who I was told had been a linebacker for the Washington Redskins hit me, like a pterodactyl pouncing, and I was nearly knocked cold.

When the clock expired in the fourth quarter, the score stood at 57 to nothing. I left the field bloodied and sore, but the secret service never pushed or bullied me again. I had played four quarters with them in what was really tackle without pads, and I became one of the boys. So it was with the boys of the 7th Cavalry. Because we lived and shat in the dirt with them, shared the MREs, asked no privilege, and didn't cut and run, they adopted us as their own. We still perceived ourselves as objective and detached, but the fine line was not understood by the soldiers who increasingly seemed not only to enjoy our company but also delighted in having their unit's story told.

Captain Lyle assembled half a dozen or so Bradleys, several tanks, and our Humvee Old Betsy, and off we went, paralleling the railroad tracks that ran east-west along the southern edge of Al Samawah. To the south were a few farmhouses in the desert along the divide created by the railroad embankment. Any one of those farmhouses could have concealed Iraqi reconnaissance squads watching us, radioing to someone ahead. Just to the west was a well-kept railroad track, high up on an embankment that shielded our flight from Iraqis in Al Samawah itself. We passed a recently abandoned railroad station, newly built, and except for a few shot-out windows, ready for customers. There were feeble attempts at gardens, with some scraggly rose bushes and some neglected shriveled-up orange- and rust-colored marigolds. On the west side of the road was an abandoned cache of artillery shells, unexploded, dangerous, and hot. There must have been two-dozen khaki-green boxes of 120 mm shells. We did not need to be told not to go near them. We suspected they might be booby-trapped to blow if we left the road and approached on foot.

After paralleling the railroad track for several miles, we came upon a black-and-white poster venerating Saddam. In this neighborhood, the villagers were too frightened to change their loyalties just yet. Taking the poster down prematurely or manifesting any enthusiasm for the American invaders could easily have gotten an offending Iraqi killed as a collaborator after the 7th Cavalry moved on to its next objective.

Farther ahead was a collection of houses, too small to be called a hamlet. These were squat, flat-roofed dwellings in such disrepair we couldn't tell if they were inhabited or not. More importantly, however, we discovered there was a road through the village that ran under the railroad tracks, opening a window, if not a door, on Al Samawah. Through the trestle under the railroad tracks, we were startled to see a lush green world on the other side.

Several of the armored vehicles in our patrol growled past us crossing under the railroad tracks. On the other side was a collection of well-watered farms with the heavy foliage of banana and palm trees. A few men and boys worked the fields, and some of the farmers waved at us. At least one tank had climbed up the railroad embankment and taken up a position resting atop the railroad tracks. Another Bradley stopped on our side of the trestle just in front of Old Betsy. Its crew discovered a volleyball-sized boulder wedged into the treads. A heavy crowbar was retrieved from the side of the armored vehicle, and the crew labored mightily to remove it, predicting unless it was extracted, it was likely the tread would break, and their vehicle would probably have to be abandoned.

Paul, Charlie, and I dismounted from our Hummer and cautiously walked through the underpass. A small stream flowed alongside the road that ran under the trestle. Charlie dutifully shot some video of the nearby hamlet and landscape while I looked about for signs of trouble. Paul also sniffed the wind. Each of us relieved ourselves of the early morning tea, and I thought what a helluva time to get shot. Yet, it looked safe enough, and it might turn out to be an alternate way to bypass the Iraqi soldiers who were blocking our primary route through Al Samawah. The problem was we just couldn't see much, yet we knew that the palm groves, mud homes, and far outbuildings could also have hidden a full Iraqi army. There were no signs of trouble, but I went back to the Humvee and waited for the others to join me.

A few Iraqi men and boys gathered in the settlement where some of the 7th Cav's scouting patrol remained to protect the rear. The Arabs were staring at the parked Bradley that had the rock extracted from the tread by now. Atop the Bradley, the turret gunner was looking down his gun barrel at one of the Iraqi men who started walking toward his vehicle as the older men retreated. I stopped the approaching Iraqi about thirty-five yards from the Bradley and tried to talk to him in the few phrases of Arabic I remembered, such as "*Anna sahaffa*," "I am a journalist." He knew a few phrases of English and began grinning, revealing a mouth full of black teeth. "Don't worry, I speak English," he said in pidgin. He was lank and disheveled and tried to tell me how much he disliked Saddam. I thought he protested too much. He was just too enthusiastic in his denunciations of a man whose boots he probably would have licked two days earlier.

He proceeded to tell me how happy he was to be liberated, as was everyone else who had been on the scene. His enthusiasm now had propelled him to within twenty-five or thirty yards of the Bradley. Glancing back over my shoulder, I could see the machine gunner training his gun right at my back and this guy's chest. It did not occur to me that the Iraqi with the black teeth could have had an explosives belt strapped to himself, but I knew if he took many more steps toward the Bradley to express his gratitude for his liberation from Saddam, he was certainly a dead man, and I did not want that to happen. I threw out both arms like a school crossing guard and in loud anxious English said, "You go any closer to that vehicle, and they will kill you."

I was now physically restraining him, at about twenty-five yards from the muzzle of the machine gun. For some reason, he desisted. I started to walk him back in the direction from which he had come. When we were both some distance from the machine gun, he disappeared, and I, too, turned around. I walked past the Bradley, returning to Old Betsy, and the machine gunner thanked me for stopping the guy. I told them I knew the Iraqi was a dead man if he got any closer to them.

Yet, it was we who nearly became dead men. In a matter of seconds, Iraqi mortars began once again falling about us. They were thunderously loud, and one was so close I could feel its concussion and heard incoming bullets whizzing overhead. Jeff stated the obvious, "We are under attack." Someone else was shouting, "Back to your vehicles! We are under attack! Get out of here!" The heavy engines of the Bradleys and M1A1s were growling and revving up big time now, carving up the earth in the scramble to pull back.

That grinning Iraqi with the black teeth and pidgin English who had professed hatred of Saddam was almost certainly another forward artillery observer calling in the mortars and the RPGs, the rocket-propelled grenades.

Captain Lyle was cursing the Iraqi farmers on the other side of the bridge who had seconds before been smiling and waving, knowing that hidden in their homes and fields were soldiers now pouring fire down on us. The captain was a Texan, and the farther he was from Texas, the more suspicious he was of people. As a result, the local Iraqis were about as despicable a lot of humans as he could imagine, and his vision of liberating an oppressed Iraqi populace fell victim to those mortar attacks.

It is amazing how fast a person can move when he is getting shot at. I recalled that soldier the previous day running through a wheat field with that M-16 in both hands over his head. Once again, we were out of range in a matter of seconds, and that was fortunate, because increasingly, we were having battery problems with Old Betsy. Starting the engine had become a roll of the dice. This time, it was seven-come-eleven, and we were out of there. The heavier element of the patrol, the M1A1 tanks, withdrew in a more desultory fashion. The sixty-nine-ton monsters were engineered to survive nuclear blasts on a European battlefield during the Cold War, so they had less to fear than our Humvee with its thin plastic doors. The farther we got from the site of the shelling, the slower all of us moved until we again stopped at the cases of abandoned artillery whose markings clearly showed they'd been made in Russia.

The net result of this sortie was that we still had not found a way to pass through Al Samawah to locate our bridge across the Euphrates. If I were an Iraqi, I would have begun dynamiting the bridges, slowing the American assault. It was time for the American generals to reconsider the 7th Cavalry's dilemma. We had been in the Al Samawah's environs over twenty-four hours and remained stalled and blocked by an ancient river. Captain Lyle was ordered to withdraw a few miles into the desert into what must have been the Al Samawah city garbage dump.

It is sad that burning garbage and a perimeter of plastic trash bags have become the hallmarks of so many Arab cities in the Middle East. The 7th Cavalry now found itself rolling through the flotsam and jetsam of Al Samawah. These deserts of Arabia are awash in blowing plastic garbage bags, black, white billowing plastic, like sails filled with desert winds that also fill one's nostrils with the stench of half-burned garbage. In Iraq, the U.S. Army was fastidious by comparison, burying or burning nearly all of its litter as it went along. By contrast, there appears no concern for the environment or aesthetics in these desert cultures. My Arab friends explain that most Arab cultures are so underdeveloped they simply do not understand elements of infrastructure like garbage removal. Additionally, burdened with serious overpopulation, these desert towns and cities now stand in danger of becoming prisoners of their own walls of garbage. There are few exceptions to this filth that pollutes the Arabian peninsula's deserts. The Gulf Arab states seem to escape it because they have plenty of oil money and smaller populations. The other exceptions tend to be the most draconian cities of the Arab world like Riyadh, Saudi Arabia, and Damascus, Syria, where corporal punishment, beatings, and thrashings await local litterbugs.

The only oasis we could find from the blowing garbage was an elevated area of sand dunes, and that is where the 7th Cavalry now formed. Part of our stop at Al Samawah was warranted to give the men some sleep after a more than seventy-hour drive, almost nonstop, between Kuwait and the Euphrates River. It gave some a chance to clear their heads of dust and purge their bodies of exhaustion. By late afternoon when we arrived, however, we were told there would be no sleep this night. The fuel trucks had again been summoned to fill the thirsty tanks and Bradleys. A violent wind was whipping up another sandstorm, and this time the silicon grains were cutting our faces pretty badly.

At one point, Captain Cote's Humvee had a flat tire and no spare, so the crew approached us, and the bartering began. We didn't have much the army needed, but we did have a spare tire. They offered us a five-gallon Jerry can filled with motor oil in exchange, and we struck a deal. Besides having a failing battery, Old Betsy was burning oil, although she was still the best of the reconditioned Humvees CNN had purchased from King Hummer, back in Kuwait City. We were sure the newly wealthy King had moved on to better things and was by now certainly basking in his new, CNN-financed palace in Saudi Arabia, with the other billionaires and war profiteers. They were probably having a good laugh about us sods with sand in every orifice, driving about their deserts, getting shot at to make their worlds safe again. In the middle of the latest sandstorm, Colonel Ferrell had summoned his officers to his Bradley again, and increasingly, we were permitted to eavesdrop and even ask questions about the 7th Cavalry's next marching orders. We never dreamed of becoming this embedded, sitting in on briefings on operational orders. Recognizing that I was a reporter and not a soldier, I always waited until the end, after the junior officers asked their questions, to inquire about the unit's next combat operation. Most often, I would ask if the helicopters would be out in front as scouts or whether we would have close air support. I never did question tactics or strategy openly, but I got the impression that if we didn't ask a stupid question, Colonel Ferrell let us ask anything we wanted. Paul, Charlie, Jeff, and I were welcome at each of these briefings that surveyed the maps of the road ahead. Colonel Ferrell was that dedicated to seeing the Pentagon's marching orders about accommodating embedded journalists were obeyed. He may have hidden something from us, but I never detected it, and I don't recall his refusing to answer any question about the unit's objective, our route, or the time frame in which he hoped to get to Baghdad. We came away from that meeting having learned that the 7th was giving up on Al Samawah, leaving that to the 3rd Infantry Division or some other trailing unit. Nothing behind us mattered. We were to be off and scouting again that night, looking for yet another bridge upstream in a less heavily populated area where the 7th would not have to shoot its way through a town. The cavalry still had to find a way to cross the Euphrates River canals and ultimately the river itself to resume the rush to Baghdad, and we were along for more than just the ride because those orders essentially became our orders, too. We could not turn back or bail out. Detaching from the 7th Cavalry at that point was unthinkable. We could not be left behind deep in enemy territory. Besides, we were having fun. It was a graduate seminar for Boy Scouts, except there were real guns.

During one evening prime-time live shot with anchor Aaron Brown, I let slip on air that I was having quite an adventure, saying the campaign was actually quite a bit of fun. Brown, a decent fellow, seemed surprised that I would describe a military campaign with its death and destruction as fun. When he asked me if I had misspoken, I quoted Winston Churchill's line, "There is nothing so exhilarating as being shot at and missed." Former NATO commander and four-star general Wesley K. Clark was on set with Aaron and came to my defense. Clark held bronze and silver stars for bravery in Vietnam, and he knew exactly the adrenalin high of which I spoke. I owe Clark for backing me up.

Standing in the still-blowing sand and with anal sphincters getting taut again, a shot echoed above the wind in the desert encampment, and we all dived for cover. Bradleys had gone out several times that afternoon to check reports that the Iraqis were sending units to probe our position. None of us was sure whether that shot signaled that an Iraqi infiltrator had made his way into our temporary encampment. We laid low for a few minutes before someone shouted, "All clear." It turned out the shot that came in our direction was from one of our own soldier's accidental discharge of his weapon. "Friendly fire" is what it was called, an absurd term, especially to someone wounded or killed. That shot was a precursor to a wild evening.

4

Ambushed

I have a rendezvous with Death
At some disputed barricade.
—Alan Seeger, "I Have a Rendezvous with Death"

We knew we were in for it that night, "headed for the shit," as soldiers are fond of saying. Each of us in the CNN vehicle wore our full protective gear, the Kevlar body-armor vests, and helmets. The Iraqi Republican Guard and Fedayeen resistance at Al Samawah had not been insurmountable, but it was sufficiently strong for a small cavalry unit to bypass it, leaving it to larger follow-up forces to confront. As I have noted, cavalry lacks dismounts, that is, infantry, and thus while its tanks can blast their way through a city, it has no troops to support it in house-to-house searches or street-to-street fighting. Somewhere ahead lay a collection of bridges yet to be crossed, some spanning irrigation canals as broad as the Euphrates River itself. They were perfect chokepoints for Iraqis to ambush the convoy. I kept thinking we of CNN were traveling in the only soft-skinned, unarmored vehicle, easily penetrated by even a halfway-decent pellet rifle.

The last hours of light that day were a dull and reddish gray as the remnant of the sandstorm blew itself out. Pulling out of our afternoon encampment, we passed again through a blowing curtain of plastic garbage bags to escape the Al Samawah environs. We took the only exit we had in order to swing back on to a hardtop road. At several junctions, clusters of Iraqi civilians stood and waved. We were not totally unwelcome in this dry and thirsty land. I thought these were anti-Saddam Shiites, but on reflection, they might have merely been saying good riddance.

Every time I saw Iraqis gathered, I scratched my head in disbelief that an American president would think this was fertile ground for democracy. To me, the attempt to bring democracy to Iraq was akin to attempting to grow hybrid tea roses in the Yukon. The Iraqis had been told by Saddam Hussein that the American army was coming to kill their husbands and rape their women. The Iraqis didn't give a damn about democracy. They just wanted to survive and like most humans preferred a return to the comfortable status quo. Democracy seemed as alien to these waving Iraqis as scrubbing floors would be to the Queen of England. The 7th Cavalry didn't have a clue as to how to sow seeds of democracy in Iraq. Later, it would seem an abuse of fine soldiers to impose that assignment upon them. They were men trained to fight and kill, and despite mouthing the occasional catechism about bringing democracy to Iraq, what they really cared about was getting to Baghdad as fast as possible so they could rotate home faster.

I had become disoriented because of the absence of sunlight or stars the previous day and night. Our convoy emerged from the Al Samawah dump, and I thought we were swinging downriver, to the southeast, looking for a bridge closer to Al Nasiriyah. We were actually headed north-northwest, in the direction of Ar Rumaythah and beyond that to our objective to take up a blocking position at An Najaf. The weakening sandstorm left nightfall scowling down on us.

I was aching. During the earlier rains, I had climbed on the back end of the Humvee to retrieve something from the roof rack. The sloping back end of the Hummer was greased with mud, and I slipped and fell four feet to the ground landing on my hip. My left knee was also bothering me again. I had injured it the previous autumn covering a foxhunt in Britain. Now, unless I extended the knee, it was painful as I sat doubled up in the back of the Hummer with its sandbags on the floor. I never said anything to CNN about the knee for fear they would disqualify me from front-line combat duty. I was also mildly concerned that if CNN ever stopped to think about how old I was, management might have decided I should not be riding around in combat with a bunch of kid soldiers, many of whom were fifteen years younger than my two adult sons. Indeed, I was somewhat horrified that Aaron Brown, our New York anchor, announced on his news prime-time news program one night that I was sixty-two. I would have preferred that went unnoticed, fearing someone, perhaps in the Pentagon, would have decided I was a little too old for the army. Usually I keep up with people twenty years younger, and I look ten years younger than I am. Still, when Aaron joked on his program about my being the sixty-two-year-old Scud stud of the war, the public reaction was both surprising and gratifying. The disclosure generated bags of fan mail from CNN's rather large audience of over-sixty viewers, who, as newfound fans, cheered me on. I honestly do not believe CNN gave a damn how old I was during the war as long as I produced. Still, the war also demonstrated the error of those who would put out to pasture the over-sixty generation without realizing how fit and capable we can be and still are.

Riding along at thirty to thirty-five miles an hour on the hardtop road, I again opened the back door of Old Betsy and began flutter-kicking my legs, thrashing them in the air. We passed marshlands, scrapes where migrating waterfowl gathered for their spring trips north. Green sandpipers and red-wattled plovers hopped about on the margins. Other waders, too small to be identified with the naked eye at dusk, also gathered on the margins of these marshes, taking aim on Turkey and Russia. Most common were the elegant black-winged stilts on their rickety legs, probing the mud for mollusks, worms, insects, or whatever those puddles held. At that moment, I wanted very much to go birding in Iraq. I am ever "birding" in my head, and I found myself muttering, "If wishes were horses, beggars would ride." I was riding and still felt a bit of a beggar badly in need of a bath and a chance to watch birds.

When the last light of day was extinguished, the M1A1s, Bradleys, Humvees, and other vehicles of the 7th Cavalry ahead and behind us turned on their headlights. It bespoke an undue confidence in the as yet unscouted region through which we were traveling. We actually came to within fifteen or twenty miles of An Najaf before the Iraqis began shooting at us again. Like many military operations of some size, the opening shots were desultory and deceptive. We had just turned north, making a dead-run for the Shatt al Atshan waterway, a major irrigation canal as wide as a medium-sized river. There somewhere in the dark a few miles ahead of us lay the first substantial bridge to be crossed since we had left Kuwait.

We began taking incidental small-arms fire, mostly from Kalashnikov rifles. It almost certainly came from foxholes and small rifle pits dug back from the road 150 to 200 yards on both sides, and I debated the best way to protect myself. The heavy Kevlar protective plates in the body armor covers vital organs front and back. But the incoming fire was coming from our flanks, leaving only marginal protection in the vests along the side seams from the waist to the armpits. Sometimes, it seemed a good idea to shed the vest and put its protective plates between myself and the direction from which the fire was coming. In front and behind us, larger, armored vehicles protected our vehicle. But we were vulnerable to attack from the sides of the road, and that was the source of the incoming Iraqi fire pouring down on us now. In Baghdad after the war, with the advent of roadside bombs, invariably I preferred not to wear the body armor in the car but used it as a flanking shield from those improvised explosive devices. It's common for someone under fire to have all sorts of arguments with himself in combat about how to make himself less vulnerable and smaller. Perhaps the ultimate debate is what to do with the helmet. I hated the ill-fitting chin strap on mine, and it came down to "Do I wear it on my head, or do I sit in it to protect the family jewels?" Still, the latest generation of helmets is capable of deflecting a rifle round.

From the darkened fields on both sides of the road, the Iraqis now began pouring down fire. The noise was thunderous: rocket-propelled grenades roaring toward us, heavy machine-gun fire raking our column, automatic-rifle fire zinging about us, a blizzard of hot lead. It was now a full-fledged and ferocious ambush. I don't recall ever feeling so naked and helpless. That sense of helplessness is endemic to combat. I imagined it was like a B-17 bomber crew flying through dense anti-aircraft fire over Germany in the Second World War. A B-17 traveled too damned slowly. The crew couldn't bolt and hide. The plane had to stay in bomb formation. The crew couldn't show fear. They just had to grit their teeth and endure whatever hand the fates dealt them. That was the hand we were dealt now.

Light flashed off to our left, but it was what I saw in front of us that was most alarming. Fifty-caliber machine-gun tracer shells were slamming into the turret of Captain Lyle's tank twenty yards in front of us, and beyond that, they were slamming into the Bradleys in front of him. It was happening up and down the line of our convoy. These red-hot tracers were bouncing off the sides of the turrets and then ricocheting skyward and back at angles of forty-five to eighty degrees. It was the Fourth of July with no rules, and it was loud. I was reminded of a New Year's Eve I once spent in a provincial French town, when all the young men shot fireworks off, aiming their skyrockets horizontally across the town's central square at people on the other side. The French revelers targeted anyone foolish enough to be out on the street. The difference here, of course, was that the rockets and tracers now being fired at us were lethal not celebratory.

If one of those fifty-caliber shells hit our Humvee, we were dead. I believe the Iraqis were also firing guns, mortars, and 20 mm anti-aircraft bursts. The guns on the Bradleys, Abrams, and other tracked vehicles were now returning fire furiously, slashing into the dark farm fields on both sides of the road. The U.S. soldiers had the advantage of being able to see in the dark although I suspect their night-vision goggles had turned the entire battlefield into a greenish horror film. Later, they told us there were truckloads of Iraqis out there shooting at our convoy, which had now slowed to a crawl.

An M1A1 Abrams battle tank, "armed & dangerous" painted on the gun barrel, waits for ammunition supplies before the 19 March invasion, 13 Mar. 2003. © copyright Jeff Barwise.

A supply of tank shells comes in on tractor trailers for handloading into the tanks, 13 Mar. 2003. © copyright Jeff Barwise.

Tank crew members handload tank shells, 13 Mar. 2003. © copyright Jeff Barwise.

Charlie Miller, freelance photojournalist and former British Army captain, films a full-on exercise of crossing the berm, 15 Mar. 2003. © copyright Jeff Barwise.

Jeff Barwise, CNN field-broadcast engineer, models the full chemical-weapons suit that he wore. CNN driver Paul Jordan wore the same type. Most suits of U.S. Army's issue were desert camouflage brown, 17 Mar. 2003. © copyright Charlie Miller.

At the line of departure, close to the Kuwait-Iraq border, Jeff Barwise rests on the tailgate of the CNN Humvee. Walt Rodgers is to the right, 19 Mar. 2003, the day the war began. © copyright Charlie Miller.

Just outside Al Samawah, the 7th Cavalry embarks on a reconnaissance mission. The soldiers talked to some local people and also were ambushed by two men near the bridge, 24 Mar. 2003. © copyright Jeff Barwise.

The morning after being ambushed on the road to An Najaf, the CNN crew wakes up in this area. Fierce fighting broke out in a nearby palm grove when a couple Abrams tanks and a fuel truck got stuck and blocked Old Betsy's path forward, 24 Mar. 2003. © copyright Jeff Barwise.

The 7th Cavalry pauses on the way to cross the Euphrates River to secure a bridge farther north. The bridge was rigged with an unexploded bomb that was diffused by B Troop, 3/7 Cavalry. Later, the convoy drove through machine-gun alley, 25 Mar. 2003.

The 7th Cavalry stops off the road on the way to some R and R, 27 Mar. 2003.

At the R and R area for maintenance and ammunition resupply, twenty miles to the rear of the advance, some of the men gather around the CNN Humvee during a live shot. An enemy rocket is headed here. Everyone had to run for cover in the middle of the interview. Capt. Clay Lyle is wearing dark glasses near center; Sgt. Todd Woodhall is second from right, wearing the holster; Charlie Miller is walking at far left, 27 Mar. 2003. © copyright Jeff Barwise.

Soldiers of the 7th Cavalry inspect one of four enemy anti-aircraft guns captured along with radios and a bunker after the unit made contact with about twenty Iraqis. One or two got away in a taxi cab. Capt. Clay Lyle ordered a tank to drive over the guns to destroy them. One of them fired, and its projectile cut the captain's right ear. The engineers were called up to destroy all parts and ammunition with C-4 explosives, 2 Apr. 2003.
© copyright Jeff Barwise.

A Scud-missile buster works its way closer to Baghdad, 3 Apr. 2003. © copyright Jeff Barwise.

Iraqi prisoners who were taken by another U.S. Army company wait behind barbed wire, 3 Apr. 2003. © copyright Jeff Barwise.

On one of the major highways, wreckage marks previous fighting, 3 Apr. 2003.
© copyright Jeff Barwise.

Alongside the road are uniforms discarded by Iraqi soldiers who wanted to blend in with the civilian population. Most of the bunkers were completely empty except for uniforms, 3 Apr. 2003. © copyright Jeff Barwise.

A dead Iraqi soldier lies next to the Abu Ghraib Expressway (Route 1). The 3/7 Cavalry destroyed nine enemy tanks in a force-on-force engagement that went on into the morning here. This area of operation was still hot. The 3/7 was fired upon numerous times throughout the day, 4 Apr. 2003. © copyright Jeff Barwise.

On the Abu Ghraib Expressway (Route 1), an MTLB APC (a Soviet-era armored personnel carrier) and one of the dead Iraqis are in the foreground, and the CNN Humvee is in the background. This photograph was taken just before Jeff Barwise discovered that one of the "dead Iraqis" was actually alive, 4 Apr. 2003. © copyright Jeff Barwise.

One of the KIA Iraqis is badly wounded rather than dead. Paul Jordan, security guard for CNN and former Australian Special Air Services commando, provided life-saving emergency medical treatment for him until the 7th Cavalry could transport the Iraqi back to the campsite from the Abu Ghraib Expressway (Route 1). He survived as far as is known, 4 Apr. 2003. © copyright Jeff Barwise.

A T-72 main battle tank is one of twenty-two enemy vehicles on the Abu Ghraib Expressway (Route 1) that were taken out by Apache Troop less than two miles from where the CNN crew had slept, 5 Apr. 2003. © copyright Jeff Barwise.

On the Abu Ghraib Expressway (Route 1) sits a Chinese command vehicle YW701, one of twenty-two enemy vehicles demolished by Apache Troop less than two miles from camp, 5 Apr. 2003. © copyright Jeff Barwise.

Two T-72 tanks, part of twenty-two enemy vehicles destroyed by Apache Troop on Abu Ghraib Expressway (Route 1), burn less than two miles from where the CNN crew stayed at night, 5 Apr. 2003. © copyright Jeff Barwise.

On the Abu Ghraib Expressway (Route 1), a T-72 main battle tank, one of twenty-two enemy vehicles destroyed by Apache Troop, is in a ditch less than two miles from the 7th Cavalry's camp, 5 Apr. 2003. © copyright Jeff Barwise.

A T-72 main battle tank, one of twenty-two enemy vehicles taken out by Apache Troop on Abu Ghraib Expressway (Route 1), is stopped in its tracks less than two miles from the troop's camp, 5 Apr. 2003. © copyright Jeff Barwise.

The CNN Hummer and military vehicles sit among archaeological mounds whose tops the Iraqis cut off for gun platforms. Bomblets are everywhere in the foreground; decaying corpses are about four hundred yards away. This is the last position the CNN crew shared with the military before leaving the 7th Cavalry to head to Baghdad, 7 Apr. 2003. © copyright Jeff Barwise.

The Apache 3/7 controls an area previously occupied by the Iraqi army. The U.S. had mortared the holding, 7 Apr. 2003. © copyright Jeff Barwise.

Posing for a snapshot are civilians the U.S. Army would not let cross the railroad tracks. They asked if they had permission to kill any Fedayeen still in the neighborhood, 8 Apr. 2003. © copyright Jeff Barwise.

The man on the right, who really wanted his picture taken, poses with an American soldier. The local people were amazed to see themselves on the screen of Jeff Barwise's digital camera. This is the area where an old man told about a buried American soldier, 8 Apr. 2003. © copyright Jeff Barwise.

On the way back to camp after meeting the civilians at the railroad tracks, the CNN crew sights a Paladin artillery vehicle, 8 Apr. 2003. © copyright Jeff Barwise.

While looking for WMD, the 7th Cavalry inspects Iraqi equipment found at a weapons storage center. Numerous empty carriers were found, 9 Apr. 2003. © copyright Jeff Barwise.

Jeff Barwise leans on an Iraqi short-range ballistic missile at the weapons storage center, the "water-purification" plant. The missile had been examined by UN inspectors, 9 Apr. 2003. © copyright Charlie Miller.

Satellite dishes, trucks, and international journalists crowd the front of the Palestine Hotel, Baghdad, 17 Apr. 2003. © copyright Jeff Barwise.

It seemed insane at the time, but we were all riding with our white lights, our headlights, on. Jesus, Mary and Joseph, we were presenting ourselves as an illuminated target, and the Iraqis were obliging, hammering us with an ever-increasing hail of tracers and small-arms fire. And in our poor unarmed Humvee, the only thing we could do was sit there and take it. There was no escape and no place to hide. We could not break formation, and in any case, there was no place to go.

A huge flash of light exploded about twenty yards ahead of us at the right side of Captain Lyle's Abrams tank. "RPG," Paul observed, tension in his voice. There was not the slightest betrayal of any fear, yet each of us surely felt it. Another rocket-propelled grenade roared directly over Old Betsy. It was a miracle that with all our sleeping bags, backpacks, boxes of MREs, and a satellite dish up there, we didn't get whacked.

With clenched teeth, we muttered, mused, and grumbled about why the hell we were traveling with headlights on. If we couldn't outrun the ambush, the least we could do was shut off our white lights. What in the hell were we doing in the middle of a ferocious, nighttime firefight driving with headlights on helping those in ambush target us? Later, I learned the decision to travel with white lights, even in an ambush, was made earlier by Colonel Ferrell and his junior officers. There was an assumption, the kind that can be disastrous even on more equally matched playing fields, that another U.S. unit might have already preceded us down this same road en route to the waterway canals. So, despite the seeming madness of going to war fully illuminated, the headlights stayed on, just in case we bumped into a friendly unit somewhere in the dark ahead of us. Even when it became apparent no friendly American units had gone before us, the officers kept their headlights on because it was now just as obvious that because no one had scouted the road in front of us no one had a clue what lay ahead by way of booby traps. And so, on a moonless night, the running lights helped us see where we were going even as they helped the Iraqis target us.

Charlie, like the rest of us, wondered aloud why we now stopped in the middle of the ambush to return fire instead of trying to run through it as quickly a possible.

"I was scared," the dour Scot later said, "but I don't think death came into my mind." Rather, "I just said this is how it's going to be."

With the detachment of his engineer's mind, he was also able to remove himself from our predicament and enjoy it with awe and amazement— enjoy the overwhelming American firepower being poured out into the bunkers, attacking Soviet-era BMPs (armored personnel carriers) and the pickup trucks in those fields. There was nothing to say, no time for chatter. Besides, the firing was so loud we couldn't hear anything anyway. Still, in my head, I was having a debate about whether it was better to draw myself into a tight fetal position, knees under my chin, or splay myself out trying to reduce my body mass. Jeff, who had been shot at in Somalia, had seen nothing like this before. He, too, in his laconic, soft, Southern accent later admitted he was initially afraid.

"I just said, 'I hope I make it out of here alive,'" he added.

We all shared that hope but without a surplus of confidence.

The noise of the firefight was so disorienting I couldn't tell where the shooting was coming from. It turned out that it was coming from all around us. The Iraqis were firing on us from the right and left side of the road while in front and behind us, the 7th Cavalry was shooting back at them. Without the luxury of night-vision goggles, Charlie, Jeff, and I were effectively blind. Paul was pretty taciturn so even with his night-vision goggles he didn't say much. Later, however, the soldiers told us their targets were substantial Iraqi units off in those fields—four hundred to five hundred soldiers shooting mortars, RPGs, machine guns, and rifles at us. Not being able to see more than twenty or thirty yards, we did not know the soldiers in their tanks and other vehicles were shooting at waves of Iraqis charging us from out in those fields. It was the first but not the last time that we encountered seemingly fearless Iraqi soldiers making suicidal charges at the 7th Cavalry's machine guns. In the midst of this ambush, we were only moving at about three miles an hour by Jeff's recollection. It might have been slower. The column would periodically stop and start and stop again in a crawling battle with each side continuing to fire on the other.

"It was unreal . . . unimaginable," Sgt. Paul Wheatley, who commanded one of the Abrams tanks somewhere in the night ahead of us, later said of the ambush. "You're constantly paranoid. You are paranoid about every turn, every person, every building, and it's a little nerve-racking at times. If you could have done anything about it, it would have been terrifying, because we were trapped in the middle of it, helpless. You just gritted your teeth and watched the night explode and burn around you."

Through their thermal-imagery optics, the army crews could see the Iraqi infantry running along the side of the road below the shoulder, and Sergeant Wheatley's gunner started cutting them down with the 7.62 mm machine gun on the left side of the turret. Later when I asked him how many Iraqis his tank alone took out in that ambush, his response was, "I wouldn't even begin to guess. Probably thirty to thirty-five on that one stretch of road."

Sergeant Wheatley compared the sounds of incoming Iraqi machine-gun bullets bouncing off his tank as "like someone throwing rocks." In the midst of that, the feeling of being blind and helpless inside the now-stopped Humvee was more than I could take, and Charlie and I got out to watch the show, which kept reminding us of a huge fireworks display, except it was everywhere, over us, in front and in back and above. And it was deadly. Charlie started taking pictures with his weenie cam, but there was so much going on he never could really focus on any of the exploding ordnances, it was happening so quickly. Flashes of light, streams of tracer fire everywhere amid the darkness, and then more darkness. Streaming tracers so impressive to the naked eye were just light blips across the videotape. Our Humvee offered no protection. We could only watch in awe. In retrospect, doing so was stupid. But the battle was visually compelling, and I was there to report on it. None of us was about to close his eyes and wish it was over. In truth—certainly in retrospect—we were enjoying it. The main battle tanks were firing platforms with machine guns blazing and cannon booming. There was definitely more outgoing fire than incoming, but the Iraqis had not lost their nerve nor had they run out of ammunition. Jeff speculated we were deliberately going slowly to dare the Iraqis to stick their heads up, but the Iraqis did not need daring. They were motivated, and they were brave. They didn't give an inch. Iraqi soldiers were making these suicidal charges because many had been told their families would be executed if they did not.

It might have been safer for us to lie on our bellies in the road to watch it, but none of us had ever seen anything quite like it before. Certainly we had not been in anything so intense. This was the mother of all firefights, and there was no one with a gun on either side who was not banging away. Then and throughout the rest of the war, I watched Capt. Clay Lyle atop his turret, firing away at Iraqis with a vengeance. When he was not firing his fifty-caliber machine gun, he was firing his M-16 rifle. He thoroughly enjoyed combat. It seemed what he was created to do. Later, he was nominated for and received the Silver Star for bravery.

The closing movement of this symphony of death was the summoning of close air support to suppress the Iraqi fire, which was still ricocheting off all the armored vehicles and whining in the air over our heads. I thought that seeing the incoming tracers slamming into the tanks and Bradleys was about as dramatic a spectacle as combat gets. I was wrong and soon would experience more and worse. The 7th Cavalry was getting hit hard, but it was surviving and surmounting the enemy ambush. Charlie and I were now sticking close to the back end of Old Betsy, walking about cautiously on the road when we heard the jets overhead. Previously, I recall too often having parroted a line from my old army friends who used to say, "You take what the air force says it can do and then divide by ten." After that ambush, however, neither I nor anyone in the 7th Cavalry ever was critical of the air force on our push to Baghdad. The men of the 7th Cav would reprove the marines and mock the army's own much-vaunted Apache hunter-killer helicopters, but there was never a disparaging word about the U.S. Air Force again. I felt they saved us that night, but perhaps I exaggerate.

The planes were up there. We could hear them although it was unimaginable the pilots could see any more of the attacking Iraqis than we with no night-vision goggles could. Two or three vehicles behind us, however, were several air force sergeants invisibly calling in the planes and identifying the Iraqi targets all around. Suddenly, and like the denouement of some violent drama, came the startling noise of what seemed a dragon heaving, about to vomit its fiery guts. Someone said, "A-10 Warthog." When those airplanes fire their 30 mm Gatling guns, the effect is terrifying even if they are on your side in a battle. To our rear, Iraqi soldiers were still shooting at us from the fields. The dragon's heave was now a huge belch in the dark overhead. The fields suddenly lighted up like a huge fireworks factory, exploding with probably tens of thousands of white phosphorescent 30 mm shells flashing, sparkling all at once. I do not exaggerate. The scene was a blanket of sparkling silver fireworks laid down on the earth, except no one walked away. I have a vague recollection of cheering because I knew no one was going to be shooting at us from that part of the field again. The A-10 made several more passes, and each time, the Iraqi fires decreased exponentially.

On the west side of the road was an elevated ridge, black against the sky, from which the Iraqis had been firing on us as well. Everything was generally detected by sound, because the light from the explosions came only in flashes. We could hear another jet making runs on the Iraqi targets. Later we learned it was a U.S. Air Force F-16. Again there was the roar of a huge bomb being released with a growling sound, and I wondered if the Iraqis about to die ever had a moment to think about what was happening to them. Still, I felt no sympathy for those who, moments before, had been trying to kill me. They wanted me dead, and I wanted the same for them. That night, the gods favored me. The bomb detonated less than a quarter mile away was so powerful it blew our Humvee door closed on the driver's side. As the Iraqi fire decreased to a persistent snapping, our confidence returned, and we foolishly walked about our stopped Humvee with too much bravado.

There was still plenty of shooting, but we had become almost blasé about it, even as Specialist Marcutio Posey on the tank just in front of us was still blazing away with his 7.62 mm machine gun atop the turret. Posey was swinging his gun around wildly seeing things, killing targets we never saw. The air force had just put on such a spectacularly loud display of firepower we failed to notice this light machine gun still at work. It wasn't until the following day that another soldier related the details of the closing minutes of the battle.

That soldier suggested I might want to buy Posey a drink or take him to dinner after the war. I asked why.

"When you and your cameraman were outside your vehicle," he said, "two Iraqi soldiers were taking aim on you with their Kalashnikovs, and Posey cut them in half for you."

I still tremble thinking about that, the Iraqis who had been invisible, hiding in the ditch on the west side of the road. They had been only fifteen yards from where we had been standing. I still want to hug that shy, retiring African American from Alabama. Captain Lyle later nominated Specialist Posey for the Bronze Star with a citation for valor. For some reason the army dragged its feet on the additional citation for valor. My personal recommendation was that Posey at least get the Congressional Medal of Honor for saving all of CNN's embedded journalists that night.

As vulnerable as we of CNN were, some of the soldiers toward the rear of the column driving those five-thousand-gallon tank trucks filled with petroleum were actually the bull's eye in this ambush. Jeff later talked to the tanker truck drivers, who told him they were terrified that night. No sane person sitting on that much fuel would have been otherwise. Later in the war, the Iraqis would learn to let U.S. armored units pass unopposed and then open up fire on the softer supply vehicles, including the highly flammable fuel trucks that were following in the train. In this ambush, however, the Iraqis' enthusiasm for a fight far exceeded their intelligence. They never had the discipline to wait. If any of those fuel trucks had been hit, much of our column would have gone up with them. But it was the forward elements in the column, where we in our Humvee were, that took the brunt of the fire in that night ambush.

There is no rational explanation for why Old Betsy was not riddled with fire. It was as if the Iraqis decided to lay all their firepower into the most impregnable vehicles in the squadron, the heavily armored main battle tanks and Bradleys. Stupidity is also a strong component on most battlefields. There was a story that surfaced months after the war that the Iraqis had been told the American tanks were made of wood; that the M1A1s were not only big targets but soft ones as well. From my tenderfoot perspective, it is also possible that the Iraqis were aiming a little high. Still, I will always be amazed that we were not hit. In our case, even with our headlights on, it was as if the Iraqis never knew we were there. We were twenty to thirty yards in back of Captain Lyle's tank and thirty yards in front of the air force's tracked vehicle. The Iraqis shot at the tanks and Bradleys in front of us and at the tanks and Bradleys in back of us. But we had become invisible to them. Not a scratch.

The firing ended as it began, with some sporadic shooting from the darkened fields. Some small fires from the A-10's cannon were still smoldering behind us, but that was the only light. When the guns fell silent, we noticed that the stars were out. We could also see the silhouettes of isolated, primitive mud farmhouses and outbuildings. And then there was nothing but the night. The Fertile Crescent of my grade school lessons was as dark and timeless as in the nights when Nebuchadnezzar or Hammurabi ruled this violent land.

The bridge over the Shatt was quiet. No one was shooting at us when we crossed, and no one had sabotaged it although I worried that explosive charges might have been laid and then remotely detonated when there were enough vehicles on the bridge. It did not happen.

We rolled slowly forward toward a small, darkened village, a collection of houses set about among large groves of date palms. Colonel Ferrell had hoped to avoid villages like this, hoped to avoid another situation where the Iraqis could take human shields and fire upon the 7th Cavalry. He would have to shoot back, and that would mean certain civilian deaths.

A few hours closer to dawn, we learned that one of the unit's Bradleys had killed two Iraqi children during the ambush. Saddam's defenders had taken a position in a darkened building along the road and blasted away at the convoy. The 25 mm cannon on the Bradley's turret responded and knocked down the wall, crushing the children. Again, the Iraqis had taken their own kind as human shields, this time children. A covering of gloom fell over Apache Troop when word worked its way through that two children died because of U.S. fire in that ambush. One soldier I talked to was deeply moved, saddened by what had happened although it wasn't his gun that killed the Iraqi children. Perhaps battle causes soldiers to feel things more deeply than they might otherwise. Later, I checked with Colonel Ferrell about the story, looking for double sourcing.

"Yeah," he said, without hesitation, "it's true. We feel bad about it."

I think he did, or as bad as a commander could allow himself to feel, having just emerged from such an ambush. I do not know if the Iraqis who were responsible felt any remorse, if they survived.

Almost immediately after crossing the Shatt waterway, the 7th Cavalry's probing armored column turned west along a narrow, single-track lane into some thick palm groves. It was another unscouted road, and I had to remind myself that the cavalry was the scouts, the ones with the "balls of steel." This unit was clearly the advanced guard for the 3rd ID somewhere miles behind. The orders were to find a quick, out-of-the-way route for the following force, a route to An Najaf, perhaps twenty miles northwest of where we now were. The decision was made by Colonel Ferrell to avoid the main road through the village just beyond the bridge, so we turned west into what was to become a minor debacle. No one really knew where we were going. We were just given to believe the 7th was casting about for a back route to An Najaf, a town on the north bank of the Euphrates. The Iraqis were showing an inclination increasingly to fight madly, if not bravely.

We suddenly found ourselves in an improbable jungle in the Euphrates River Delta. Amid the forbidding shadows and silhouetted palm trees, at night, this could also have been somewhere in the Philippines or Southeast Asia.

The maneuvering of huge tanks on the narrow, paved farm road with huge trees and a few mud houses on either side was the greatest operational challenge the tank drivers had so far encountered. Previously, the 7th Cavalry had simply rolled through deserts. The ambush from which we had just emerged a half hour earlier involved driving down a straight farm road. Now we were in an ancient delta with thick foliage. On such narrow tracks, tanks do not turn like cars. Certainly, they would not turn without difficulty trapped as they were between columns of big date palms. If we ran into another ambush, the tanks could not even swing their turrets either to the right or left to fire. The columns of palms blocked the barrels. So confining were these roadside columns of large palm trees one tank commander began mowing them down with his Abrams. Worse, there were deep irrigation ditches perhaps six or eight feet deep just off the road itself so even if the trees had not been there, the convoy could not have maneuvered well. And, from deep in the bowels of the tanks and Bradleys, drivers could not see the ditches on either side of the road, and any miscue, any dozing at the controls and the tank would roll over on its side and be lost in village sewage. Any Iraqi armored force familiar with the countryside would have had the foreknowledge that this was not a good road to run tanks down. The night was still so dark that what little we were able to see beyond the rows of date palms appeared to be a rice paddy or a recently irrigated grain crop.

On our left, between the convoy and the river, were a few squat mud houses, but the Iraqis who lived there had the good sense to stay inside and keep their heads down. For them, this had to have been a terrifying night. Children on their sleeping mats that night would have been frightened by the whining, growling noises of steel monsters at the ends of their dirt driveways. Iraqi women hid in the woods, certain they would be attacked by the infidel Americans. War is a nightmare for anyone in its corridor, and through several millennia, these people had been ever in the path of some invader.

It was only slightly less frightening for us, the terrifiers. The tanks had to to and fro around the palm trees in every bend in the road. None of us could see more than three or four armored vehicles ahead of us. We were inevitably bunched together, making inviting targets. There was much revving of the turbine engines amid the maneuvering. We never seemed to move very far forward. Looking out the opened back door of the Humvee into the palm trees and grain fields, the thought of Vietnam also kept occurring to me. The palms and paddies made the comparison inevitable. I couldn't get rid of those apprehensions. I just kept thinking, "If the Iraqis are reforming out there, we are dead ducks. We can't go forward, and we can't go back. We can't turn. We are trapped."

We hadn't gone half a mile up this uncharted farm road before it became evident I had not overestimated our predicament. In later conversations, I found out that most of the soldiers in Apache Troop had also sensed our dilemma. We could only move forward very, very slowly through this forest of towering date palm trees. We could not go back, because the entire rest of the 7th Cavalry—Bravo-Bone-Crusher Company and Charlie-Crazy-Horse Company—was stacked up on the road behind us. The question became, "Who scouts for the scouts?" The answer that night was "No one."

Somewhere ahead in the inky darkness lay our crossing point—a small, concrete bridge that spanned the formidable irrigation and sewage ditches that paralleled us on our right and left. After clearing the earlier ambush that slowed forward progress, the unit was again moving but more slowly now. The silence of the night was almost as unnerving as being shot at. Everyone's nerves were banjo tight, especially when our forward progress stopped again. We were deep in enemy territory, and we just sat there, going nowhere in the middle of nowhere. I got out of the Hummer, ran up to Captain Lyle's tank, and asked what the holdup was now.

"One of the forward tanks just collapsed the bridge ahead of us," Captain Lyle replied, with considerably more reason to be irritated than I.

Six of his armored vehicles had crossed to the other side of the deep drainage ditch before the bridge collapse. They were now off on their own in hostile Iraqi territory in the middle of the night, having just passed through a serious ambush. The senior soldier on the other side of the fallen bridge was Sergeant Wheatley. He had three main battle tanks with him and three Bradley fighting vehicles. What he lacked was orders on what he should do next now that his group could not pull back because of the collapsed bridge. The order came through from Colonel Ferrell: "Continue to scout ahead on your own without the rest of the troop, and check out a route to a bridge across the Euphrates." The colonel was constantly on the radio with his sergeant asking, "How you doing, White Four?" as if the colonel were trying to bolster the morale of Sergeant Wheatley and his crew. It was an especially anxious night for that scouting party who while not lost found themselves alone and deep into enemy territory without backup.

"I had a very bad feeling," Sergeant Wheatley said later. He, too, was thinking about Vietnam as his scouting patrol moved among the black silhouettes of palm trees.

The rest of the 7th Cavalry, however, was stopped, going nowhere. Having successfully shot its way out of a blazing ambush, Apache Troop found itself gridlocked, still south of the Euphrates River. Complicating matters, our retreat was now totally checked by one of those five-thousand-gallon fuelers that had also insinuated itself up that dark road that wasn't wide enough for two Volkswagens to pass each other.

I was still unclear why we had come down this road, but the route seemed to have been dictated by Colonel Ferrell's decision to avoid passage through Iraqi towns if at all possible. That option went down under the weight of the tank ahead in the ditch. The tank was now going to have to be destroyed.

There was no choice but to turn around the other tanks and the rest of the convoy and get back to the main road. Then a tank behind us slid off the road and into the drainage ditch. Getting Apache Troop out of that narrow road became a difficult night maneuver in hostile territory. The huge tanks and armored vehicles hemmed and hawed around the palm trees, into and out of driveways, and finally managed to extricate themselves skillfully in a way that could never have been practiced at any armor school in the States. Some Iraqi housewife's petunias may have been ground into the earth, but the tanks didn't bulldoze a single palm tree. As we returned on that same mile or so of dark road, two other vehicles were not so fortunate. One of the tanks from Bravo Company behind us also slid off into the irrigation ditch and later had to be destroyed by the engineers. The big fuel truck that was trying to stay close to the tanks went into the ditch, and the driver suffered a broken arm. After withdrawing down that road to a more open area, we sat and waited until daybreak to regroup.

It was a bad night. The 7th Cavalry had now lost precious time in its race to An Najaf. Three tanks and a fuel truck had been put out of action in the jumble of that night. By now, the Iraqis surely knew where we were.

Fourteen hours after we had launched out of the garbage dump, we were parked beside the road with a gaggle of about a thousand scrawny Iraqi men from the village curiously staring at us. I don't think any of us had slept, and with dawn came the dull, thudding headache from another uncomfortable night. Looking out over the village that morning, I stared at the narrow passageways among all the adobe buildings and at the occasional emaciated chicken scurrying about. At the end of the street, the civil affairs unit and the only Arabic speaker in the company kept telling the older Iraqi men and younger boys to stay back on the other side of the road and away from the tanks.

There was a singular absence of any young men of draft age in these towns. Whether they were hiding from us or fighting for Saddam, we did not know. There was never a woman in sight. In Afghanistan, no women outside the home was generally the norm, but in Saddam's secular Iraq, Sunni women outside the home were not uncommon except in the presence of an advancing army. Whatever enthusiasm the older men demonstrated at seeing the Americans also seemed feigned. And while they paid attention to us, most of us, except the 7th Cavalry's pickets, were disinterested in them. We were weary and suffering from yet another night without sleep.

Looking out over the village that morning, I began walking among the soldiers lounging about their tanks. I was trying to gauge morale after what was for nearly all of them their first baptism under fire. They seemed enthusiastic, as if they had survived a rite of passage. They were swapping stories about the ambush, about their vehicles being hit, and about the number of Iraqis they had killed. One soldier said he'd killed "sixty I-raqis" from his tank turret. Later, after the enthusiasm of the blood lust wore off, I suspect that number declined somewhat.

For Paul, Charlie, Jeff, and me, it was amusing to see these young soldiers' reactions to their first real firefight. Having survived and still on an adrenalin high, they really seemed to enjoy it, a sensation familiar to soldiers everywhere. They had tested their manhood and proved themselves and their training. My impression was that the ferocity of intense combat surprised them, and some of them seemed a little disappointed when they saw us older men, the embedded journalists, taking it in stride. Some asked us, "Have you experienced anything like that before?" It was obvious one of their senior officers had not. The SCO's executive officer, Major Brad Gavle, confessed candidly, "I hope I never have to go through anything like that again."

Practicing my craft, I chatted with a couple of other soldiers whose tanks were parked on the shoulder of the road outside the village we had hoped to avoid. They spoke of the confusion that ensued as they followed Apache Troop across the main bridge the previous evening. Some remnants of the Iraqi forces that Apache had battered during the ambush tried to stage a counterattack closer to the bridge over the Shatt. When they opened fire on Bravo Company, some of Bravo's return fire spilled over into the rear elements of Apache, which had preceded them, illustrating the genius of the phrase attributed to Karl von Clausewitz in the immortal phrase "the fog of war." But it was not fog so much as another sandstorm that still lay ahead of us.

I approached one soldier whom I had interviewed earlier in Kuwait, a driver for Sgt. Matthew Chase's tank. He was Christopher Reed, a large, beefy African American from Tuscaloosa, Alabama. Nearly all of these young men were younger than my sons. After exchanging "hellos," I asked him how he was doing, and he admitted he was pretty down having heard about the two Iraqi children killed in the previous evening's ambush.

"Well, you keep your head down, soldier," I admonished.

Without missing a beat, he lifted his arms out of the driver's portal in his tank. He was clutching a large, black leather book in both hands.

"I'll be just fine, sir," he replied, holding the Bible in the air. "I'll be just fine as long as I got this."

5

Machine-Gun Alley

Now God is in the strife,
And I must seek him there.
—Siegfried Sassoon, "A Mystic as Soldier"

Many years earlier and five thousand miles from Iraq in a remote mountain village in southern Japan, I walked into a wood-carver's shop. He only carved one thing: heads, chiseled out of the local cypress. There must have been eighty of those wooden heads on the shelves, looking off to sea as on Easter Island. Primitive in their artistry, the heads varied little in size and shape. It was as if the carver was ever trying to get them right and never quite succeeding. They were not quite full-scale human heads. I thought of offering to buy one, but the wood-carver spoke no English and I no Japanese. He was deep in thought, almost meditating, indifferent to my presence, so I turned and departed his shop. His work was beautiful but I did not wish to bother him with the labor of haggling.

Later that evening at a local banquet I was attending, this wood-carver and I were at the same table but a few seats apart. He was tall, not stooped with age, at least eighty years old. He was gaunt, with golden skin and long, flowing, white hair and beard. Through a translator, I asked him about his work.

The old man began a haunted soldier's tale. He had been a private in the Imperial Japanese Army in 1937 in China, in Shanghai and Nanking. Without looking at me or anyone else at the dinner, he spoke as if addressing spirits in another world. He told of having been with an army unit that was later mauled by Mao Tse Tung's forces when the war went bad for the Japanese. Most of his comrades, he said, were killed in China. He was evacuated from China by the Imperial Command and transferred to the Philippines to fight the Americans. By war's end, he lamented, he was alone, the only one of his unit left standing, left alive. Then without betraying the slightest emotion, he said, "I carve a head for every one of my comrades I lost in the war."

74

No one present spoke. I was grateful that I had not earlier haggled or tried to buy one of his carvings.

"I should not be here," he said. "I shouldn't be alive."

In Iraq, I came to know what he meant.

As I now reflect on what happened after the 7th Cavalry's march toward Baghdad, the old Japanese soldier's words still haunt me a dozen years later. "I shouldn't be alive." But we were. There were the bodies of hundreds of dead Iraqis along the road, but no one in our troop suffered a scratch.

In the dark of the previous evening, we had been trapped on that narrow road in canyons of palm trees deep inside Iraqi territory on what was to soon become the Euphrates River defense line. Bone Crusher and Crazy Horse Companies had also crossed the Shatt waterway that night right behind us and now clogged the road with vehicles and soldiers, partially blocking the route we were assigned to use on our push northward. From their tanks and Bradleys parked on the shoulder, soldiers stared at us with faces that showed disorientation and with eyes that spoke of bewilderment about where they were. A few waved limply, but mostly the soldiers of Bravo Company just watched as Apache Troop began to roll past. Most of the men looking on were just grateful it fell to someone else to blaze the trail into the villages of the delta ahead.

In military campaigns throughout history, knowledge of the route of march and what happens next is the province of the few at the head of the column. But in our Humvee and in the bowels of the armored vehicles, most of us knew and saw little more than the vehicle ahead, assuring ourselves that somewhere up ahead someone knew more than we did. Tactics and strategy are above most soldiers' pay grade. If the enemy began shooting at a soldier, training kicked in, and the soldier returned fire like an automaton. In the absence of shooting, the 7th Cavalry's soldiers did what soldiers from the Roman legions through the present have always done: They simply followed the soldiers, chariots, wagons, or tanks in front of them.

Following Capt. Clay Lyle's tank and piloting Old Betsy are where Paul found himself again, short on sleep and adrenalin after the night before. By now I had changed my opinion of him. He was a good soldier, a fine soldier, and a perfect fit for our TV crew. I am not sure he had arrived at the same conclusion about us, but I was considerably older than he, and sometimes perspective comes more easily after sixty.

The road north was straight through farmland and endless date palm groves. Mud houses sat not far back from the road, but Iraqis civilians have it in their genes to disappear at the first sight of trouble. We should have divined from the absence of farmers and other civilians that the indigenous population smelled another battle coming, and they discreetly disappeared, not so much because of the American armored column that was passing through their villages but because they knew an invisible Iraqi army was taking up positions along the road ahead.

Ahead of and above us, a sickly yellow sky was continuing to brew up another dust storm that had already reduced visibility to less than a quarter of a mile. Ahead was the outline of a steel bridge across the Euphrates. The old, riveted girders reminded me of one of those toy bridges that as a boy I used to lay down for my electric trains, only this bridge had rusty and rickety steel girders, rivets, and bolts. Every sixty-nine-ton tank that passed over it made me wince at the thought of a collapse. Downstream, the water seemed low. Steep mud banks were along both sides of the Euphrates. Just the same, there was plenty of water in the river for us to drown in if the Iraqis decided to blow up the bridge as we were crossing or if the weight of the 7th Cavalry's armor taxed it. The fall from the bridge itself would have been lethal to any of us.

On the far side of the river were more date palm groves. Hidden deep in the foliage, Iraqis began popping off automatic-rifle fire at us. It began as a crackling sound from within Old Betsy with the diesel engine growling, but there was no determining how effective or accurate the Iraqis' shooting was. Being shot at was unsettling as we rolled across that damned bridge and wondered about explosive charges underneath the girders and at what point the Iraqis would decide to detonate them. Any one of our tanks or armored vehicles would go to the bottom of the river in a matter of seconds, trapping the entire crew in a steel sarcophagus had the Iraqis the foresight or the will to blow the bridge. How many vehicles would they allow across before they decided to do so?

The Iraqis, we later learned, had placed explosive charges all over the bridge and were planning to detonate them, killing us and denying a crossing to the following elements of the column. What spared us was that the charges were either not wired or wired too hastily and could not be detonated. Scrunched up in the back of the Humvee, I visualized all of this in a kind of second sight because of an increasing hail of rifle fire as we crossed the bridge. Army engineers who examined the bridge after Apache Troop and the following units were on the other side later confirmed the charges had been laid.

The Iraqis clearly knew where we were. They were pouring small-arms fire and RPGs down on us with steadily increasing fury and vengeance. It was as if they became more wrathful because the bridge could not be detonated. At that point, I decided we should go up on the videophone and try to do some real-time war broadcasting. The shooting was loud enough for viewers to hear. Although we were banned by the Pentagon ground rules from panning our camera right or left in a way that might betray our location, I thought we could at least say we were across the Euphrates and show the tank in front of us, even if we were forbidden to show the dense palm thickets from which Iraqi fire was coming.

It was "bulletin" news, maybe even a "flash," the first American unit to have taken a bridge, shooting our way across and moving again, now in central Iraq, in the general direction of Baghdad. The 7th Cavalry had breached the Iraqis' Euphrates River defense line. The army, at least, had made a mockery of all those BBC reports that the Americans were bogged down. Our next objective was An Najaf, just an hour's drive south of Baghdad. I knew that clearly, but it would have violated the Pentagon's ground rules to disclose that on the air.

With bullets hissing around us, Jeff dialed up Atlanta on the sat phone. Charlie was using a camel's hair brush to try to keep the blowing dust from clogging his small video camera. In these broadcasts from the front, I never had a script. I never wrote a script during the entire war. I just narrated into a microphone what I saw and heard about me. Perhaps it was the exhilaration of the moment.

The words, the descriptions just flowed out. After the war, people often told me they felt as if they were right there amidst the battles. I don't see how. The mortars and RPGs and rockets were landing all about us with such rapidity, I don't think I could have accurately depicted the scope of everything exploding about us.

Each of us, Paul, Charlie, Jeff, and I, was again in full battle dress—helmet with uncomfortable chin strap snapped tightly and the hugging body armor. Atlanta threw us on the air in seconds, thanks to a wonderful "minder" named Eileen Hsieh, who gave new definition to the word *efficient*. This woman seemed to simply order higher-paid executive producers to put us on the air whenever she told them, "We have news."

Our convoy was by now across the bridge and rolling toward a three-way intersection surrounded by a forest of date palms. If the Iraqis were half as intelligent as the Japanese snipers of World War II in the Pacific Islands, they would have had a dozen snipers hidden in the tops of those palms shooting down on the soldiers who had to stick their heads out of the turrets of the Bradleys and the tanks. The snipers could also have cut us up in our soft-skinned Humvee.

Instead, the Iraqis were on the ground and aimed nearly all their fire laterally, on the same horizontal plane, from both sides of the road at the same time. The only exception to that incoming fire was the arcing mortars they were lobbing down on us. Everything else, the rocket-propelled grenades, the machine guns, the AK-47s, and the old Soviet 20 mm anti-aircraft guns, were stinging us from both sides of the road. As Paul turned left following the tank in front of us, I had my back door of the Humvee open while trying to broadcast some of the war noise, which was now gawdawful loud. A mortar fell in the palm grove off to my right about thirty yards away. The jagged, lethal fragments pruned palm fronds as they blew upward, and moments later, the same shrapnel rained and rattled down through the palm fronds as it fell back to earth. I don't know why a single exploding artillery shell like that froze itself in my mind, when there were so many explosions going off on either side of Old Betsy. Perhaps it is because the mind cannot possibly record the entire canvas of a combat engagement so it seizes one nearby moment and holds on to it.

This ambush was akin to having a hundred or perhaps a thousand hornets trying to sting at once, but the victim could only ride slowly forward through the intensifying fire. It was not a quickly resolved ambush. It lasted thirty to forty-five minutes. The Iraqis had dug foxholes a hundred yards back from the road, perhaps thirty yards apart. In each of these, two or three soldiers were blasting away with automatic rifles.

Again, you couldn't run. You couldn't duck. You couldn't hide. Paul, with his strapping six-foot-five frame, had the hardest time of the four of us trying to make himself small while driving that unruly vehicle. And unlike the previous night's ambush when the Iraqis fired from the darkened fields alternating from the left and then the right and back again as we moved forward, this time the fire was coming from right and left simultaneously, machine guns belching at us out of the yellow clouds of blowing dust.

The noise was horrendous. I was broadcasting on a lip mike, a heavy, hand-held microphone designed to filter out all ambient noise more than three feet away, improving the broadcast quality of the correspondent's voice. Earlier, when we rolled across the desert, the lip mike was excellent for reducing and eliminating extraneous noise like the Humvee's diesel engine or Jeff's coughing. At some point during my live narration of this running battle, I explained to the audience the gap between the shooting and explosions I was hearing and seeing all around me, assuming that the lip mike was not picking up the exploding mortars and RPGs. In my ear, down the I.F.B. (interrupt fold back) satellite phone circuit live from Atlanta, someone told me, "They can hear it, they can hear it. Keep talking." The fact that the explosions could be heard despite the ability of that microphone to filter out most other ambient noise attests to the ferocity of that deafening firefight. I kept telling myself, "Don't hype this, Walt. Don't exaggerate it. Stay calm." In truth, I deliberately and consistently understated all my live reporting under fire. It would have been unprofessional to sound excited in such a descriptive narrative, even when people were trying to murder me. Sports reporters are allowed to get excited about goals, touchdowns, and home runs. But it seemed wrong for me to get excited even when tracers, machine guns, and rocket-propelled grenades were slamming all about the convoy. I deliberately remember understating the entire half-hour broadcast of that ambush just after crossing the Euphrates, figuring no one would believe we were in the midst of this firefight and still surviving. Like that old Japanese soldier had said, "I shouldn't be alive. I shouldn't be here."

Because Paul was driving and being shot at, he didn't get to enjoy the luxury of looking left or right. He knew the Iraqis were dug in on both sides of the road and blazing away. He more than the rest of us had to look straight ahead to make sure Captain Lyle's tank, which was firing away with both its 7.62 mm coaxial and .50 caliber machine guns, didn't stop suddenly, and we would go piling into it. Jeff and I knew it would. Behind us, the "chugah, chugah, chugah" thudding of the .50 caliber on the USAF armored vehicle was firing constantly again. For those poor guys who might have joined the air force thinking they would avoid infantry and armor battles, they sure got it wrong. Still, that air force noncommissioned officer never flinched and never pulled his head down within the relative safety of the steel shell in which he could have hid. The NCO just kept ripping the Iraqi soldiers' bodies apart with heavy machine-gun fire.

In the months after the war, I was repeatedly asked, "Were you afraid?" and I thought back to this ambush more than any other moment. I do not believe any of our crew was close to panic. That was never an option. During the thick of it, I remember asking myself, "Well, are you afraid now?" And the answer was always "No." But I was quite concerned and darned uncomfortable. The most basic instinct that I felt, however, was wrath. Something deep inside me wanted nothing more than to grab a rifle and shoot back at the Iraqi bastards who were trying to kill us. I did not like being shot at, and at that point, I liked even less not having a gun with which to shoot back. Shooting back seemed the "American thing" to do. At that moment, I didn't give a fig for the canons of journalistic ethics that mandate journalists must not bear arms in combat. I grew up an American kid.

I had fired rifles since I was a teenager, and I wanted nothing more than to shoot back at those who were trying to kill me.

The sandstorm blowing about us was so dense that I could not see who was shooting at me such that I could not have shot back. I might have felt an awful lot better, however, to have banged off a couple of rounds. This was a full-scale gauntlet we were forced to go through. The air was filled with bullets for miles up and down the road. The yellow dust storm denied us any close air support, which had bailed our asses out in the previous night's ambush. The air force tactical observers in the vehicle behind us were along just for the ride at this point.

Apache Troop completed the ninety-degree turn at the intersection, and Bone Crusher and Crazy Horse units followed. The battlefield now had a ninety-degree angle to it. The Iraqis had positioned themselves in the inside of that angle in the woods and fields and for miles ahead along both sides of the road. Those Iraqis who were caught between both legs of the 7th Cavalry's column were dead meat. But in destroying the Iraqis in the hinge, Bone Crusher's Bradleys were also firing into the flank of Apache Troop, which had already turned left at the corner. (The full extent of the friendly fire wasn't known until later when several of the main battle tanks were discovered to have .25 mm holes punched through them. The Bradleys' .25 mm guns using uranium-depleted shells hit Apache Troops' tanks.)

On a battlefield there is not just one war but one war for every combatant. Each of us has his own mental video playback tape in his head of the little he saw from his respective vantage point in the ambush.

Ahead on the driver's side, Paul was hugging close to Captain Lyle's tank and wanted to slip in beside it for protection, except there was no lee, no shelter, with bullets everywhere on both sides of the road.

"Hey, Paul, you're our security advisor," I said nervously. "Should I sit facing the incoming fire because that affords my chest the greatest protection, or do I just sit facing forward, presenting a slightly slimmer profile?"

In the shooting I never heard his answer, but I suspect each of us was at that point hoping whatever wounds we suffered would be minor, an arm or a leg, so we could be Medivaced out in a hurry—except, of course, helicopters were grounded in the blowing sand and dust. In the movies, the soldier who gets wounded is Medivaced to a field hospital. If any of us had been wounded in that sandstorm, with no aircraft flying, we would have just sat there and held our guts and died.

At some point in running the Iraqi gauntlet, we stopped broadcasting and focused on staying alive. At the time, I thought the dust storm rendered us even more vulnerable. For the Iraqis, the low visibility was a perfect cover for them to charge out of the palm groves to stand within fifty yards of us, and fire off twenty- or thirty-round magazines from their Kalashnikovs.

There had been no let-up in the firing for at least half an hour now. I imagined myself one of those grinning tin ducks in a shooting gallery. We just had to keep riding along on that little track and hope no one hit us. And like those tin shooting-gallery ducks, I could not fly away. We just followed the tin duck in front of us. We were trapped in machine-gun alley, creeping forward at twenty miles an hour, hoping the covering fire from the Abrams tanks and Bradleys would spoil the aim of the Iraqi brigades out there in the fields and palms hiding in the blowing clouds of dust.

Hunkering down as best we could, none of us said much. In those circumstances, maintaining any focus is the ultimate discipline. I remember trying to recite the Ninety-first Psalm in my head, the same one the chaplain had read fragments of the week before in Kuwait just before we embarked. I had grown up in a Christian Science Sunday school as a kid, and by God, you learned how to pray there. Making some of those verses hang together in sequence, however, was difficult, especially when exploding mortars and RPGs punctuated every other verse. The staccato machine-gun fire seemed to have become ellipses between the psalmist's passages.

"He that dwelleth in the secret place of the most High shall abide under the shadow of the Almighty," I mentally recited just fine.

"I will say of the Lord, He is my refuge and my fortress: my God in him will I trust—"

Bang! Boom! Palowie!

Things were still hanging together until I got to:

"Thou shalt not be afraid for the terror by Night: nor for the arrow that flieth by day."

I never remembered that pestilence that walketh in the darkness bit and skipped instead to "the destruction that wasteth at noon day."

Then another RPG slammed into the shoulder of the road beside us, and I had to start all over again. I'm not sure I ever got all the way through it, but I think it helped. We did not get whacked.

I complained aloud about that damned dust storm making it so easy for the Iraqis to charge out from the fields and thickets and blast away at us from the sides of the road. Paul, however, also remembers the Iraqis attempting a frontal assault on the column. They charged straight out of the blizzard of yellow desert dust, down the road in an old kamikaze bus. Paul was the only one in our vehicle who could see them.

"It was," he said of the Iraqis, "suicide, pure and simple."

They seemed to come from nowhere out of the storm.

"Like crazy men, they suddenly jumped out of this bus and, standing their ground, began firing their Kalashnikovs at the 7th Cavalry's armored column," Paul said. "In a matter of seconds, someone swung a machine gun from one of the turrets of a tank or Bradley in front of us and like a scythe cut them down."

The sandstorm, which I had cursed, actually worked to our advantage, giving the Iraqis a false sense of security, I later learned. One of the unit's officers subsequently called the storm "a Godsend."

"The Iraqis had dug in about a hundred yards, the length of a football field, from the road on which we were traveling," he said. "But because of the blowing grit, they never could really see us. Instead they were firing blindly at the noise this heavily armored company was making along the road."

The visibility was really never more than forty yards. That meant the Iraqis in their foxholes could not even have been certain of the correct angle at which they should have been firing. They never could have led their moving targets in their gunsights because they couldn't see us.

Sometimes, the Iraqis would be lulled into a false sense of security in the limited visibility and come out of the cover of their foxholes fatally exposing themselves, because unbeknownst to them, the U.S. soldiers had thermal-imaging capability on their guns that gave them extended visual sighting, enabling them to pick off Iraqis they could not otherwise have seen at ranges of up to 150 to 200 yards. It was a slaughter, except this time it was Custer's soldiers doing the slaughtering. Upon hearing later of the imbalance of the battle that raged about us, another line from Psalm Ninety-one drifted into thought, "A thousand shall fall at thy side and ten thousand at thy right hand, but it shall not come nigh thee."

Forty-five minutes or so down the road, the firing seemed to abate. In the sandstorm, I couldn't tell whether the Iraqis had run out of fight, the U.S. Army had run out of Iraqis to kill, or the Iraqis had run out of ammunition and crawled back into their foxholes. Whatever way, I was grateful although that awful yellow sky continued to glower at us and spit cutting sand into our faces. We rolled through a four-way intersection that a few hours later would become the scene of more bloody carnage. The paved road that took us north was welcome relief after three or four days of rolling across open desert, dry *wadis*, and moonscapes. We were getting closer to An Najaf and ultimately Baghdad with every minute.

Another twenty minutes or so north, we slowed at a small collection of Iraqi farm buildings nestled in a date palm grove on our right about fifty yards from the road. Once again, it appeared the local inhabitants had abandoned their homes to get out of the way of the advancing American army. A large dirt apron on the side of the road was to be our staging area for the next sixteen hours. Colonel Ferrell's Bradley pulled off while some of Apache Troop's tanks rumbled a little farther up the road, swallowed up in the blizzard of sand and dust.

When we emerged from our vehicles, anything not nailed down blew away. Most of us were wearing ski goggles to protect our eyes. I made the mistake of putting my goggles down on the hood of the Humvee and turning my back for only a second. The goggles blew away forever, and my eyes suffered painfully for this carelessness. My tear ducts were running dry from the constant reflex of trying to wash out my eyes. But it was hopeless. Tear glands have their limits and soon run dry. Later that night, the problem became acute. I dozed off. Tears tried to cleanse my eyes, but the ever-blowing dust melded the tears into a paste that dried on my eyelashes. When I awakened later, in the middle of the night, my eyelashes were painfully plastered shut and could not be opened without ripping out a few.

The end of the afternoon brought renewed confusion. The wind was howling so everyone had to shout to communicate, but the sound was carried away before anyone could hear anything. There ensued more confusion manifesting itself in the form of fifteen very large tanks and other armored vehicles trying to pull into the same small parking lot at once. Each driver wanted to position his tank or Bradley in such a way that nothing obstructed a quick getaway if the Iraqis attacked again. In the meantime, every one of us needed to stretch his legs and breathe through makeshift masks after the run up through machine-gun alley.

Swapping near-miss stories, we discovered the other soft-skinned Humvee, which belonged to Captain Cote, had some scary bullet holes in it. One of the soldiers inside emerged to display bullet holes in his jacket and trousers. Everyone laughed because he was badly in need of a new chemical-weapons suit because his present one was now quite ventilated. The soldier himself was unscathed.

Out of the blowing grit, the three-man crew of the air force's forward-air-control vehicle came striding toward Old Betsy with great purpose.

"Show us the holes," they demanded. Their vehicle was right behind ours on the entire passage through the Iraqi gauntlet.

"What holes?" Jeff asked.

"The bullet holes! We saw them hitting all around your Hummer. Show us the holes."

"We didn't get hit," Jeff said.

They wouldn't believe it. I was reminded of the Apostle Thomas adamantly refusing to believe in the resurrection until he could see the nail holes in Jesus's palms, except Old Betsy had nothing to show.

"You have to have holes. We saw the bullets hitting you. They hit all about you."

There were no bullet holes in Old Betsy, Jeff insisted.

The air force NCOs couldn't believe it and just shook their heads. Every other vehicle in the convoy had been shot up. Bullets were bouncing off the armored vehicles like hail on a tin roof in a July thunderstorm. But Old Betsy was untouched, still a virgin. Maybe ole King Hummer had sold us a magic car.

Word was passed throughout the assembled troops that we would probably be spending the night here. Night was fast falling, and there already was no visibility in the blowing sand. Even with thermal imaging, no one could see a quarter mile. Besides, we were where we were supposed to be, a few miles northeast of An Najaf. Again, the 7th Cavalry was "hanging out," way ahead of the 3rd Infantry Division still off to our rear somewhere. The 7th Cavalry's objective was to hold the bridgehead about two hundred yards up the road across yet another major waterway and prevent Saddam from sending any reinforcements south from Baghdad or Al Hillah. Again, it was a classic cavalry operation, race forward, seize an objective (in this case isolating An Najaf), and prevent reinforcements. Then wait until the 3rd Infantry Division with its dismounts and much-heavier armored columns could take over the city.

An Najaf was probably as "safe" an Iraqi city as the Americans could capture because of its overwhelming Shiite population, long persecuted by and alienated from Saddam and his Sunnis. But again the 7th's marching orders were to not enter the city but instead to stake out a position to the northeast and hold a line at the large, modern concrete bridge just ahead, preventing any relief of An Najaf.

None of the men of the 7th ever got close enough to the city to begin to fathom how important An Najaf is to the Shiias they had come to liberate, which is a pity. It is home to one of the most beautiful shrines in Islam, the golden-domed Mosque of Imam Ali, spiritual leader of the world's Shiite Muslims. He is buried within. Many Shiias believe the biblical Adam is also interred there along with Imam Ali. The blue and white and gold tiles that adorn the exterior of the mosque are exquisite. An Najaf is sacred ground for Shiites, and millions of them through the ages have sought to be buried near that mosque. Shiites believe the gates to the fabled Garden of Eden and the gates to and precincts of the mystical Paradise also lie somewhere within that mosque. The cemetery at An Najaf dates back to pre-Koranic times and has more horizontal inhabitants than An Najaf has living residents. Many of the dead are buried in layers, atop of each other.

Because of the dust storm, the fabled Hanging Gardens of Babylon might have been just across the road, and none of us would have been aware of them. Still, the convoy had parked for the night, and despite the blowing dirt and falling light, we had another chance to broadcast the tale of what the 7th Cavalry had just endured, the run through machine-gun alley. While Charlie and Jeff prepared for our transmission, I did a check around our encampment. Our location seemed ill advised. About thirty-five yards away, an Iraqi multiple-tubed rocket launcher was pointing skyward, still armed with half a dozen or so tactical missiles.

Paul, who had fought in Africa, guessed they might have been South African in origin. An earlier U.S. air strike had killed the missile battery's crew, and the charred remains were still there. Bits of scorched fabric and scraps of charred human flesh lay about on the ground. That there were not more body parts seemed odd until I realized the local farm dogs abandoned as the Iraqi farmers fled would have made do with the remnants of Saddam's soldiers. Ever since we'd arrived, these same farm dogs could be heard barking threateningly at us from off in a nearby copse. Arab dogs have the good sense to stay out of sight among strangers. Few creatures are viewed more contemptuously in the Arab world than dogs; they are persecuted and killed randomly. We wanted no part of them either but for quite different reasons. Each of us had been warned that Iraq is one of those places where rabies is rife, and befriending an ill-tempered Iraqi mutt was a risk none of us intended to take.

Just beyond our new encampment, I discovered that somehow amid the misery of the blowing sand and with the 7th Cavalry breathing down their necks, three Iraqis had decided to surrender. In the greatly restricted visibility, how they managed to capitulate without being shot and killed will ever remain a mystery. Now, there they sat with their hands strapped behind them and seemed a miserable lot. A couple of U.S. soldiers guarded them. By now I was a familiar face in Apache Troop, so I was allowed to talk to the Iraqis. I tried to assure them they were going to be all right. The American soldiers looked on with disdain. I wasn't sure if the prisoners were frightened at this point. They were a scrawny, undernourished trio. Surely, I told myself, they had to be relieved the war was over for them. But then I caught myself and remembered that my reaction was Western, American, and these were Iraqi Muslims. Imposing similar cultural assumptions on Arabs is part of what got the U.S. into this war in the first place. After all, where were all those hordes of Iraqis hungering for democracy and freedom that our soldiers had been promised would greet them? These POWs could just as easily have felt humiliation and shame.

Charlie, our cameraman, had also spotted the three Iraqi prisoners squatting in the dust and came over on the double with his camera. In retrospect, identifying POWs violated one of the military-embed rules, but given the fact we had heard on the radio that the Iraqis were executing U.S. prisoners of war, marines in southern Iraq, I was not greatly troubled by the video we took. Rules break down quickly in war, especially those made by TV executives or officials in pinstriped suits back in Washington, D.C. In truth, journalists and soldiers tend to interpret the rules as they go along, much of the time as circumstances dictate.

After grabbing some video of the miserable POWs, Charlie and I decided to hike over to the long, concrete bridge that spanned the Shatt, a waterway northeast of An Najaf, to get an overview and some bearings. We hiked up to the apex of the bridge, and below us appeared to be a broad watercourse big enough to handle barge traffic although there was no evidence of that. The bridge was a piece of world-class engineering, paid for with Iraq's oil money. Along the banks, a few narrow, wooden rowboats were drawn up. To the northwest, a few more abandoned, mud brick homes were nestled back in the date palms. Up the road in the direction of Al Hillah and Baghdad, the lead elements of Apache Troop with Sgt. Paul Wheatley out in the front took up positions for the night. The sergeant's instructions were that the position had to be held. There would be no retreat. Sergeant Wheatley and his men were assigned to stand guard in their Abrams and Bradleys for the rest of Apache Troop. Nothing was to pass that position. The coming frigid night spent in their armored vehicles had to be among the most miserable of their lives: biting cold, gale-force winds, and vicious sand slashing away at any exposed skin. Captain Lyle offered us the chance to spend the night with Sergeant Wheatley, on the other side of the bridge on point, and we declined for reasons of cowardice and discomfort. Besides, we could not have gotten any pictures in the night in a sandstorm.

Charlie and I retreated across the bridge to where the prisoners had been last seen. They were now stashed away for the night in a nearby farm shed.

The South African rocket battery still stood silent sentinel, leaving me even more apprehensive. If an incoming Iraqi shell detonated one of those abandoned rockets, we would be dog food like the original rocket-battery crew. The missiles were a stone's throw from where Colonel Ferrell had dropped the tailgate of his Bradley and set up camp. A young black and white puppy was running about with a collar on his neck and trailing a tether that he'd obviously slipped. He was a fur ball, charming and frisky—one of the boys. The puppy's girth increased rapidly, filled with scraps thrown at it by soldiers. Overcoming any concern about a rabid dog, I untied the rope around his neck, because I worried he would snag it on something and starve somewhere among the deserted farm buildings. War or no war, this dog was having a fine time; for one night, he had the nickname Napoleon in honor of the French.

Our efforts to broadcast from this encampment had landed us in some trouble with military censors for reasons we could never really divine. We had been extraordinarily careful about what Charlie showed on air. We knew the bridge would have driven the censors mad so we avoided showing that. The camera's capability in the sandstorm was next to worthless. The lens showed little more than my face and form in the low light and sandstorm. Virtually nothing else could be seen other than shapes and shadows. We never pointed the camera toward the bridge. There were no road or route signs about. Still, somebody at the Pentagon knew where we were, and they were nervous about it. We had broken no rules, but still we were ordered to shut down.

I nosed about the encampment trying to discover which stricture we had transgressed but never got a straight answer. It was suggested we had shown the bridge over the waterway northeast of An Najaf but that was patently false. Charlie had done no such thing. Several other specious excuses were floated, and they, too, were untrue. Atlanta was angry at us being shut down, and someone mentioned telephoning the Pentagon to complain. The army's decision seemed formulated more on whim than a matter of principle so I urged Atlanta not to make an issue out of it. Atlanta did not, it seemed, because they were fascinated with the pictures of the yellow sandstorm we had been sending them. For us that evening, the sandstorm became the war. Charlie, Jeff, Paul, and I were overwhelmingly thankful just to be alive that evening. We reminded Atlanta there was almost no light available to broadcast. In truth, we just wanted to put all our gear away to protect it from the blowing grit and batten down for a very frightening night. I successfully persuaded Atlanta to revisit the issue of censorship in the morning, if we lived that long. That was becoming an issue of increasing concern.

That may sound a bit melodramatic now, but it was very real that night. We were listening to the intelligence reports Colonel Ferrell was receiving over his radio inside his Bradley. The colonel had orders leading him to believe the Pentagon very much wanted the embedding process to succeed so he allowed my crew and me to sit around the back ramp of his Bradley fighting vehicle and eavesdrop. An American spy plane, using thermal imaging, flying in the dark above the dust clouds and swirling sand, had spotted a convoy of "a thousand trucks and armored vehicles heading south from Baghdad."

Suddenly, I found myself more alarmed than when we were being shot at earlier. Actually, being shot at is more exhilarating and less frightening than the anticipation of being overrun by an Iraqi armored column somewhere miles ahead of us coming our way in the night. From the intel reports, we gathered we were probably in great danger. The radio read out grids, "Five, zero, two, six." Another voice crackled, "Thirty-eight Romeo, November, Victor." Captain Lyle again ordered Sergeant Wheatley's tank and several other armored vehicles across the bridge to make the initial contact with the incoming Iraqi units.

Captain Lyle asked Jeff, Charlie, Paul and me if we'd like to go forward for the night and stand point with Sergeant Wheatley's unit. I quickly thought of about three reasons to decline. First, in the middle of the night, we couldn't really get any pictures of an engagement. Secondly, there was the discomfort factor; I stood a heck of sight better chance of getting some sleep closer to the main body of Apache Troop. And thirdly, there seemed a fair chance we would be overrun, and that was more risk than I wanted to take.

"No, thank you," I told Captain Lyle.

What I did not know was that Sergeant Wheatley had a few moments earlier radioed Captain Lyle.

"Apache six, this is White four," Sergeant Wheatley said. "How would you like to come across the bridge and spend the night with us over here?"

Sergeant Wheatley like the rest of us was shivering cold in the frigid sandstorm and was looking for company.

"No, thanks," Captain Lyle radioed back declining the same offer I had just declined from him.

A few moments later, the 155 mm Paladin self-propelled guns to our rear began hurling lethal, high-explosive shells over our heads toward the north.

"North of Al Hillah, a thousand vehicles moving south," the radio again crackled.

South was us. More grid numbers came over the colonel's radio.

"Moving thirty to sixty kilometers an hour [nineteen to thirty-seven miles an hour]. . . . They are wearing American uniforms," the radio reported.

That was truly alarming if true. This was the reinforcement effort of An Najaf that the generals anticipated and that the 7th Cavalry had been ordered to block.

"We believe we'll probably come under attack sometime this evening," I reported.

And everyone in Apache Troop thought the same. The generals also believed an Iraqi attack imminent and ordered the 3rd Infantry Division, which was behind us, to link with the 7th Cavalry by morning. Crazy Horse Troop was, we were told, getting hit off to our flank.

There were no reinforcements that night, however. If the Iraqis came, it would be just Sergeant Wheatley and his tanks and Bradleys on the north side of the bridge and the remainder of Apache Troop on the south side. We were alone, and the situation was becoming more tense. In the dark, soldiers gathered around the rear ramp of Colonel Ferrell's Bradley. It was difficult to discern who said what to whom, but someone reported there was a B-52 or a B-1 bomber in the air preparing to drop its bombs off in the distance. Someone else spoke of a smaller fighter-bomber that was dropping laser-guided JDAM (joint direct-attack munition) bombs as well on that Iraqi column. Soon, I could not separate intelligence from speculation.

Broadcasting on the satellite phone, I alluded to the 7th Cavalry's predicament. Wolf Blitzer began questioning me about the veracity of what I was reporting, especially given that a similar Iraqi convoy a day or so earlier had been reported to be heading toward Coalition forces over in Basra or Nasiriyah. That had turned out to be a phantom column existing only on a radar screen.

Colonel Ferrell's soldiers were told they would be facing the Iraqi Republican Guard, one of Saddam's better-equipped and better-trained units. It was, we were told, moving at between nineteen and thirty-seven miles an hour through that same sandstorm in which we had been struggling.

A day or two later, the Pentagon indicated I had overstated the size of the approaching Iraqi force. But, in truth, I was merely reporting the intelligence that was coming over the army's own closed-circuit radio, intelligence that was being passed to commanders on the ground only moments before I broadcast it. Colonel Ferrell believed it that night, and so did all of his officers. My reporting was only as good as the army's intelligence, which the Pentagon later downplayed, suggesting in retrospect the army was getting some inflated reports from the spy planes overhead.

Responding to those same intel reports being broadcast over the speaker on the left rear side of the SCO's radio, we soon heard the army's MLRS (multiple-launch rocket systems) roaring out over our heads in the direction of the reported Iraqi armor column said to be coming our way. There was talk on the radio of "blowing the bridge" as a last resort. But Apache Troop had been assigned to hold the bridgehead all costs. Destroying the bridge would have required approval of the Central Command, and no one there that night believed we would get that permission, even if the 7th Cavalry was being overrun.

"I am not going to collapse this zone," Colonel Ferrell muttered. He knew the 3rd Infantry Division was coming up and would reinforce the 7th Cavalry by daybreak. Under those circumstances, Colonel Ferrell could hand over the bridgehead to another reinforcing unit from the 3rd ID as long as (1) the Iraqis did not attack at night, and (2) if they did, the 7th Cavalry held its position.

The thought of being overrun by angry Iraqis was not very pleasant. Each of us was stumbling about in the desert darkness with his own worrying thoughts. I was hatching my own escape route if indeed we were overrun. Earlier that day, when we crossed the Euphrates River, I'd noticed the banks littered with those primitive wooden rowboats the locals used. Some even had outboard motors. With a couple bottles of water, a compass, and my knife, if I was separated from the unit, I planned to hike across country, steal one of those boats, and float downstream until I hit Nasiriyah and the marines. It was sheer fantasy. But like planning to survive detonation of that heavily mined bridge across the Euphrates earlier, I always had a plan B. If nothing else, my plan was an exercise in self-comfort. Surely, that old Japanese warrior, who told me he shouldn't be alive, stayed alive because he always had a plan B, a bolt-hole, an escape route.

Plan A, however, was simply to go to sleep. Paul, Jeff, and Charlie had learned to sleep in the Humvee, but with my aching knee, I had to stretch out somewhere, preferably not in the open sand where scorpions abounded. With outgoing artillery now banging away over our heads and bursts of MLRS rockets roaring outbound as well, I found a small, concrete-block farm outbuilding with a good supply of hay in it and decided that was where I would stretch out. I burrowed into the hay, spinning it about me like a cocoon. A corrugated-metal door kept out some of the wind and dust, but it banged throughout the night until the gale blew itself out. The blowing and banging metal door was more annoying than distant explosions of bombs and artillery. All night, I would awaken from cold and try to draw more straw about me. As I lay in the haymow, I remembered there were at least five varieties of venomous snakes in Iraq, and I assumed they probably all inhabited the same haymow as I, looking for rats. I tried to reassure myself snakes are cold-blooded creatures, and the cold front which was driving the sandstorm would probably have driven the vipers and cobras deep into the ground. Death by snakebite or death by bullets. In the end, however, it was the bitter cold that kept me awake more than concern about dying. In retrospect, despite the cold, I know I got a pretty good several hours' sleep in the hay, especially after the wind dropped and the corrugated metal door stopped banging.

I might not be alive the next morning, but as under such circumstances in Sarajevo or Beirut during shelling or now in central Iraq, I simply assumed I would be. Morning has a way of taking care of itself. Therefore, the most intelligent thing to do was simply shut my eyes, even though I knew it would result in the dust and tears painfully gluing my eyelashes together again and that trying to open them in the morning would involve peeling away the crust of adobe sealant before I could see what the sunrise had brought.

6

R and R

Our birth is but a sleep and a forgetting.
—William Wordsworth, "Ode: Intimations of Immortality"

Paul came to fetch me from the haymow.

"Come on, we're moving," he said.

It was barely daylight but clear and cold after the passing of the sandstorm. We were still alive. It was quiet now, no artillery, no bombing, just a cerulean-blue winter sky. It was as if the murderous run down machine-gun alley, the sandstorm, and the terror of the Hammurabi division taking aim on us the night before had never happened, a bad dream. I began to wonder how much of what I remembered of the previous day was a delusion. If the brigade of 3rd ID reinforcements, which moved up overnight, had not parked all of its tanks and armored vehicles along the road right in front of us, I might never have known there was a war on this the morning after. The previous night, many of us had wondered if we would live to see the next sunrise. Now, as far as the eye could see, from the bridge northeast of An Najaf and for miles back down the road, there was an American infantry brigade of armored vehicles across the horizon, more tanks and Bradleys than I could count. They were like a stalled, long freight train, waiting for us to get out of their way. The 7th Cavalry had orders to withdraw and relinquish the tip of the spear.

The previous evening's estimates of "a thousand Iraqi armored vehicles" had been consistently downsized by "intelligence sources" through the night to about five hundred vehicles while I had shivered half asleep in the haystack and worried about the vipers of Iraq that might snuggle up for warmth. An air force surveillance, targeting, and battle-management plane known as the JSTAR system, flying above the sandstorm and in darkness, was by midnight reporting that elements of that same Iraqi Hammurabi division had begun peeling off, disappearing from the highway. During the long, cold night, officers of the 7th Cavalry deduced that the Iraqis had decided against a force-on-force confrontation and instead were opting to establish numerous defensive sectors all the way between An Najaf and Baghdad. If that turned out to be the case, it was a shrewd strategy, for it would require the advancing American units to do battle all the way to Baghdad. It seemed a plausible option. Earlier, all along the Euphrates River defense line, the Iraqis had demonstrated they were quite capable of putting up a respectable fight, and it was now a reasonable assumption this might be what they were planning, a fighting retreat to a Baghdad perimeter.

In retrospect, the previous night's threat raised important questions about a journalist reporting basically what was raw intelligence data coming out of the squadron commander's radio. The army allowed us to be privy to the data and report it. I had seen the 7th Cavalry preparing for an assault by the Hammurabi division. Every soldier there believed the threat was materializing and was heading our way. Thinking back, however, I am not sure exactly what happened that night or the extent to which that threat ever existed. The 7th Cavalry's commander had received intelligence reports of an Iraqi armored column taking aim on us the previous night. I listened to the raw intelligence coming in over the squadron commander's radio and still have my notes of it. I heard Lt. Col. Terry Ferrell reading out his unit's coordinates, talking directly to the pilots of the B-52s overhead. He was concerned the air-force–sent B-52s might mistake our tanks for Iraqis. When the bombs began to fall, those Iraqi armored vehicles not "killed" by the B-52s were widely presumed to have scattered, going cross-country to hide in copses and date palm groves. Sgt. Paul Wheatley, who spent the previous night way out in front of Apache Troop in his tank, remembers the bombs from those B-52s shaking the earth and his tank. He never had any doubt either about what the Iraqis were throwing up against him that night. None whatsoever.

A day or so earlier, however, there had been a similar intelligence report that an Iraqi armored column was moving southeast out of Baghdad, moving in the direction of Basra or Nasiriyah. That turned out to be specious. The military later acknowledged the report of an armored column headed from Baghdad to Basra was an error. It was a phantom threat by a spectral division that did not exist. It was later concluded from evidence we saw on the road from An Najaf to Baghdad that many of those advancing Iraqi units that night outside An Najaf just went AWOL the moment the B-52s started to pummel them. Cutting and running increasingly became the operational orders for the Iraqi army in the latter days of the war. I did not blame them, and however ignominious it may seem, it was a clear-cut victory at that point in the war for the Pentagon's much-vaunted policy of "shock and awe."

The 7th Cavalry spent weeks after the fall of Baghdad scouting out these abandoned Iraqi armored vehicles. What had been heralded in the world press as "elite" Iraqi units had simply gone over the hill. This Arab army, like most others, showed scant inclination to live up to its reputation of being crack soldiers but instead demonstrated remarkable good sense. They packed their kits and went home rather than face total U.S. control of Iraqi airspace as well as the U.S. Army's total dominance and firepower on the ground. If any foolhardy Iraqi soldiers needed additional incentives, the abandoned and bombed-out vehicles that other units encountered later along the road to Baghdad attested to the convincing power of the 7th Cavalry's 155 mm Paladin guns and the persuasive ability of the U.S. Air Force to kill targets on the ground at night even when sandstorms reduced visibility to less than the length of a football field.

Still, the Iraqi army's dwindling appetite for a fight had not been obvious to any of us the previous evening amid regular intelligence reports of that thousand-vehicle convoy headed our way. Charlie Miller, who had been an officer in the British army, later told me his "imagination ran riot that evening. We were spread pretty thin. It seemed obvious the Iraqis knew where we were, and they were coming our way." He also confessed that after listening to the squadron commander's radio, he, like me, had a plan B for escape, although he admitted that his was not nearly so imaginative as mine of stealing a canoe and floating down the Euphrates to the marines in Nasiriyah. It turned out that each of us feared we might be overrun, and that in the confusion and darkness, we would get separated from each other or lost. Charlie's plan was to "climb aboard the back of the nearest American tank and hang on for dear life."

In the midst of the previous evening's sandstorm, Captain Lyle had ordered the Company to form a defense line at the bridge. He had to decide whether to try to slug it out on the north side of the hundred-yard-long bridge or on the south side. He opted for the south side. Toward the rear of Apache Troop's column, Sgt. Todd Woodhall was waiting with the medics and three fuel tank trucks. To forestall an attack from the rear, Sergeant Woodhall strung three coils of concertina wire and had the engineers bulldoze large mounds of dirt on either side of the road to prevent the Iraqis from coming up from behind.

Sergeant Woodhall remembers graphically his fear of an Iraqi counter-offensive that night. The air force was bombing in the dark.

"It was awful, loud and awful close to you. . . . and the bombs going off, and you're wondering how close they're going to get, how close that enemy is getting to you," he told me the following day. It was "very nerve-racking, exciting but scary. I got everything set and prepared for the worst and hoped we could pull through that thing."

He fingered his rosary regularly throughout the night.

Two younger soldiers asked Sergeant Woodhall, himself now approaching retirement age, if he thought the three seasoned sergeants up by the bridge, Chase, Gerry Gilmore, and Wheatley, with only a handful of tanks and Bradleys would be able to blunt the thrust of an advancing Iraqi Republican Guard division. Most of us were expecting the Iraqi tanks to pop out of the sandstorm at any moment.

"Everything depends on how many vehicles the 7th Cavalry can take out in the initial assault," Sergeant Woodhall tried to reassure his youngsters. "If the U.S. tanks can block the road from Baghdad with burning Iraqi tanks, then the outnumbered cavalry would have a chance. If not, if the Iraqis broke through, then, it's going to be bad for everyone."

Waiting in the dark, in their M-113 tracked vehicle that night, Sergeant Woodhall, a Roman Catholic, a younger soldier who was a Baptist, and another Catholic all prayed together that the Hammurabi division would never make it to the bridge.

Up at the bridge, on the turret of his main battle tank, Sergeant Wheatley remembers praying, too, praying "that the air force . . . picked up the convoy, and I knew they were moving, and I was hoping and praying artillery and aircraft could take some of them out so they would either split up and disperse and run the other way, so, at the very least, we would not have to fight off a thousand vehicles."

Everyone's nerves had been on edge from our run up machine-gun alley, and the coming night had exacerbated our fears. Within the relative security of his steel box, Sergeant Woodhall and his young charges had spent most of the previous afternoon listening to Iraqi machine-gun bullets and small-arms fire "pinging and dinging" off the sides of their armored vehicle. They said the fighting they experienced was not nearly as intense as what we had encountered at the front of the column, right behind Captain Lyle's tank; but still, the Iraqis had shot off one of the medical kits lashed to the side of the M-113 medics' vehicle, and they, too, had run a gauntlet of rocket-propelled grenades exploding all about them.

It was small wonder most of us had dull headaches when we awakened the next morning and were told we were moving again. The baking heat of the Iraqi desert in summer was still several months away, and the early-morning sun seemed in no hurry to climb above the horizon. But if the sun seemed tardy, the same could not be said of the army, which seemed never anything if not early. None of us, Charlie, Paul, Jeff, or I, said much to each other the morning after. We had spent the night not on point, like Sergeant Wheatley and his crew, not at the rear exposed to an attack there but inside a fairly secure circle of tanks and Bradleys. The previous day, we had been through what should have been a terrifying experience, but it had not fully registered mentally yet. Still, if we were not yet ready to acknowledge the near-miracle of our experience, emerging from machine-gun alley without a single bullet touching our soft-skinned vehicle, Captain Lyle, Sergeant Woodhall, and some of the others had begun to talk among themselves, describing the CNN crew as "charmed." To them, it seemed almost as if we had an invisible and impermeable shield around Old Betsy.

"I don't know how Walt and his crew could do that thing unscathed. It was," Sergeant Woodhall later told Captain Lyle, "amazing."

Charlie, Jeff, Paul, and I were not soldiers in uniform although it would have been difficult for the Iraqis to distinguish us from the real soldiers in a firefight because we all wore the army's desert camouflage MOPP suits. For the Iraqis, if we were with the U.S. Army, we were the enemy. In the eyes of officers and men of the 7th Cavalry, we had been continuously tested under fire, day after day, and not been found wanting. We never panicked, never complained, never asked to fall to the rear or to a safer position. Like Uriah the Hittite, we were placed in the hottest part of the battle, at the very front, amid half a dozen lead tanks and Bradleys. Charlie, Jeff, Paul, and I never publicly made an issue that we were the only unarmored vehicle in the column of steel-plated tanks and other fighting vehicles. It was not so much that we had become mascots; rather, we found ourselves being adopted. We were "their" embedded journalists, and in an ill-defined way, we came to belong to a proud fighting unit as a kind of oddity. This change of attitude only slowly became apparent to us, but in coming runs through other Iraqi gauntlets on the approaches to Baghdad, we discovered Captain Lyle and his men now took closer care of us. Even in the midst of later force-on-force confrontations with Iraqi tanks, head to head, the 7th would draw its tanks and armored vehicles about Old Betsy, shielding us from incoming fire. It came to be a badge of honor to be counted among this "happy few, this band of brothers" in the coming days. Increasingly, soldiers would ask, "You sure you volunteered for this?" We would reply "Yes," and they would just shake their heads and walk away. Of course, so had they.

Apache Troop, with its CNN embeds, now having survived again without a casualty, was ordered to head back in the direction whence it came.

In its place, a line of tanks and Bradleys had taken up positions overnight. This brigade of the 3rd ID had little resistance coming up from the rear, along the gauntlet of the previous day. At the next crossing of the Euphrates River, it would be these soldiers who would take the wrath of those Iraqis who chose to put up a fight. The 3rd ID would leave scores, perhaps hundreds, of scorched and dead Iraqis lying beside the road. That was okay with most of us. I, for one, had little use for anyone who was trying to shoot me. So, if some soldier on a Bradley chose to dispatch Saddam's soldiers to a Muslim paradise with seventy virgins waiting for him, well *"min-fad-lak,"* as the Arabs say, "Please," be my guest. Later in the war, when the Iraqi body count mounted, I came to see the dead Iraqis as someone else's son, brother, father, or husband, but after our experience of the previous night, my sensitivity enhancement was still a hundred miles up the road.

For the moment, however, we were headed to the rear, wherever that was, to refuel and refit. In theory, it was R and R, rest and recuperation, for the soldiers who had not slept more than an hour or so at a time for more than a week. It was now only about an hour after our rapid pullout that morning, and we had had no time even for our meals-ready-to-eat breakfast. MREs come with a small, chemical, heater packet, which when mixed with several ounces of water gives off heat in the exothermic reaction that does a passable job of warming a meal. Trying to heat an MRE in a closed vehicle on the move, however, was out of the question. The chemical reaction gave off noxious fumes that would make a person very ill. Paul didn't even have time to brew his beloved cup of tea, and the stubborn sun lagged in warming the frosty layer of air that had moved in to replace the previous day's sandstorm.

Our stomachs could wait. I was weary of my usual chicken cavatelli MRE breakfast. Actually, MREs never really distinguish among breakfast, lunch, or dinner. Because the army runs on Zulu (Greenwich Mean) Time, it's always dinnertime somewhere. Most of the meals could be made palatable by drowning them with McIlhenny's Tabasco pepper sauce, which came from a tiny bottle included with the MRE. I used the sauce regularly to jump-start my sixty-two-year-old body. I had come to believe Tabasco sauce could make almost anything palatable until the "hot meal" the army promised us for lunch somewhere back over the horizon finally came along.

We now passed U.S. tanks that had taken up positions at intersections that the previous day the 7th Cavalry had had to shoot its way through. This day, the machine-gun nests had GIs manning the guns, securing strategic crossroads. Some very courageous Iraqi soldiers had died in those fields less than twenty-four hours earlier and for no good reason except the glory of an Arab despot who probably couldn't even have named the units who fought and died for him there.

Along the side of the road, skirting east and south of the town of An Najaf were dormant farm fields. Planting would have been a risky option for farmers at this point in the war. In the distance, the farm buildings seemed untouched, at least along this stretch of road, and the farms themselves appeared deserted. The farmers may have been in hiding, waiting to stick their heads up until the Iraqi army retreated, and the Americans departed pursuing them. One could imagine wheat and barley being planted on either side of the road but only after yet another army had passed through this ancient land.

Overhead, on telephone or electric wires, the occasional white-breasted kingfisher ignored the rumbling of the Cavalry's column along the paved road and concentrated on dive-bombing whatever lizards or frogs were just beginning to shake off the morning chill. I wondered who would get to the Iraqi corpses first, the burial parties from the local mosques, the dogs, or the vultures? In the far distance, a raptor of some sort, perhaps a harrier, was gliding on angled wings low over the fields. Having been grounded the previous night by the sandstorm, it would resume its pursuit of voles and passerines. The bird was perhaps hungrier than we were for nothing flew in that sandstorm that grounded both hen harriers and helicopters.

After the previous day's run up machine-gun alley, I heard a ratcheting-up of complaints and grumbling among the men about what they saw as the much-overrated Apache helicopter gun ships that were never there when they needed them. And while the soldiers of the 7th never questioned the courage of the pilots of the smaller, lightly armed Kiowa helicopters, which, weather permitting, scouted for them at treetop level until just before we approached the southern suburbs of Baghdad, the same admiration did not hold for those who flew the army's vaunted Apaches. That aircraft came to be seen as next to worthless in the eyes of men I knew who had been shot at hour after hour, slugging their way ever closer to Baghdad. The manufacturer boasts the Apache can engage more than twenty targets at once, but we never saw one engage anything. Having lost more than a few of these gold-plated, rotary-winged planes and crews a few days earlier in the war, the army's commanders became more careful about losing them. And, we were given to believe, a new, much-higher minimum operational ceiling of eight thousand feet was imposed, making them less than useful to us. I was later told even Colonel Ferrell was overheard to dismiss the Apache attack helicopters as "next to useless" in the kind of fighting the 7th Cavalry was engaged in. A soldier told me he heard Colonel Ferrell complain the damned things wouldn't even fly protective cover for medic missions.

What none of us was fully aware of at that point, however, was that a day or two earlier, a detachment of Apaches hovering at low altitudes had flown through small-arms and machine-gun fire thrown up effectively by the Iraqis, and the army considered it too risky to throw any more of the choppers into the kind of slugfest the 7th Cavalry was encountering. The Iraqis up near Karbala were firing anti-aircraft and machine guns at the Apaches from residential neighborhoods, and the choppers were being mauled. Many of them had returned to base with between ten and twenty bullets in them. One Apache was downed, and its crew lost.

Bouncing about in the back of Old Betsy that morning, my bruised rear complained dreadfully again, and my knees rubbed against my chin because of the sandbags lining the floor. I could almost have been persuaded to take a ride in an Apache to Baghdad rather than continue in the cramped Hummer. Still, we were headed away from the shooting, and that was new and welcome. And besides, in moments like this, I could always put my legs out the back door, holding them above the ground, flutter-kicking into the wind just to keep the blood circulating. I also assured myself it was but three more months until I would be salmon fishing in the Labrador Sea off Canada, standing hip deep in sub-Arctic rivers. I found that emotionally safer than allowing myself to think about my wife and sons. After the events of the previous three or four days, there was no guarantee I would live to see them again. More journalists would be killed in the days ahead as the battle neared Baghdad. Some were friends. It was not so much that I expected to die as that I was not so terribly sure I would live.

Once a day, I tried to telephone my wife, back in London, to let her know I was okay. It had been another spring that I was not home to celebrate her birthday. To her undying credit, even with gunfire crackling in the background and artillery going off, clearly audible through the satellite phone, she never conveyed any sense of fear or panic. Still, as eminently practical as she is, I knew she would be mentally planning for what she would have to do if I were killed in combat, a suggestion she later confirmed. Those phone calls became almost a joke between us. And she, like Captain Lyle and Sergeant Woodhall, came to believe we CNN journalists with the 7th Cavalry were leading a charmed life amid the firefights.

Few of the soldiers enjoyed the luxury the CNN crew had of being able to call home once a day although each of us shared our phones with as many of the soldiers as we could. This campaign was being waged in the middle of the NCAA basketball championships, and I was regularly on the satellite phone to the international news desk in Atlanta, getting the previous evening's basketball tournament results for the soldiers engaged in daily combat. The University of Kentucky score was the one most in demand. Kentucky was home to more than a few soldiers in Apache Troop. Getting home was all this war was about for most of the soldiers I talked to. They knew they wouldn't get back home until they had fought the war. President George W. Bush's argument that this was a war to make safe the folks back in America had little resonance in the day-to-day combat we encountered. If anyone was fighting and dying to make their homes safe, it was the Iraqis, and they were losing.

Yet, for the soldiers I was with, the pull of home was an ever-present force in everyone's mind. In one of the other tanks in our column, Master Gunner Sergeant Matthew Chase had, before we left Kuwait, written a farewell letter to his German-born wife, whom he adored. He, more than most, seemed especially nervous about whether he was going to make it through the campaign. That last letter to his wife, in case he did not survive, was entrusted to his friend Sergeant Woodhall to deliver. Sergeant Woodhall resisted, but Sergeant Chase wouldn't take no for an answer. At that point in the war, we still expected the Iraqis to put up a goal-line stand at the gates of Baghdad. We anticipated it would be savage, bloody, street-to-street fighting, the most dreaded of all manner of combat. Doubts lingered about who would live and who would die.

When the 7th Cavalry moved now, Old Betsy had pretty much become a fixture following Captain Lyle's tank. We were like an ugly junkyard dog that hung back a couple of steps behind its master in the main battle tank in front of us. The odd thing was that although we had a satellite dish on the roof and could dial up most anywhere in the world, we had to communicate with Captain Lyle's tank with hand signals from a few yards back above the screaming of his turbine engine. It was in this position we traveled for the rest of the war or at least until Baghdad fell.

Bouncing along, now going away from the front, I happened to peer into the front seat of the Hummer and observed, without comment, that we had acquired a couple of AK-47 semi-automatic rifles the previous night. The guns were lying between Paul and Charlie, each fully loaded with a twenty-round banana clip. I later learned a couple of 7th Cavalry soldiers had offered them to Paul after they took them from the three surrendering Iraqis the previous day at the bridge. The American soldiers were aghast to discover CNN had no weapons in its Humvee, that we had come through several ambushes and other firefights without any way to defend ourselves if the Iraqis had gotten the upper hand. It was Pentagon policy that no journalists were to be prancing about in this war with guns. But some of the soldiers of the 7th Cavalry, now showing a distinct fondness and admiration for us, wanted us armed and "to hell with Defense Secretary Rumsfeld and his deputies in the Pentagon."

In retrospect, the rifles raised an interesting ethical question although at the time, not one of us said anything. My reaction was that I was damned glad we had acquired the two AK-47s from the Iraqi POWs the night before, and I was rather sure the National Rifle Association would have supported us on this issue. The guns were, after all, in Paul's charge, and he was being paid to protect us. There was no question of Paul's ability to use them. I had already checked myself out on the basics of AK-47 operation just in case anything happened to Paul. If our vehicle had been hit during the ambushes and skidded off the road, we might otherwise have been defenseless. The solders were too busy defending themselves and in the thick of things might not have even noticed we were missing. Even when those two Iraqis stalked Charlie and me during the first night's ambush, Paul had no firearms to protect us. So, even if he had seen the Iraqi soldiers locking and loading on Charlie and me, he would have been helpless to defend us. The army's policy expressly forbidding embedded journalists, as opposed to security guards, from carrying guns was, in my judgment, wise. CNN also mandated that we not be allowed to carry weapons. The gray area was, of course, private security guards assigned by CNN to our crews. They were not journalists but retired military. In Paul's case, he had been Australian SAS, which is to say a trained killer with notches on his belt, who had spent time in Rwanda, Africa.

CNN expected the security guards they hired to protect us with firearms under dire circumstances. Thus, when Paul asked about acquiring a couple of "liberated" Kalashnikovs the previous day, the soldier's response was, "Sure, help yourself." The lowest-ranking soldiers of Apache Troop did not concern themselves with the Pentagon's niceties. They saw themselves not as arming journalists or as even offering us the option of defending ourselves. Yet, having seen what we had been through with them, a couple of these army good ole boys, with a wink and a nod, simply countermanded the Secretary of Defense. They correctly reasoned they were not giving captured weapons to CNN journalists but to Paul, a fellow soldier from the Australian SAS. At that point, it seemed a fine idea to all of us. I do not believe any of the officers of Apache Troop knew anything of it until the end of the war when Paul returned the two AK-47s.

About ten days later, it was quite a different story for my CNN colleague Brent Sadler and his camera crew up in Tikrit, Saddam Hussein's hometown. Sadler, who was traveling outside the army's bubble, said he was unaware the city Tikrit had not been liberated by the allied forces, and so he tried to enter Saddam's hometown. In a matter of moments, he said, his camera crew, acting independently of the army, came under intense fire from Saddam loyalists. Wheeling their convoy about, they hauled out of town with an Iraqi vehicle in pursuit, firing at the CNN crew with pistols. Will Scully, the driver and security guard assigned to that CNN crew, noticed in the rearview mirror that one of the pursuing Iraqis was locking and loading an AK-47. Driving with one hand, Will returned fire with his Hoechler Koch MP5 out of the driver's window, pointing it at the pursuing vehicle, which had now closed to within thirty feet.

Scully, according to Sadler, fired off twenty-four rounds from a twenty-seven-round clip, apparently hitting the driver of the Iraqi car, because it ran off the road. Months later, I asked Brent what would have happened had not his security guard been armed.

"I wouldn't be talking to you now," Brent said. "I would be dead."

Nearly a year later, another CNN convoy came under fire from insurgents with a less fortunate outcome. Two CNN employees, an Iraqi producer and his driver, were killed in this shoot-out. Two of my colleagues in that same convoy, Michael Holmes and Scott McWhinney, escaped death, again because they had an armed security guard in their vehicle, and he shot their way out of the ambush. Neither of these two incidents occurred with embedded journalists, but they demonstrate how quickly things can get out of control for unarmed journalists in shoot-outs in particular and combat situations in general.

Two years earlier in Afghanistan, Fox News' Geraldo Rivera boasted he was carrying a pistol and was itching to use it on one Osama bin Laden. Most of us recognized that as bravado, if not stupidity. In twenty years in and out of war zones, I have never known a Western journalist to pack a gun although there were moments in Afghanistan up around Al Qaeda's Tora Bora preserve where just carrying a gun might have made a statement of sorts to the various warlords' thieving armies roaming the countryside. The difficulty, of course, is that one journalist with a gun is almost always outgunned. In the final analysis, a sharp wit is probably a more effective weapon. More importantly, if you aren't prepared to kill someone, you should never even think of having a firearm. Killing someone should be left to Paul and Will, trained soldiers. For them in Iraq during Gulf War II, guns were never a debatable issue. After the war, however, the issue of journalists with weapons became more problematic.

There was no telling how many Iraqi soldiers' corpses were lying off out in the fields through which we passed. I admit I didn't look very hard although the bodies close to the road were hard to miss. There were several sprawled in the unnatural configuration of death inside a badly shot-up bus beside the road. As the war moved closer to Baghdad, increasingly the Iraqi soldiers would commandeer these vans and the like and use them as kamikaze buses to attack the 7th Cavalry, always with the same suicidal and futile result.

As the previous day's slaughter became increasingly apparent, I invoked one of my long-standing rules, to wit: Try never let your eyes fix upon a dead person. That way I don't remember what I see. The gore is thus not fixed in the camera of the mind for life. I learned that trick in Sarajevo in February of 1994 when a single Serb mortar shell slammed into a crowded marketplace, killing sixty-eight men, women, and children doing their grocery shopping. Later, in a makeshift morgue, those corpses were all neatly laid out like felled timber on the cold, stone floor. Standing there beside CNN cameraman Mark Biello I never focused on any of the mangled bodies so as not to be haunted by the carnage. I let my eyes wing back and forth like radar, always moving the focus.

That morning in Iraq, Charlie violated Walt's Rule and is still stalked by the vision of death along that road. One Iraqi soldier wearing a paramilitary uniform was lying in the middle of the median strip. We assumed he was Fedayeen. Charlie recalls this corpse as the first dead guy he had seen close up in the war, the others having been killed at considerable distance. For some reason, the sight of this particular Iraqi hit home for our cameraman.

"This is for real," Charlie remembers saying, staring at the dead Fedayeen. "He was in his early thirties with two bandoliers of ammunition crisscrossed over his back and chest."

My notes reflect I, too, noticed the corpse, but what I saw has long since been deleted from my mind.

For many of the soldiers in Apache Troop, the carnage of this campaign was the first glimpse they ever had of what the weapons of war do to the human body. Not long after this, Sgt. Kendrick Moore was sent out in fighting closer to Baghdad to conduct intelligence reconnaissance from his tank among the Iraqi dead who littered the road. The commanders were keen to know what uniforms the dead Iraqis were wearing, whether the black of the Fedayeen irregulars or the more traditional military uniforms of the

Republican Guard or Medina division regulars. Normally, they would have searched the pockets of the dead for written orders or anything else that might be of value to military intelligence analysts. But more than a few of the dead Iraqis bodies were too charred to search. Many in the squadron remember Sergeant Moore leaving his radio open as he navigated his tank through the corpses and repeating over and over again, "Oh my Gawd, I am scarred for life. I am scarred for life; this is horrible."

Riding in the back of Old Betsy, I was looking forward to a few hours of R and R, simply being outside of that damned Humvee. I wanted to stand down, walk a little in the desert, and sleep. Taking a nap on any flat patch of sand seemed idyllic. To hell with the scorpions and sandflies. I had long since shut out any concerns I had about scorpions. If they wanted me, I was theirs, just as long as they didn't waken me.

We had no idea what our R and R site would be like or where it was, but at least we would get the opportunity to dig into our backpacks on the roof. Each of us desperately wanted to put on some semiclean clothes and especially some less-than-rancid socks. I confess I was a failure at taking care of my feet and had started to get boot rot. Charlie, by contrast, was fastidious. Nearly every day, he had his boots and socks off and bathed his feet, washing between his toes. He also washed his socks at every opportunity with a plastic wash pan Jeff had fortuitously purchased before we left Kuwait City. In basic training in the British army, Charlie had learned well the lessons taught by all the sergeant majors, who would order soldiers to remove their boots in order to inspect their feet during training marches. It was wise. But with Charlie, cleaning his feet was an obsession. He seemed to forget we were riding with the cavalry, not marching with the infantry.

Good personal hygiene was simply not possible. I did carry one of those alcohol hand washes in lieu of soap and water. Our skin suffered terribly in the desert from the sun, the aridity, and the dirt. We were never really able to clean ourselves, and I was horrified to see my hands and arms assuming the contours and colors of poorly tanned lizard skin. I wanted to smear moisturizing lotion on myself, but that was futile because it would have merely turned the encrusted dirt to adobe. I honestly wondered if my dry, cracked, wrinkled skin would ever heal. Baby wipes, those perfumed, moisturized tissues, were a luxury we saved for our faces and were all I had to remove the filthy coating of TV makeup, dirt, and sunblock from my face. I hoarded my handiwipes nearly as jealously as I rationed my water. I counted out enough handiwipes to last until war's end or at least until May 1, whichever came first. They were the most valuable items in my kit.

My most worrisome desert affliction was a growth that had been swelling on the left side of my nose. I could feel it, and it seemed an unsightly and frightening wart. It bothered me the entire course of the war. Given the intensity of the desert sun, some were all too eager to pronounce the wart as a cancer. It wasn't until some months later, I discovered the "cancerous growth" was more accurately identified as cutaneous leishmaniasis, a parasitic disease transmitted by the desert screw-worm fly, one of which had bitten me along the bridge of my nose. The fly deposited a cluster of eggs in my skin. The eggs' growth causes lesions and disfigurement. U.S. soldiers dubbed the wart-like growth "the Baghdad boil," and hundreds of soldiers suffered the same affliction. At some point on the final approach to Baghdad, my growth simply crumbled and fell off, and I was left with a small pockmark, a crater-like scar.

Mercifully, the R and R encampment came into view. It was little more than a plot of open desert transformed into an unpaved parking lot. For Charlie, the Brit, and Paul, the Australian, it was the first opportunity to see just how big this American operation was. Jeff and I, being Americans, took "big" for granted. There were rows and rows of vehicles drawn up, and our small troop disappeared into the midst of them. Finding our place in this expansive desert parking lot was challenging. We never knew for sure exactly where we were supposed to be or if we were in the right place. At times like this, embedding seemed a fuzzy concept. Paul, who was doing all the driving, correctly concluded that for a couple of hours, it didn't really matter where we parked among the tanks and Bradleys. Like hundreds of others there, we just sort of spilled out on to the sand.

While Charlie's first priority remained his feet, mine was to discover if one of those tents on the horizon had showers. The thought of washing off the caked dirt, sun block, and dried-up skin lotion became my obsession. The army was extraordinarily generous about letting us use its facilities, as long as we waited in line like everyone else. Out of deference, we almost always waited until everyone else's needs were attended to. It was no different at the shower tent. We arrived at what was still "the women's hour." It seemed like two hours. More and more male soldiers queued up, and we stepped farther and farther back in the line. We were scrupulous throughout the war in our efforts to avoid any appearance of privilege. Finally, some plump NCO suggested to the women inside the shared shower tent that perhaps they remember there was a war on and that perhaps their beauty hour had become two and that perhaps it was time for them to get their buns out. They did not need hair dryers; in the midday heat, their hair would be dry in fifteen minutes.

A military shower tent in the desert is not a five-star establishment. It was steamy and tropical and smelled bad. The water is either scalding or frigid. Everything is coated with the scummy residue of shampoo or soap. From deep within the fetid canvas tent, I heard a soldier exclaiming from a shower stall, "Gawd damn! First the Iraqis try to shoot me, then they try to blow me up, and now the motherf—— army is trying to boil me alive!" He recounted to his companion, "At least this is the first time in a week I have been able to shit without someone trying to shoot my ass off." I could not help but laugh. Everything he recited was "spot on." The common water line in the shower tent was turned to scalding, and I wondered if the displaced women soldiers, irritated at the men, had thrown a switch on the heating tank somewhere.

None of us could stand in those showers without being boiled like a Maine lobster. We turned scarlet just trying to clean ourselves. In the end, we simply cupped our hands and splashed scalding water over filthy bodies. Shampoo was liquid soap in the desert. I used it to wash and shave throughout the war. And it was no mean trick to perform those ablutions without being boiled alive. In a commercial hotel, one could sue the management for that shower. But this was the army, and we were grateful for an opportunity to bathe even if the process was painful. No one who ever took a shower in the desert that day will probably ever forget the army trying to parboil us.

The soldiers had also been promised hot meals that day at the R and R stop, a change from the MREs we had lived on in the previous week or more. Like the showers, no one who partook of that hot lunch will ever forget it. A year later, everyone still remembered the only things edible were the canned peaches and vanilla pudding. At the other end of the edibility scale were the rhinoceros-hide hamburgers. After lunch, Charlie, Jeff, Paul, and I decided to forego the offer of a hot dinner that evening and went back to our tried-and-true MREs.

Soldiers are forbidden to denounce their commander-in-chief and other top government officials, and they did not. But Jeff, our engineer, was not bound by any such oath, and he had some pretty unflattering things to say about the vice president of the United States, Dick Cheney, who used to be chief executive officer at Halliburton, the parent company of the firm that was getting rich supplying to the soldiers what passed as food. Given the chance, I think all of us would have hosed down Halliburton's board of directors in the showers from which we had just emerged scalded.

Cleaned and fed, we went back to Old Betsy and would have been delighted to have the afternoon off to nap, but the network in Atlanta was anxious for us to put on the air anything we could give them. The request would have been more than reasonable were our bodies not crying out for sleep. The easiest thing to do was grab a couple of soldiers whose acquaintance we had made and simply let them talk on camera. I may have become the face on camera of the 7th Cavalry, but I knew the best storytelling at that point in the war would be done by the soldiers themselves, especially the NCOs who had the confidence of command but who were not inhibited by fears of how what they said would affect their chances of becoming senior officers.

Sergeant Wheatley was one of those absolutely natural soldiers, tall, handsome with a chiseled face, usually with a plug of tobacco in his cheek. He was a decorated tank commander, spending the previous night out in front of everyone, waiting for the Iraqis to attack, sitting in the blowing sand and darkness listening to B-52s dropping bombs.

"I was hoping and praying artillery and aircraft could take some of them out," he said, "so they would either split up and disperse and run the other way, so, at the very least, we would not to have to fight off a thousand vehicles."

These live shots putting soldiers on the air served another purpose. Their families back home would know their soldiers at work were okay. Early in the war, we began to get feedback from Atlanta that soldiers' spouses and parents had developed a network, such that whenever we went "up on the bird" and began broadcasting, they would notify other families to let them know their loved ones were okay. Captain Lyle's wife had a support group who stayed up all night in Fort Stewart, Georgia, to watch what would have been middle-of-the-day broadcasts for us from the Iraqi desert. Whenever the 7th Cavalry had been in action, I had developed the technique of including in a broadcast or a live shot information that went something like "and to the best of our knowledge, no soldiers in Apache Troop of the 7th Cavalry have been injured." Later, after the war, I received endless messages of thanks and gratitude from families of soldiers for those little asides. It was so easy to do, and so appreciated by the folks back home.

Shortly after commencing, my interview with Sergeant Wheatley was suddenly interrupted with the whoosh of rockets roaring overhead and white contrails just above us. The rockets were clearly audible on home TV sets. Because we were not sure if these were incoming or outgoing rockets, I stopped broadcasting.

"I think we're going to break off this live shot for the time being," I said. "We're not sure what we see up there. See you. Good-bye."

Throwing down the microphone and camera, we piled into the nearest army vehicles. I ended up with Charlie in the back end of someone's overcrowded Bradley just as they were about to retract the rear ramp. It was all soldiers, all elbows, knees, and rifle barrels, check-to-jowl in the midnight darkness inside a Bradley. Jeff and Paul had dived alongside another Bradley. At the last moment, some rather decent soldiers let down the loading ramp again and dragged Jeff and Paul inside with them. The safest shelter for all of us would have been inside an Abrams tank that had been designed to survive a nuclear battlefield in Europe, but the Abrams couldn't accommodate anyone other than the tank's four crewmembers. We were relying on the hospitality of some soldiers we never knew or saw before and now in the dark but with whom we became closely acquainted during this latest rocketing scare.

The 7th Cavalry was getting closer to the Karbala Gap where the commanding officers believed Saddam's generals might use their chemical and biological weapons if they intended to use them. The large R and R encampment with its massive concentration of troops and armor was the perfect target for an Iraqi chemical-weapon attack. It offered perhaps the best opportunity yet for the Iraqis to take out a brigade-sized unit of U.S. forces. Many of us at the encampment knew how to distinguish between incoming and outgoing artillery shells, but when rockets were zipping overhead, we had less experience at determining whether they were Iraqi or U.S., and we didn't know whether the warheads were high explosive or the much-feared unconventional weapons. There was enough uncertainty among all of us, soldiers included, that everyone just dove for cover.

Moments before, we had been on the air with Bill Hemmer, one of CNN's news anchors, who bade us a temporary adieu.

"The embedded reporters are often giving us valuable information from the battlefield at the same time the Pentagon is receiving it," he said. "It's never been done this way before."

He got it right on both points, and Washington was clearly watching the battlefield in real time for the first time.

When the all-clear was sounded, Sergeant Wheatley emerged from his tank where he'd taken shelter also in the belief the rockets might be incoming Iraqi rockets, either Scuds or al Samouds. He resumed his interview, reminding viewers what we'd been through for the previous seventy-two hours.

"You're constantly paranoid," he said. "You're paranoid about every turn, every building, every person, and it's a little nerve-racking."

What he was saying was at least as important for me to hear as it was for CNN's audience. Personally, I was feeling a strong need for validation of everything that I had experienced during the previous week. I needed to know that I was neither imagining nor exaggerating all the RPGs whizzing over the top of our Humvee. I needed to know those mortars were not figments of my imagination and that the bullets splattering all about us were not fantasy. So much had happened, and I was not sure I could fathom all we had been through. This validation was something I needed to do for months after the war as well to assure myself I did not make any of this up or that I was embellishing anything that had happened to us.

I asked Sergeant Wheatley about the night ambush before we crossed the Shatt after leaving Al Samawah, "What did you see?"

"Just a blaze of tracers coming from both sides of the road and mainly from the left side of the road, and like I said, I went behind the sight with the gunner, and we engaged everything we could engage."

"Did it take courage to stick your head out a tank turret to start shooting in those conditions?"

"Yes, sir. Very much for loaders and tank commanders." He described the noise. "It was almost like somebody was throwing rocks, like against the side of your car when you kick up rocks. They were probably 150 meters away, so, their AK-47s wouldn't do too much damage to a tank."

Sergeant Wheatley estimated that in that first night's ambush and firefight he killed thirty to thirty-five Iraqis with his machine gun.

On the road to this R and R encampment, Sergeant Wheatley had also seen some of the carnage of the previous day on the run through machine-gun alley: the bodies in the fields, the twisted forms lying in the kamikaze buses and pickup trucks. There was gentleness in the voice of this reluctant warrior as he spoke of dead Iraqis.

"It was sad they were forced to fight against odds that they would never have a chance to overcome, shooting rifles at tanks," he said. "They are driving Toyota pickup trucks at Bradleys and tanks. War is often beyond human reckoning. I could never explain it."

None of us could. But we had lived it. As the hours and days went on, it became increasingly difficult for many of us to recall how much of what we experienced was real and what was imagined. Perhaps it was easier for soldiers. But, not long after Baghdad fell, Charlie, Jeff, Paul, and I would go our separate ways, and we would not have the mutual-support group soldiers in a unit have to talk about what they experienced. Still, one needs to know the difference between reality and imagining. In retrospect, I think it was even more real than we admitted at the time. I suspect the human mind, the senses, capture and record only a sliver of what is happening: mortar shells falling and exploding in the drainage ditch a few feet away, a rocket-propelled grenade going over head and exploding in the field beyond, kicking up dirt, machine-gun bullets splattering in the dust beside the car. It helps to marry what a person *believes* he saw to what others *say* they saw and remember; then there emerges a much more encompassing tapestry of shooting, killing, and death—bigger than one man's mind alone can register. And this is how we create memories, which are really the things we remember. The additional validation was important for our sanity. I had to know I was not making up any of this. The truth is, four different soldiers sitting inside the same tank witnessed four different wars.

During one of our live TV interviews, the viewers got an added taste of the reality of soldiering. I was broadcasting live and on camera from the middle of our desert encampment when right in the middle of my broadcast and clearly just a few yards in back of me, a soldier, totally oblivious or indifferent to the fact he was on television, unzipped his MOPP suit and commenced urinating for all the world to see. I never knew it at the time. I don't think the soldier knew, either. But the control rooms in Atlanta had a wonderful laugh over it. War in real time is multifaceted and at times wonderfully human.

Journalistically, a certain casualness in living with the soldiers increasingly worked to our benefit. If they felt comfortable peeing on camera, they were also at ease sharing the hottest camp gossip. At about this same time, one soldier trying to be helpful approached us and said, "Have you guys checked out that Iraqi truck over there? It's full of rockets, and the chemical guys are climbing all over it."

I grabbed Charlie, he grabbed the camera, and trying to appear casual, we sauntered over to the Iraqi truck. It was a vehicle that had been captured at the bridgehead at An Najaf, twenty or so hours earlier. In the sandstorm, we hadn't even noticed it. Still, the camp gossip now had it that the Iraqi truck had chemical weapons inside. Behind the canvas were twenty-five or so twenty-foot-long missiles. What made the rockets so interesting to the army was that the documentation papers had been signed by an Iraqi officer attached to a chemical-weapons unit. The chemical-weapons team attached to our company had thoroughly inspected these rockets.

"I guarantee you," one of the soldiers told me, "if there had been something bad in those warheads, we wouldn't be standing here now. If there was a blister agent, the soldiers would have been affected by now."

In the end, except for some good video, we never reported any of this. It was simply too risky to talk about Iraqi rocket shipments signed for by one of Saddam's chemical-weapons officers. No one would have heard anything beyond "chemical-weapons officer," and my disclaimer that there was no evidence of chemical warheads would have been lost. Television viewers hear what they want to hear, and over the years I have found, even in the face of contradictory evidence, viewers believe they have heard reported things that never were said. So, the battered old, green, Iraqi army truck with its twenty-five missiles sat there unreported. I doubt younger correspondents or some-one from Fox News would have made the same judgment call. But I am descended from a long line of conservative Republicans, and erring on the side of caution is intuitive. And the fact was, this was a cache of twenty-five conventional short-range, surface-to-surface missiles with high-explosive warheads and not much more. In the larger context of the war, it wasn't much of a story.

I don't recall eating that evening. All of us needed sleep desperately, and we had been denied that during the day, so at sunset, I spread my sleeping bag on the hood of the Humvee and made ready for bed. The ritual was always the same. First, I put down a foam thermal pad to insulate and soften the bag from whatever was under it. Then, I set out my flashlight, putting it within reach on the windshield wiper for easy access. I climbed on to the hood of the Hummer and unlaced my boots, keeping them well off the ground so no scorpion would sneak in. I placed my body armor and helmet beside me on the hood to keep me from rolling off. They were also there for quick access in the event we took incoming. Then, I stripped to my underwear, often shivering in the desert night air, peeling off the chemical-weapons suit's trousers and jacket and rolling them up beside me, again for quick access in the dark of night. And then, I slithered into a sleeping bag ballooning with goose down, and I dropped off, letting the missiles and the artillery overhead do their work over the horizon. In my state of exhaustion, there would be no dreams or even nightmares. My mind would do a total shutdown. This would be "a sleep and a forgetting."

7

The Karbala Gap

May my heart always be open to little
birds who are the secret of living.
—E. E. Cummings, "May My Heart Always Be Open"

Rest and Recuperation, R and R, was a bit of a misnomer during the Iraqi campaign of March and April 2003. For the 7th Cavalry, there was little of either. Time was too short. The desert heat would soon be upon the liberating—or invading, depending on your politics—Coalition armies. There loomed the genuine concern the soldiers would yet have to fight outside the gates of Baghdad in chemical-weapons suits at a hundred-plus-degree temperatures. The mighty American army was now fewer than a hundred miles from those gates.

For the Cavalry, R and R came to mean only "refuel and refit" before the final push. For embeds as well as some soldiers, one might add a third R: reflection. We now had a little downtime to reflect on what we had seen and what we would yet face as we approached what would be the denouement of this war.

On 27 March, the first full morning of our R and R, soldiers were using compressed air to hose down the air filters they removed from their tanks. Great billowing yellow clouds of dust spewed forth out of the filters. I realized that morning that we would now no longer be on point, because Colonel Ferrell had new orders to move to the edge of the battle where we would be guarding the flank of the 1st, 2nd, and 3rd Brigades of the 3rd Infantry Division. After An Najaf, we had pushed as far and as deep toward Baghdad as command wanted the 7th Cavalry to go. Powerful as it was, the 7th Cavalry would not be the mailed fist that would slam into the Iraqi capital, making mockery of the Iraqi government's claims that the allied forces were still in Kuwait. The people of Al Samawah, An Najaf, and soon Karbala knew better.

I had ambivalent feelings about what I was sensing. Part of me was quietly delighted. I wasn't being shot at every day at point-blank range. That part of me needed a day off. But another part of me missed the battle, that wonderful exhilaration of bullets and noise and danger. George Washington, writing of that exhilaration, observed, "I have heard the bullet's whistle and there is something charming in the sound." I had already gotten myself into editorial hot water in a live interview with CNN anchorman Aaron Brown in the opening days of combat operations. He again asked me how I was bearing up. In retrospect, I think he expected a ponderous response reflecting on the horror of war, the death and destruction and brutality. Perhaps showing poor judgment, I again told the truth, which is to say, "I am generally having a good time, and it is a lot of fun."

War, in a metaphysical sense, is immoral. But it is also one helluva adrenalin high, a defining moment, often a germinal event in a person's life. Perhaps that is why old soldiers are forever holding reunions. It is why after the war, so many old soldiers messaged me saying, "Gawd, I wish I could have been there with you." Ask the dwindling numbers of survivors of the Second World War. For those who have been there, despite the terror of some of those moments, it is out-of-this-world spectacular. I have never done drugs or booze or anything that induced a buzz to equal being shot at. It is mind-blowing every time you survive it. Sometimes, afterwards, it frightens me how much I enjoyed it.

Once in the mid-1980s, after spending a couple of days with Soviet troops in Afghanistan during Moscow's war there, it took four days to scrape me off the ceiling when I came home. During that sojourn with the Russians, we lived in considerable danger close to Soviet troops. The last night in Khost we came under a heavy mujahideen artillery barrage. Running down the dirt airstrip toward our Soviet Antonov 26, I could feel the concussions of exploding incoming artillery rockets buffeting my face. Moment later, we took off from Khost in total darkness save for the flashes of incoming artillery explosions on both sides of the runway outside the plane. Taking off and climbing with incoming all about you and huddling inside a darkened aircraft, there is an uncontrolled exhilaration that comes from being able to remind yourself you are still alive after having been under fire. It is that same exhilaration, that rush, that comes from being shot at that I tried unsuccessfully to convey on Brown's show.

The idea probably seemed warped to Aaron. On reflection, perhaps it is perverse.

During the R and R, we came under only peripheral fire and usually at long range. I telephoned Atlanta and told them, "Nothing is happening today," which, compared to the previous week, was absolutely true.

"We need rest, so we won't be broadcasting," I said.

My estimation was that we had been temporarily sidelined on the march toward Baghdad. Unbeknownst to Charlie, Jeff, or me, however, our adventures had become a hot-ticket item for CNN viewers. Families of the soldiers in the 7th Cavalry wanted to know where their men and women were. The problem for embeds like myself, however, was that there were twenty-four hours of airtime to fill. The 7th Cavalry, coming through ambush after ambush without a combat injury, had become a charmed unit viewers wanted to see. Old army cavalrymen were wedded to their TV sets. Col. George Armstrong Custer's men were being redeemed on global television.

Tom Johnson, a former president of CNN and a really decent, honorable television executive, jumped in on one of those telephone calls to congratulate us on what we had been able to broadcast of the 7th Cavalry's engagements. Tom was extraordinarily well connected inside Washington's power elite, having years earlier started as an intern in Lyndon B. Johnson's press office. Later, as president of CNN, Tom had entree into all of Washington's corridors of power, having for decades adroitly cultivated much of official Washington. So, when I heard Tom's voice on the sat phone telling me, "Walt, they are watching you in the White House and the Pentagon. They are watching you closely," I quickly understood we were going to be broadcasting during R and R regardless of my own preference for sloth and sleep.

Eileen Hsieh, one of our long-suffering and often brilliant "minders" in Atlanta, also reminded me we had developed quite a following back in the States, and even if we weren't being shot at today, perhaps we could give the viewers a video tour of Old Betsy, where we slept and worked. Thus, despite my saying "We won't be broadcasting" today, we did. Jeff put up the satellite transmission dish. Charlie and Paul dragged out the generators to power up the transmission, and I wracked my brains for something to say.

Old Betsy, our Humvee, had become our office, our studio, our living room, and my bedroom on the hood. Charlie pointed the camera at the Hummer, and I began talking, ad libbing.

"This is our recycled, second-hand, U.S. Army Humvee, which any bullet will pass through, even a .22 caliber bullet. You can see our body armor draped on the door. This is where we have actually been living. This is the kitchen when we're down," I said, pointing to a bumper with some MREs and a teakettle. "And we're very fortunate because we have a teapot."

Pointing to the open right rear door, I said, "That's my cubby hole. It's extraordinarily cramped because Paul Jordan sandbagged the floor [I point to sandbags] in case we hit a mine. That's all the space we have to eat and sleep in."

I then pointed to the spacious hood of the Humvee, describing that as my bed. I should have made mention of the incline and that I had to brace myself with boots to keep from rolling off at night. I also noted that Charlie, Jeff, and Paul had scrounged some cots from the army, which were, in a way, the ultimate in decadence. Most of the time, I preferred the hood of the Hummer because it was such a struggle to put up the cots with their rigid tension bars on the ends. I could get two of the three support bars in place, but when Paul with his youth and strength had difficulty wrestling his into a correct assemblage, I did not feel so humiliated. I took the lazy way out and continued to sleep on the hood.

"Now let me hold the camera," I continued, showing our audience the rest of the crew.

Charlie handed me the weenie-cam, and I introduced my comrades without arms except for Paul, who discreetly kept our AK-47s out of sight during the tour.

"On camera left is Charlie Miller. He has been our superb and intrepid cameraman. On our right is Jeff Barwise, a brilliant satellite engineer. That's the crew that brings you these pictures." Then, moving on, "And this is Paul Jordan, our security guard and driver through thick and thin."

One of the defining moments of this break from the war was absurd but, in retrospect, amusing. I gave the tour of our encampment wearing a filthy, gray, athletic t-shirt. This is not standard on-camera apparel for television, but it was genuinely what many of us, soldiers as well as myself, stripped to in the midday sun. Our desert ordeal had knocked some twenty pounds off me, and I was slim again. I forgot any self-consciousness I had about humiliating myself in a jock's locker-room t-shirt, because when I looked down, my paunch was gone. The filthy-gray t-shirt was to become my "signature" garb throughout the war. My wife was shocked, watching the TV and seeing me appear on camera in that dusty, sweaty tee. She queried me, in our next telephone conversation, but then she is ever conservative and hesitant about risk-taking of any stripe. Soliciting a second opinion among the women on the Atlanta news desk, however, I got the impression they thought it was pretty cool for an old codger to go on camera like that. Their vote, in chorus, was, "Wear it! Wear it!" I was later told some of the young women on the news desk had given me the nickname "stud muffin," which was as flattering as it was absurd for a sixty-two-year-old duffer. My wife lost. The t-shirt won. One of those infamous t-shirts now sits in my closet, and only the mothballs among the sweaters overpower the rancidity; the other is lovingly and dutifully worn to this day by my younger son, Timothy.

The R and R also gave me a chance to wander about the encampment and talk to some of the weary soldiers, many of whom had not slept lying down in more than a week. We were short on news and badly in need of color to share with viewers about the soldiers' lives at this juncture in the war. Leaving Charlie and his camera behind, I grabbed my notepad and took off. One of the puzzling things I had occasionally observed when we stopped was that the trail of the 7th Cavalry was littered with unopened Charms Candy packages that were included in some of the MRE meals. As I strolled from tank to tank, I noted there were even more of these rainbow-colored packages littering the ground. I couldn't figure out why the soldiers had thrown them away. They were a good, hard candy to suck on, a sugar fix, in the absence of some decent chocolate that would only have melted in the desert heat. Charlie, Jeff, Paul, and I swapped Charms and traded them among ourselves for breakfast Pop-Tarts or M&M's or whatever appealed at the time.

I asked some soldiers who were at ease.

"Charms are bad luck," they said. "Never eat them."

"Throw away the devils," other soldiers told me.

I did not stop sucking the darned things when I found them in my MRE food sacks, but I was just cautious enough not to pick up any of the discarded Charm packages.

Charms candy was just one of many superstitions faithfully assumed by soldiers who seemed at least as credulous as sailors. Nosing about further, I was also told to never eat M&M's on a tank.

"Why?" I asked.

"Bad luck" was the reply.

In our Humvee, these morsels of chocolate were so prized that Charlie, Jeff, Paul, or I would have scrounged them off the ground, had we found any. Soldiers' superstitions aside, we freely traded other morsels for M&M's. Faced with a choice between my craving for chocolate or superstition, it was chocolate hands down, in or out of a tank.

I began compiling pages of notes on the superstitions of modern soldiers at war.

"Never mention the sun," I was told. If you did, it would surely rain. "Always call it the big orange ball."

"Never, never say the *r* word, or you will be up to your axles in mud," another tank crew member said about rain.

I think it was Sergeant Wheatley who mandated that his tank crew "never, never eat dried apricots aboard the vehicle." I was never sure when anyone got a package of dried apricots anyway, and that "superstition" probably had more to do with the flatulence apricots produced in the close quarters of a tank than on any premonition of good or ill luck.

Never touch the gun barrel after realigning it.

Never eat potato chips on your tank.

All "very bad luck."

Other soldiers told me, and this seemed a universal superstition, "Never pee in the tracks of your tank. Always urinate in another crew's tank tracks." Well, that made sense, kind of.

Certain tanks I looked at were considered lucky or unlucky, not unlike ships at sea. Lucky and unlucky tanks were determined by the name painted on the gun barrel and how the sentiment painted there matched the temperament of the crew inside, especially the commander. All of these tanks had been pre-positioned in storage in Kuwait. The soldiers did not travel with their own tanks. They did not get to name their tanks but instead picked them up as they remobilized in theater, much the way a navy crew acquires a "new" ship. When soldiers acquired a tank before this war, they inherited it with a name on the barrel, and they wanted to be certain the name on the barrel "fit the crew inside." For example, "Antique IV" had to have an older soldier as part of the crew for it to be a fit. "Armed and Dangerous" on the barrel had to have a crew member perceived as slightly mad. "Any Last Words" on the barrel had to be manned by a crew with swagger. A bad name translated into a bad tank.

Lastly, yet another tanker warned, "Never, never talk about breaking down," because it would surely come about. Being anything but superstitious myself, I shook my head and smiled, taking the notes dutifully.

In truth, the greatest talisman against the "evil eye" in this outfit was the superb maintenance that had been done on these tanks before the war. All of the "pre-pos" were in excellent states of repair. After the war, the officers of the 7th Cavalry said the vehicles they picked up were like new. Captain Lyle later remarked that when one of his Company's tanks went down, it never stayed out for more than an hour or two. The usual repair time was two or three days, sometimes even as long as five days. But some nameless but brilliant army mechanics in Kuwait before the war started had those

M1A1 Abrams tanks and Bradley fighting vehicles running like Patek Phillippe watches. That accounted for the stunning rapidity and success with which the army was able to move from Kuwait to Baghdad. I doubt that anyone ever thanked those mechanics.

During this refitting stop, tank and Bradley crews got out their manuals and went through a two-hundred-point check of their vehicles, literally by the book. There were 150 preventive-maintenance checks alone. The manuals told a soldier how to check every item. Each check was graded accordingly: (1) shortcoming: has a problem but will last longer; (2) dead-lined: won't work any longer, have to have part for the tank to continue to function; and (3) "broke," in the words of one sergeant. The four-man tank crews worked in shifts during this resupply and refitting period near An Najaf. One crewmember got to sleep; the rest worked checking the vehicle's suspension, tracks, and seals and tightening bolts and valves. As the vehicles sat parked, they were supplied with a new box of MREs lashed to the sides along with cartons of two-liter water bottles. Many of the supplies that had been on the Bradleys and tanks at the outset of the campaign had either been consumed or shot off during the ambushes of the previous three or four days.

At one point during this pause in the desert, I was wandering about and chanced upon what appeared to me a three-star general. I hesitated for a moment, reflecting that in my sweaty gray t-shirt and filthy cargo pants, I was hardly dressed to meet a "three-star." Still, I greeted him.

"Hello there, General. How are you?"

His name patch said "Wallace." Later, learning his first name was William, I knew I had correctly surmised "a good Scot," whose forebears had for centuries been the backbone of the British army. The commander of the Vth Corps of the 3rd ID glowered at me without speaking, thinking I would wilt in the presence of "command." But I often fish with U.S. Air Force retired "four-stars," some who flew B-24s in World War II and others who fought and won the Cold War, so I was not intimidated.

"Hello there, General, my name is Rodgers. I am the embedded journalist with Apache Troop."

There is nothing so much like God on Earth as a general on his battlefield, and General Wallace was clearly feeling pretty deific that day. But my attitude was, "What the hell, no one had been shooting at him for a week." Besides, the worst thing he could do was send me home. Make my day, General Wallace.

"How do you think the embedding process is working?" I proceeded. My question was totally self-serving.

"I think it's the best innovation of this war," he growled, ending the conversation and walking away.

I later learned he had been looking over the unit, and this unit inspection had a personal side to it. He was checking on a friend's son. One of the lieutenants commanding one of Apache Troop's Bradley fighting vehicles was Matt Garrett, a fine young officer who happened to be the son of General Wallace's roommate at West Point. When the general found him, Lieutenant Garrett was chatting in the shade of the vehicle with Sergeant Wheatley about the previous week's fighting. General Wallace slapped both the lieutenant and the platoon sergeant on their backs, congratulating them and saying, "You sonsabitches killed some real shit." Sergeant Wheatley later recalled, "He was real happy with what we had done."

After some more small talk among soldiers, the general told the sergeant, "You take care of my boy, you hear?" Then the three-star general hugged the sergeant, "putting his arms around me," Sergeant Wheatley said. The image of that three-star bear hug makes me chuckle a year later. Then the general grabbed his college roommate's son by the arm, and they went off to have a private chat, in which he assured Lieutenant Garrett he would e-mail his mother to let her know her son was okay. The army, like the CIA and most U.S. government institutions, is nothing if not incestuous. That close, political tie between the young lieutenant and a bevy of generals up and down the chain of command did not, however, stop Captain Lyle from growling without fear at Lieutenant Garrett later in the war. I don't think there was much Captain Lyle did fear, and the more I saw him the more I knew the army was blessed to have him. The captain didn't stand much over five-foot, seven inches tall, but he fought like a grizzly bear with cubs under threat.

Captain Lyle's soldiers had until the R and R been advancing daily, but as new marching orders were coming in, there was some unfinished business in the rear that required a clean-up detail. Not that many miles back down the road over bitterly contested terrain, the 7th Cavalry had left two tanks in a drainage ditch between the Shatt—the waterway—and the Euphrates River. They had to be retrieved, and this refueling and refitting stop was the opportunity. Twice, a detachment from Apache Troop was assigned to recover those tanks, both times under fire. As the Cavalry temporarily abandoned them and moved on closer to Baghdad, the Iraqis did their duty and burned them. The first attempt to recover them had been during the sandstorm, but Lieutenant Patrick Shea's recovery team was driven off by intense Iraqi fire. During a second recovery attempt during the R and R, the Iraqis opened the tank's fuel tank, setting it ablaze, virtually destroying it. By the time the Americans finally got their hands on the tanks again, they were unserviceable. In the end, only one of them was recoverable. The incident should have been instructive. It was, perhaps, an inkling to the American army that it was not going to be all that welcome in Iraq, even though the president and his chain of command had assured the troops they would be greeted as liberators. People don't burn the tanks of their liberators.

Elsewhere in our bivouac, many of the soldiers were being reissued chemical-weapons suits. The ones they had been wearing were still serviceable, but had there been a chemical-weapons attack, the soldiers would have had to discard the contaminated MOPP suits at a detoxification center and put on new ones. The difficulty was that during the ambush and the run up machine-gun alley, the back-up truck carrying all the company's chemical-weapons suits broke down and was subsequently shot up, leaving the spare MOPP suits useless. The unit also lost its supply of toilet paper on that abandoned truck, so both replacement TP and new MOPP suits had to catch up with us during R and R. More than a few soldiers had their personal gear bags shot off their tanks and Bradleys during the run up machine-gun alley, so they were being issued new shirts and boots as well.

Embedded journalists were not issued back-up MOPP suits, and we could only hope there would be replacement MOPP suits for us in the event of an Iraqi unconventional-weapons release. What the army did not know, however, was that in addition to the camouflage MOPP suits they issued and mandated we wear, CNN had issued us our own MOPP suits that actually met higher protective and safety standards than army-issue. The CNN-issue suits were metallic silver, though, and we would have looked like turkeys in aluminum foil running about the desert if we had ever had to put them on.

So far during this war, the only use these chemical-weapons suits had served was that they were pretty good insulation in the frigid desert night. All of us slept in them, flipping up the parka hoods when it got really cold. The interiors of the Bradleys, tanks, and other tracked vehicles actually provided the soldiers more warmth than those of us in the Humvee ever enjoyed.

The final morning during our seventy-two-hour encampment, before the sun rose on that bleak stretch of desert, was so cold soldiers repeatedly started their vehicle engines to keep warm. The engines had to be restarted anyway to charge the batteries, but the whining of the tanks' diesel turbine engines interrupted a sound sleep, especially if one was already shivering. Unable to fall off to sleep again and quivering in the cold predawn, I decided to go stand in back of one of those tanks to try to get warm. Jeff, Charlie, Paul, and I had no heating unit of our own, and Captain Lyle repeatedly reproached anyone who tried to build a fire.

The back end of an M1A1 Abrams tank throws off a powerful blast of heat when the engine is running. The tank's power plant is mechanically more like a jet engine than the power plant of a diesel truck. If I gauged the jet blast correctly and stood about out twenty yards back, half of me at a time could get warm anyway. Breathing all those high-octane fumes probably was not healthy, and they don't smell very good, but the alternative was uncontrollable shivering in the frigid desert air.

None of us knew what lay ahead. Somewhere to the north was what the army called the Karbala Gap, a stretch of desert in between the city of Karbala and a large, fresh-water lake known as Razzazah. The gap "somewhere ahead" became the next most likely place for the Iraqis to target our forces with chemical weapons. Within that narrow ten-mile stretch, there would be a fairly large concentration of troops gathered, a perfect opportunity to strike a blow for a dying tyrannical regime.

Prior to the war, diplomats posted in Baghdad believed Saddam either stored or dumped chemical-weapons stocks in Lake Razzazah. Fueling that surmise, a number of dead animals were found around the edges of the lake, and the assumption was that the animals had been poisoned drinking the waters. U.N. weapons inspectors inspected the lake, but their findings were inconclusive.

Off to the east in the tawdry Shiite city of Karbala itself, we could hear the army's MLRSs whizzing over it and into areas where Iraqis had tried to concentrate their forces. It wasn't comforting to hear all the bangs and booms, even when realizing that it was friendly fire, not targeting me. The shooting always seemed the loudest at night when I tried to sleep, but that was usually when the Iraqis emerged from their hiding places, lulled by a sense of security. Night fire also afforded a spectacular fireworks display for those of us who lay outside in our sleeping bags. And when I had enough of this sound-and-light show, I just threw that switch in my head and went to sleep, war or no war.

When dawn broke on another day, soldiers were soon punching out gun tubes with ramrods and brushes, cleaning out the accumulated carbon deposits, dust, and sand. Everything was to be ready for the orders to go again, which we all knew would come soon. We were still approximately eighty or ninety miles south of Baghdad, having pulled back twenty miles from the front into a quiet stretch of desert.

At that point in the war, mess sergeants became perhaps the most solicited soldiers at the encampment. They controlled who got the ground coffee, which soldiers craved. None of us had had anything like that for going on weeks. The mess sergeants also meted out the canned fruit cocktail, which was sweet and syrupy and delicious compared to our daily rations.

Perhaps the best scrounger was Sergeant Chase's driver, Specialist Christopher Reed. Sergeant Chase later laughed, recalling Reed's talent for talking people out of comfort food. It turns out the driver who righteously raised that Bible out of his tank's hatch after the first night's ambush was brilliant at networking, according to his sergeant. "He knows a lot of people in different support units," Sergeant Chase recalled.

In the middle of the Iraqi desert, Reed came up with wonderful aluminum trays of pancakes, Aunt Jemima syrup, and pork sausages for his tank crew. I know colonels who never ate that well during the war. Looking back, it was the most delicious-looking meal I saw the entire time I was in the Iraqi theater. I can still see those lovely brown sausages and pancakes in those warm aluminum trays. It was too much to hope that one of Sergeant Chase's crew might offer to share. They hovered over their treasures like hungry wolves over a fresh caribou kill. In their eyes, I could see I was a stray wolf from another pack and totally unwelcome while they ate. Sergeant Chase was the head wolf. At the very least, Specialist Reed could with his Bible have exorcised the worst of devils out of someone possessed. Only in retrospect was it quite humorous. I would be back home with a hot shower and home-cooking months before any of these poor soldiers would, though I didn't laugh at the time.

I should not have begrudged Sergeant Chase or his crew that breakfast. Their R and R was already cut short because earlier a tread had come off their tank, and they were six hours late getting back. Then after they arrived and repaired the tread, they were ordered to turn around and go right back out again to protect Lieutenant Shea's attempted recovery of Bravo Company's lost tanks. In hindsight, Sergeant Chase, a shrewd New Yorker from Long Island, may have been the best judge in the unit of the Iraqi character.

"A lot of Iraqi locals were pretty upset with the Americans even then," Sergeant Chase said about the frustrating attempts to retrieve the crippled tanks. "We came to liberate them, and they tried to blow up the tank we left in the ditch. They stole everything off it, tools, personal belongings, all the food, and all the water. They even tried to blow it up with a 120 mm round that was left in the gun, only they couldn't set it off."

For his unit, there was no time even to change underwear on that R and

R, no time even to wash one's feet, Sergeant Chase recalled. For most of those soldiers, R and R never added up to rest and recuperation. Run and Run seemed more like it. The unit was scheduled to move out the following morning at 4:30 local time, 1:30 Zulu or Greenwich Mean Time. Trying to juggle all those times—Iraqi local, Zulu, Eastern Daylight Time, and British Summer Time, where my wife was—required a computer. Charlie was sufficiently confused that he rousted us out of our sleeping bags now with a laconic "Time to get up," his Scottish voice odd in the darkness of the Iraqi desert. He probably should have been forgiven more quickly for wakening us an hour earlier than was necessary for the unit's renewed assault, given the various times under which we operated. Jeff, Paul, and even Charlie himself were able to close their eyes again, but I could not. I wandered about the desert looking for a tank recharging its batteries with its engines generating exhaust heat to warm myself in the cold night air.

The new orders of march caught us by surprise. As the sun was coming up, we saw tanks being loaded aboard flatbed trucks for the next push north to the Karbala Gap. Those trucks were the first chance some soldiers had to sleep during the R and R. Sergeant Wheatley was at last able to put his head in his hands, bracing himself in the turret of his tank, now riding on a flatbed truck. It was only then he had a moment to reflect on how fortunate he was to be alive. For Sergeant Chase, reflection would wait until later.

After loading his tank aboard another truck, Sergeant Chase fell asleep, precariously atop the main battle tank's turret. It had not occurred to him the truck carrying the tank would be moving again, lurching forward, and he could have been sent rolling off on to the road and under the wheels of the truck. It happened to other soldiers in the war. They lay down in front or in back of a truck or tracked vehicle and were crushed to death while they slept. It was only when the truck lurched forward that Sergeant Chase came to, grabbed the turret, and waved frantically to the driver who fortunately saw him out of his rear-view mirror. The driver stopped, and Sergeant Chase bounded down into the cab and joined the driver in laughter.

Our convoy passed more Iraqi prisoners of war, squatting forty yards off the pavement behind coils of razor wire, their hands bound with plastic binds. None of us cared. The POWs would soon be getting sleep and food. We could not foresee the time when we might sleep again. The Karbala Gap drew closer with each mile, and soon the tanks and Bradleys began fanning out into the desert and moving northward.

In the aftermath of the war, with no Iraqi weapons of mass destruction found, it seems silly to have worried about getting hit with unconventional weapons. None of us could have been persuaded of that at the time, however. As the spit of land between the Shiia city of Karbala and Lake Razzazah narrowed, our stomachs knotted. At the outset of our launch into the Karbala Gap, we had been again ordered into nearly full MOPP suits, including the galoshes. If missiles were launched at us, each of us had a gas mask and heavy rubber chemical-protection gloves within a second's grasp. I found myself wondering where Sergeant Major Gabriel Berhane was and how I was going to spend his money. He and I still had that five-dollar bet about whether Saddam Hussein would use chemical weapons against us. We were closing in on Baghdad now, and if Saddam was ever going to win me my five dollars, it was now or never.

Losing that five-dollar bill, which today is in the hands of Sergeant Major Berhane's daughter, was not a bad bargain. Chemical-weapons attacks against us did not occur, but we knew the Iraqis had used them with effectiveness against indigenous Kurdish tribes and in an earlier war against the Iranian army. Later in the day, after our uneventful passage through the gap, Colonel Ferrell stood his troops down, relaxing the sweltering MOPP-suit order. Later when I asked him why he thought the Iraqis never used their unconventional-weapons arsenal at what would have been a most advantageous point, with a large American troop concentration at a critical checkpoint, he speculated, "They were afraid of what we would do if they did use them and afraid of the impact it would have on their own people." None of us knew at that point that the Iraqis probably no longer had these weapons. But once we were through the narrowest bridge of the Karbala Gap, and they had not been used, we knew we had dodged that bullet.

It was good to be moving again. Every mile closer to Baghdad was a mile closer to the end of the war and a mile closer to home. The 7th Cavalry now had the assignment of buffer to the west of the 3rd ID; on the other side of the 7th Cavalry was the Sunni triangle. The Cavalry was now riding flank, and other units would push forward, probe, stop, and push forward again, testing the degrees of Iraqi resistance. U.S. commanders were still alert to the possibility that the Hammurabi division, thought to be north of Baghdad, might be ordered to come south and slam into the side of the 3rd ID as it resumed the race toward Baghdad. We were now drawing to within fifty miles, as the crow flies, to the southern edge of Baghdad. But, it was not a crow that was to command our attention but a small old-world warbler.

As the Cavalry arced ahead of us like a drawn bow, our Humvee hung back in the position of the bowstring. There was no point in trying to follow Captain Lyle's tank now, because he was moving laterally back and forth between his various platoons. Often we stopped in the warmth of the day and threw open the doors on the Humvee to let a breeze through, removing the stifling heat that built up behind the engine. We were in the middle of nowhere again, and Nowhere, Iraq, has a population of six million flies, which all descended on us at once. They are the same noisome pestilences that plague anyone who has spent time in the deserts of the Middle East. God sent them to punish the ancient Egyptians when Pharaoh tried to thwart the exodus of the children of Israel.

We had a bit of a start after we peeled ourselves out of the chemical suits for the last time. We suddenly saw the NBC truck—the nuclear-, biological-, and chemical-warfare truck—scooting east to Karbala. Its findings were essentially negative. At least twice during that drive through the gap, we had a scare as chemical-weapons detectors picked up traces of poisons. At first, the tests were positive, but further tests came up negative repeatedly. Still, all of Iraq is a poisoned land, as I was sadly to discover a year later.

Sitting now in our t-shirts caked with dust, we simply baked and sweated and baked and dreaded the thought of having to put on those heavy suits again in the heat of another day. But a strange thing happened; signally, this earlier chemical-weapons scare was yet another false alarm, despite the dashing about of the NBC truck scooting to Karbala. The revelation came as "an apparition heaven sent," a small warbler migrating north through the desert to breed and summer in the forests of Russia. I knew that like the canary in the coal mines, if this old-world warbler was able to flit about the desert picking off desert flies, then clearly the air was clean. At first, I thought it might have been a juvenile Arctic Warbler, but on reflection, it was more likely the common chiffchaff. It landed just outside our Hummer, in the sand close to the truck. Then the bird intrepidly flew to the top of the open door on the right front side by Charlie.

I am not sure what attracted the warbler to us. The desert was filled with a new hatch of flies. Perhaps, sitting in the shade of our Humvee, we were just quieter than the army's tracked vehicles out on the horizon. We were not shooting or making other loud noises. Perhaps we were just a convenient rest stop on the long trek north to Russia. But the warbler later came to represent considerably more to us. It was as if the chiffchaff were a spirit from another world that spoke of a gentleness we had come to forget. It was as if this tiny, buff, gray-green promise was sent to tell us we would all survive this war. Half a year later, when Jeff was back in the United States, and I was home in London, we talked on the telephone, each needing to validate the experience of the war.

"You know, Walt, what I remember most of all," Jeff said, "more than the shooting and the danger, what I remember most was that little bird."

At first, the warbler used the perch of the open door to swoop down into the nearby sand to pick off the gathering desert flies. I took notes at the time to help identify him later: low flat head, which made me think he may have been an Arctic Warbler, generally olive with a darker olive back, and a light-green eye stripe. Each of us was so keenly aware of his presence we froze so as not to frighten him away, and he showed no fear.

Having established himself on the door of the Hummer, the bird then flit-ted inside, landing on Charlie's knee, which the bird used as a perch from which he launched to pick off the flies plaguing us in the shade of the ve-hicle. The warbler on the wing was amazingly effective, darting about even inside the Hummer, picking off dozens of flies right in front of our noses. Next, he flitted from Charlie to Paul in the driver's seat. I chuckled as I watched this gentle giant of a man looking down his strong prominent nose at a bird that he could have swatted and killed so easily with his powerful hand. The warbler sat for a few seconds, flitting from Paul's arm to the steer-ing wheel and then back to Charlie's head, and then making his way to the back seat.

Jeff was transfixed, especially when the bird picked off at least half a dozen flies in Jeff's corner of the car. Then it was my turn. It landed on my naked arm and rested briefly in pursuit of the flies that would nourish him some for the flight of more than a thousand miles that he had yet to make. It was a young bird, almost certainly hatched the previous spring. The plumage was soft, understated, and like spring mist in the boreal spruce bog toward which he was headed. The tingling of the small feet on my naked arm was a sensation I will never forget. It was as if one of the wee people, a sprite, were present, only it was real. The only things that moved on me were my eyes. I held my breath so as not to frighten him away. At one point, flitting about picking off flies, he may even have landed on the side stem of my sunglasses because I felt his wing feathers brush my temple.

He was skilled at picking off flies about my legs and arms. I wanted him even closer, for I have never been so close to a free, wild bird, and this one was beautiful. No one in the car spoke. Each of us savored the moment, knowing it would not last, that we would soon be moving again back into the fight. It would be the cannon's breath, not a bird's wing, we would be feeling. The warbler was inside the Hummer for perhaps fifteen or twenty minutes although time seemed suspended when he was with us. That such a small creature could so command our attention at such a time lent credence to my musings that this was a preternatural visitor.

Having decimated the fly population inside our vehicle, the bird left as quickly as he had arrived. His course was north to his breeding grounds in Russia. North was also the direction of Baghdad, and the parallel did not escape any of us. I imagined that sometimes these creatures are sent to speak to us and perhaps to cheer us onward. Even after the bird flew off, none of us said much. But as I sat there, I suddenly remembered another story told me by an Iranian friend who was a young soldier during the 1980–1988 war between Iran and Iraq.

Jamshid Salmainan was fresh out of a Teheran high school in 1982 and pleaded with his father to allow him to enlist to fight to repel the Iraqi invaders of his country in an earlier inconvenient war launched by Saddam. Poorly trained, Jamshid and the other recruits in his platoon were ordered to be part of a frontal attack on the Iraqi army. A short while into the engagement, the Iraqis sprang the trap. The commander, radio operator, and most of the platoon "fell like leaves in the autumn wind in the course of the day." The Iraqis closed on all sides on my friend Jamshid and the few other survivors in his platoon. Pinned down and fired on from all sides, Jamshid told me he was "convinced I was going to die. I was terrified."

"I wished I had wings to fly away from the slaughter field," he later wrote. In the distance, behind him, he saw an escape route. But he said, "I knew I was dead. No one could have escaped that slaughter field. I was paralyzed." Then, "a small, common bird landed beside me" as Jamshid lay there alone and under murderous Iraqi fire. "I noticed for the first time how beautiful he was. The little bird did not seem afraid, but why should it be afraid? It had wings. It could fly away."

It was the only sign of life the young Iranian soldier saw among the entire platoon, which was now wiped out, and Iraqi bullets were splattering all about him. Then came a poignant moment. Jamshid said he forgot where he was.

"I was just watching the bird. As the shelling and shooting intensified, the bird flew off. In a moment of personal epiphany," my friend recalled, "I wasn't afraid. I was still alive. And I wanted to see birds again. I had to see them again. I had to live."

In the next instant, Jamshid said, he joined the bird.

"I jumped up and ran like crazy."

One hundred yards distant was his escape, a boulder-strewn ravine that gave him cover. Who knows whether it was the terrain or the little bird that really saved my friend's life. But now we had just been through a similar mystical moment in another desert against the same enemy, and it was then I suspected the poet E. E. Cummings, who had seen an earlier terrible war on another Western front in 1917, may have discovered a kind of truth when he wrote that these little birds are "the secret of living."

8

Once More into the Breach

All air seemed then conflicting fire.
—John Milton, "Paradise Lost"

Fire fast. The moment you see anything, fire! We are crossing the Euphrates again and moving into the Baghdad suburbs."

With those words, Capt. Clay Lyle launched Apache Troop (aka Alpha Company) on its way northward again toward Baghdad. Following Captain Lyle's tank, maps became irrelevant. We were just eating dirt, but we were again moving in the direction of the Iraqi capital and a rendezvous with what we did not know.

The desert was flat and boring and ugly. Once again, we faced crossing of the Euphrates River. The only card the Iraqis had left to play was the use of unconventional weapons, and they continued to show a disinclination to use them. It was not until half a year later the world came to believe there weren't any. The weapons were a figment of the Bush Administration's imagination. We would, however, be chasing these phantom weapons in the coming week whether they existed or not.

We had the clear sense our line of march would, if followed, have brought us west of Baghdad. The 3rd Infantry Division was moving east of us and east of the dirty little Shiite town of Karbala on a more direct route to Baghdad. Karbala epitomized all the misery Saddam Hussein had inflicted on the Shiite population of his country: squalid streets festooned with garbage, dirt, poverty, and buildings ready to collapse at the first tremor of an earthquake. We were clearly on the flank of the assault now, and it was annoying because it seemed we were spending a lot of time waiting. Waiting was not going to get any of us home sooner, and beyond staying alive, that is all any of us cared about. Some of Saddam's army was holed up in Karbala. Wisely, U.S. commanders did not slam into any of these towns with force. Rather, they played leapfrog, flanking them, much the way Gen. Douglas MacArthur in World War II island-hopped across the Pacific enroute to Tokyo. Today, the goal was

Baghdad and regime change. Indeed, the first major Iraqi city to capitulate was Baghdad, a matter of pride for some Iraqi army soldiers after the war who had held out longer than Saddam's capital defenses.

The air force tactical coordinators traveling in the M-113 tracked vehicle behind our Humvee said JSTAR surveillance aircraft, a 747, high overhead, had picked up another convoy of two hundred Iraqi vehicles in our general area, this time in broad daylight. But when the Coalition's tactical fighter planes moved in for closer examination, the company turned out to be made up of two hundred civilian automobiles trying to get away from the fighting. That JSTAR "eye in the sky" was proving a less-than-reliable source of information. On another occasion, we found ourselves racing across the desert to check out another "hostile sighting relayed" by the air force's JSTAR, and that time, the hostile sighting turned out to be a herd of about two hundred camels. I, for one, was coming to the conclusion that we weren't going to encounter any Iraqi armor until we were at the gates of Baghdad. The reports coming over the squadron commander's radio suggested the superior Coalition air power had degraded the much-vaunted Medina division by between forty-five to sixty-five percent. Iraqi commanders were already combining remnants of units, cobbling together new divisions.

The 7th Cavalry was now forty or fifty miles from Baghdad. Ahead we could see a column of U.S. military vehicles stretching across the horizon for perhaps ten miles. It was mind-boggling to see the overwhelming strength the United States could inject into a military theater. Paul, our Australian, was awed by what he saw and said so. Russians I later talked to were awestruck at the army the Americans put into the field in Iraq. It was the typical Russian admiration of things *bolshoi*—big, huge. The phrase "like a mighty army," from the old hymn "Onward, Christian Soldiers," flashed through my mind when I watched this huge armored train with its tankers and supply trucks rolling across the desert horizon as far as one could see in either direction. It reminded me of that poignant scene from the Henry Fonda film "Mister Roberts" when Lt. Roberts was sitting on the deck of the USS Reluctance watching the entire Pacific fleet pass in front of him en route to Tokyo for the invasion of Japan toward the end of the Second World War.

That overpowering American bigness may have contributed to the ubiquitous friction between U.S. troops and British forces whenever those two allies went to war together. Those Anglo-American frictions were no less in evidence during Gulf War Two. Soldiers from the 7th Cavalry, hungering for news, would gather around my short-wave radio on the hood of Old Betsy to hear how the war was progressing across the entire front. Because the U.S. Congress has, over the years, gutted the budget of the Voice of America, the only other English-language short-wave news service is the BBC. It has also come to dominate all overseas radio news coverage within the United States.

It was always evident BBC news was giving its version of the war by the swearing that came from the soldiers gathered around the radio. Vicki Barker was for three days denying the capture of Saddam (now Baghdad) International Airport, even though the 3rd Infantry Division's 1st Brigade had established its control there. Clare Bolderson's midday news reports evoked remarks from U.S. troops like, "Oh no, it's Tokyo Rose again!" But the most venom was reserved for Andrew Gilligan, whose anti-Coalition agenda was egregious. Ultimately, the BBC was reported to be on the verge of letting Gilligan go for other perceived transgressions, so he quit to be spared dismissal. To U.S. forces, Gilligan in his broadcasts seemed an apologist for the Iraqi regime, toadying up to the Iraqis to guarantee the BBC a foothold in Baghdad during the war. In one particularly offensive broadcast again dealing with U.S. seizure of the Saddam International Airport by the 3rd ID, Gilligan said, "The Americans claim they have taken Saddam Airport, but we all know the Americans always exaggerate what they can do."

Like the desert dust, these BBC news bulletins stuck in the craws of U.S. soldiers as they resumed their assault northward toward Baghdad. The terrain was changing with each mile. The desert and the occasional sand dune gave way to arid, abandoned farmland. Desertification was reclaiming what some poor Iraqi farmers tried to make arable with primitive, artificial irrigation. The natives turned huge tracts of marginal land on the edge of the Euphrates delta into an endless checkerboard of small plots about twenty yards by twenty yards. Each plot was fenced with mud walls about a foot high that baked into adobe. This spring paddies lay drained and baked, the earth cracked with fissures that had long since surrendered their moisture.

The sixty-nine-ton Abrams tanks and Bradleys crushed their way through the adobe walls, reducing them to powder. Old Betsy struggled to pass over them, and we had to slow for each hump while Apache Troop sped off into the distance. We feared we would be left behind, but we could not keep up without risking breaking an axle. Only when this patchwork of parched paddies yielded to flatter farm fields were we able finally to catch up with Captain Lyle. And just as we did, we came under fire again.

Not far ahead was an abandoned farm etched into a small copse where about twenty Iraqi infantrymen were hiding in outbuildings and among trees. The Iraqis had two mortars set up there as well as three Soviet-vintage

23 mm anti-aircraft guns. Overhead, the 7th's Kiowa helicopters rushed forward like angry bees, about eighty feet about the ground, returning fire from their rocket pods at this small group who had foolishly decided to stand and fight.

Captain Lyle called in his own unit's mobile mortar fire, and he blasted away with his tank's 120 mm gun, so powerful it rattled the fillings in my teeth forty yards away. The Bradley fighting vehicles also raced forward, firing their machine guns and their 25 mm cannon. Off to our left was a small, flat-roofed, mud-brick house that literally jumped on its foundations as fire was poured down on it. The mud bricks danced on top of each other as automatic-weapons fire punched through them. I was curious and wanted to investigate what had been inside, but embedding with a unit on the move did not permit that satisfying of my curiosity. Besides, it would have been foolish, especially if there had been a live, wounded Iraqi soldier inside who could still pull a trigger or the pin on a hand grenade.

This was not my day for foolishness but Captain Lyle's. Apache Troop quashed this pocket of resistance with a combined armored and helicopter assault in a matter of minutes, although about four hundred yards to the right I saw at least one, perhaps two Iraqi soldiers running toward a waiting orange and white taxi that must have brought them to the battle from which they were now fleeing. No one blasted that orange and white cab with the retreating Iraqi soldiers. Apparently, this was Allah's day to smile on his own. That cab disappeared without a shot being fired at it.

Meanwhile, Captain Lyle sat in his tank at the ambush site surveying the damage. Three old twin-barreled anti-aircraft guns had been abandoned. The scene was an inviting target for souvenir hunters. Some of the soldiers from the 7th began scavenging, collecting AK-47 rifles and anything else that piqued their interest from the dead Iraqis. I was quietly dismayed. Paul, Charlie, Jeff, and I certainly knew better. No one ever knows if any of these collectables has been booby-trapped. This location was still "hot," still dangerous, with weapons and ammunition lying about on the ground, but again, these were still green American soldiers who until this war had never been under fire.

The unit's adrenalin was still pumping from yet another firefight, and Captain Lyle was determined no one would ever again be able to turn those anti-aircraft guns on U.S. forces. He then did the only unthinking thing I saw him do during the entire war. He ordered his driver to run his tank over the first of the twin 23 mm anti-aircraft guns to destroy it. Unfortunately, the twin A.A. gun still had shells in the chamber. When the tank ran over the gun, there was a tremendously loud explosion, and the upwardly pointed barrel fired vertically, sending its projectile up past Captain Lyle's ear, cutting him slightly and stunning him. If the barrel had been pointed backwards, it would have blown away the CNN Humvee and all of us with it. We had been directly behind his tank.

Several of us rushed up to see if Captain Lyle was still alive. Paul grabbed our first-aid kit and demonstrated once again that this Australian was the best medic in the unit. He knew what he was doing and dressed Captain Lyle's wound, which turned out not to be overly serious. The still-dazed captain all but guaranteed we were not going to be moving much farther forward that night. Later, when word of the accident filtered up to Colonel Ferrell's command vehicle, he sent word back to Captain Lyle, whom he loved like a son, "If you think I am going to award you a Purple Heart for that, you are nuts." A day or two later, Captain Lyle was able to laugh about the incident, but that night he had the mother of all migraines, and he seemed to lose a bit of lucidity.

Captain Lyle, however, remained clear-headed enough to call up the engineers from the rear to dispose of the two remaining twin anti-aircraft guns by means other than running over them with a tank. By the book, the engineers laced the remaining twin pair of ugly green guns and some ammunition caches with C-4 plastic explosives. With a mighty roar, they blew all heavenward. It wasn't good for Captain Lyle's ringing headache, but there wasn't that much daylight left. Not much farther ahead, we made camp again, and Captain Lyle managed to get a little sleep.

Another detachment of the 7th Cavalry had a much closer call at about the same time and not too far distant. A different company had just taken a couple of Iraqi prisoners; soldiers huddled in a mud hut with a radio, trying to transmit the position of the oncoming U.S. forces. An Arabic translator was needed. Captain Rick Cote, the unit's civilian affairs officer, was summoned along with the only Arabic-speaking translator, Daoud or David, a Kurdish Jew who had fled Iraq a quarter century earlier. Daoud was ordered up to debrief the Iraqi POWs. Bouncing along in Captain Cote's Humvee, they chanced upon a truckload of Iraqi soldiers going in the same general direction. Captain Cote remembers his vehicle had only three M-16s and an AK-47 with which to defend themselves against the considerably larger number of Iraqis in that truck. Captain Cote suspected the Iraqis had an RPG that could have blown the Hummer all the way back to Fort Stewart, Georgia.

With rather quick thinking, the captain decided not to engage and instead began waving in friendly fashion to the Iraqis, who waved back. The

Iraqis pulled away without firing a shot, and Captain Cote proceeded to his destination to interrogate the POWs. The captain, rendezvousing with other U.S. troops, now gained access to a radio. He called in the last location of the truck filled with waving Iraqi infantry. Colonel Ferrell didn't hesitate for a moment to call in the CAS—close air support—as darkness was falling. In the distance, Captain Cote said he and his soldiers saw the horizon where the Iraqis were last seen light up "like a Christmas tree" when the air force took them out.

Like Captain Lyle, many of the rest of us woke up with dull headaches the next morning. We were short on sleep, constipated, and dehydrated. Still, that was far preferable to the fate of the friendly Iraqis in that truck. Throughout the entire march to Baghdad, we were roused at 4:30 A.M., which we found acceptable if there was a purpose to it. The problem this day, like several others, was that there was no purpose in getting up at 4:30. Most of the time, we just sat around and waited two hours for someone else to decide what we were going to do next. Paul boiled hot water, which I used for the instant coffee in the MRE packages. Charlie and Jeff joined Paul for predawn tea. There was no sense of urgency about camp, so cramming our sleeping bags into our stuff sacks could wait until the day's orders filtered down to us. Breakfast was leftovers from the previous evening's MREs; vegetarian pasta was becoming dreary in a campaign in which we lost track of time and dates. There was the garbage to be buried. I am not sure what it was in our Western psyches that mandated the army tend to its garbage. It was clear from the landscape littered with plastic bags the Iraqis didn't care. Paul was fastidious about it, and the slightest transgression by U.S. soldiers brought out his scorn.

This was another morning of hurry-up-and-wait, and the wait seemed that much longer because the heat of the desert was building quickly. It was now early April. The exact date never seemed to matter if you weren't an officer, and embeds were somewhere down there among the grunts. The thermometer would hit the 90s before the day's end, and, by my reckoning, we would be about twenty-five miles southwest of Baghdad once we crossed the Euphrates again. We still did not know if there would be a bloody house-to-house battle for the city, but if there was, at least I was confident the 7th Cavalry wouldn't be in it. I had "been there and done that" along the green line in Beirut in the early 1980s, and I didn't want to do it again. If it came to house-to-house in Baghdad, it was more likely to fall to the brigades of the 3rd Infantry Division.

When we finally did form a column and get underway, it seemed but a few miles before we bumped into another unit of U.S. soldiers, who looked like they had already had a very bad morning. They were lolling about on the side of the road, leaning up against some dark-green camouflage vehicles that looked as if they had been shipped into this theater from Germany rather than having been requisitioned for the war from warehouses in Kuwait. And these soldiers looked as if they would have preferred to be in Germany as well.

I was happy another unit was preceding us across the river, having to shoot its way through Iraqis hiding in foxholes and makeshift bunkers. It meant I was less likely to get shot at and wounded or die today. I do not know a soldier's thought processes, but mine were simply wanting to stay alive, and that meant I was perfectly willing that another unit lead the way today, allowing us to follow in its path.

From the road, burning Iraqi army trucks could be seen beyond the recently fought-over fields in the flood zone of the southern bank of the Euphrates River. The fight had been several hours earlier. An Iraqi unit that tried to challenge the 3rd ID was now nothing but corpses along the shoulder and in the fields and thickets. We were once again passing through jungle-like growth on both sides of the road. The air smelled of burning bodies and oil. Once again, the unit that preceded us had to get across the concrete and steel span from which it would be a straight shot north to Baghdad. Again, the Iraqi army did not blow the bridge, which, in retrospect, seems another indication most of the four-hundred-thousand-man-strong Iraqi army had decided Saddam was not worth destroying Iraq for. None of us seemed to grasp that at the time.

The crackling of small-arms fire could still be heard above the growling engines of the tanks and other tracked vehicles. It did not sound close enough to be threatening to us but rather smacked of mopping up by the 1st Brigade of the 3rd ID, which was now well across the bridge. In its wake were the remnants of the defenders: more burned-out Japanese cars, popular in this part of the world for suicide attacks on U.S. military columns. During this part of the war, these kamikaze cars, however, were embarrassingly ineffective. They became merely a passage to the Muslim paradise for the scores of young Iraqis who had been promised the world if they fought for Saddam. Later, of course, during the occupation, the cars proved effective weapons of terror. On the pavement along the roadsides and on the walkway across the bridge were stacks of abandoned weapons, helmets, and uniforms. To Captain Cote, it seemed as if the retreating Iraqis had "peeled out of their uniforms, changing their clothes or simply running away in their underwear."

More than a few of the Iraqi defenders of this bridge never had the opportunity to escape or had sadly chosen to stand and fight and die. Ten to fifteen of them lay splayed out in various degrees of cremation on the approach to the bridge. Soldiers remember seeing many more dead lying about, but those witnesses to that carnage had the elevated view from a tank turret or a Bradley. Although, as I have said, I did not look at the dead too closely, still the newly dead on this battlefield did not look like they were asleep. Again, the dead died brutally and painfully, cut up by machine-gun fire, lying in gutters, their bodies contorted. Usually, the army clears the enemy dead pretty quickly, but we were so close on the heels of this fight, no one had gotten to these Iraqis yet; no one but the flies.

We took no fire on that bridge, perhaps the first waterway crossing on our way north where we were not shot at. Still, I had my helmet chin strap tightly clamped just in case. The strap acted as a restraint to keep me from chattering nervously. I did not want to betray the anxiety or the tension I felt passing through another chokepoint over another waterway. Once across, there was yet another jungle-like thicket on the north bank of the Euphrates. More soldiers from the 1st Brigade's advance column were parked along the road on that side of the river as well. We could hear the occasional explosion among some distant farmhouses and additional sporadic small-arms fire. It was also here that we parted company with the 3rd ID, which had all too briefly been our security blanket.

As the 3rd ID swung north toward Sadt al Yusufyah, Captain Lyle took Apache Troop a short distance in a northwesterly direction along a narrow farm road that with all the dense foliage could have been in the Philippines. Captain Lyle simply turned left, getting his men over and across the Euphrates River for a second time, and then we stopped and waited again. Damn! We were always standing down, which became increasingly vexing as we got closer to Baghdad. Twenty-five miles away. Twenty-five miles closer to a ticket home, and there we were, stopped again along a poorly paved single-track road in front of some lush tropical gardens with thick hedges that could have hidden an entire squad of Iraqi snipers. Amid the recently cultivated vegetable gardens were square box-like concrete block homes with flat roofs. A few had freshly washed clothes hanging on clotheslines but seemed otherwise deserted. I imagined terrified Iraqi mothers and children fleeing at the chatter of machine-gun fire and now huddling together somewhere back in those woods.

The Iraqi's defense was militarily ill-conceived: brave Muslim soldiers and stupid or cowardly direction. They could have fought an effective resistance under enlightened leadership. On many occasions, with a good sniper's rifle instead of a cheap AK-47, they could have inflicted painful casualties on the American advance, especially had they been able to snipe at us from the dense foliage along the river. I wondered if they ever had trained snipers. After the war, I was told Soviet Draganov sniper rifles were in the Iraqi inventory, and the Iraqi army had specially trained sharpshooters but only in its special forces units.

I asked why they were never used against the Americans.

"It wasn't worth it," one former Iraqi captain told me. "We really did not want to fight for Saddam."

After the war, an Iraqi lieutenant colonel dismissed the much-vaunted AK-47 as a "piece of shit," adding that if Iraqi soldiers had the American rifle, an M-16, they would have been much more effective. Success may have a thousand fathers but defeat has a thousand excuses. There may have been more than a little bitter bravado in that claim, however, because an M-16 isn't going to stop a tank any more than an AK-47. Roadside bombs, improvised Claymore mines so lethal on American military convoys during the first year of U.S. occupation in Iraq, were also virtually never employed against advancing American forces in the spring of 2003. It was another costly afterthought for the Iraqis, who should have known better. That same weapon, imitation Claymore mines, was more than instrumental in persuading the Israelis that their occupation of south Lebanon required too dear a price in boys and blood.

In my microview of the campaign, I do not know how many Iraqi soldiers died trying to keep the American army south of the Euphrates in this final push for Baghdad the first couple of days of April. There were, however, stacks and stacks of AK-47 rifles beside the road, suggesting either many dead Iraqis or that many of the enemy simply had bailed out in the face of overwhelming U.S. firepower. The only Iraqis my CNN crew and I saw were the dead ones. Many, if not all of them, carried gas masks, as if they, too, anticipated the use of unconventional weapons. How many corpses were lying back in the jungle borders of the river was beyond knowing. They could still be rotting there, missing in action through the next millennium. And while the snapping of small-arms fire was within a quarter of a mile, and the Iraqis clearly could also have been hiding in any one of these recently abandoned concrete-block homes, it would have been suicide for them to stick their heads up. It also occurred to me the Iraqis could have been holding a dozen women and children hostages in these homes just off the road. They had done just that back at Al Samawah. But the Cavalry's mission was to pass through this rural region as quickly as possible, and as long as it was not challenged, these Iraqi homes were not fired upon. On reflection, the 7th Cavalry's personal conduct had been exemplary from the get-go in its treatment of civilians. That was another reason the Pentagon employed embedded reporters, as eyewitnesses to counter Arab allegations of war crimes committed by U.S. troops.

With our convoy parked on the side of a farm road in the midst of a dense thicket, I lay down on pavement and took a nap, observing the "Prince Philip rule of travel," to wit, "Eat, sleep, and pee as often as you can because you never know when you will get another chance." In the heat, most of us were snoozing. Each of us had mastered the art of falling asleep quickly, any time, anywhere. "Anywhere" for me was on the asphalt road between the back end of our Humvee and the front tracks of an M-113. There was ever the risk I might be run over, sleeping in front of a tracked vehicle below the eye level of the driver. As I have written, that almost happened to at least one soldier in another unit I had heard about. But I figured if the convoy restarted its engines that would awaken me, and I could roll out of the way before being crushed. Flies landed on my lips and cheeks as they did on the corpses back down the road. But I fell asleep anyway. I simply stopped caring. It was not a long nap, fifteen or twenty minutes, ended by the whining sounds of Bradleys and tanks revving their engines again, getting ready to move down the road along which we were parked. We were held up because no one knew whether American units had passed down the road ahead of us or whether there was substantial Iraqi resistance ahead.

The great concern in Captain Lyle's mind was that there may indeed have passed another American unit in front of us, and if we overtook them from the rear, it almost certainly would have resulted in one U.S. unit firing on another. The marines had had a savage firefight with themselves, over to the east of us, and the 7th Cavalry's officers were alert to the possibility the same thing could happen to us. The best way to find out what lay ahead was for a platoon of two tanks and three Bradleys to go on ahead and scout it. A week earlier, the unit painfully had learned the need to scout bridges to see if they would support a sixty-nine-ton tank, and we were once again in an area with irrigation ditches to be crossed. Our mission was to find Iraq Route 8, somewhere to the north, because it had to be opened. The highway was to be a major supply route in the post-Saddam Iraq. That superhighway ran on a slanting northwesterly tangent south of Baghdad in the general direction of the airport. Getting there required navigating our convoy across a number of small irrigation and drainage ditches that crisscrossed this broken farm country. All the while, we would be following roads that would be scouted only if we scouted them.

Occasionally, the farther we got from the bridge, we would see Iraqi civilians who looked sullenly at us. Rarely did anyone wave except for children and not many of those either. Again, this was yet another sign of the painful American occupation to come that we all miscalculated. Along the way, there would occasionally be the smell of citrus groves in bloom, a pleasant difference from most of the smells that had bombarded us for the past several miles. We had moved so quickly the stench of death had never really had a chance to settle into our nostrils. The dead Iraqis we saw were fresh kills. When we got closer to Baghdad, and the Cavalry's orders were to stand in place, the dead would lie in the road, bloated and smelly. It may be the most disturbing and offensive odor I have ever known.

When we emerged onto Route 8, an excellent superhighway designed by German engineers and paid for with Iraq's petro-dollars, I was relieved. We were off the narrow country lane with heavy copses and cover for snipers and were now into more open terrain where an ambush seemed less probable. As it turned out, it was misplaced optimism. The entire column had swung onto the highway easily enough, and it was about the middle of the afternoon when we heard the crackle of rifle fire on both sides of the road. The louder blasts of rocket-propelled grenades began to thud about us.

We dialed up the videophone connection to Atlanta as we rolled through this latest ambush. These were the kinds of pictures Atlanta craved: A CNN crew getting shot at, and Captain Lyle's main battle tank in front of us, banging, booming, and popping as we rolled in toward the Baghdad airport. We had to be careful what we broadcast here, so as not to telegraph our position. We were just beyond the southwest suburbs of Baghdad. If Charlie panned to the right with the camera, villages and mosques would instantly betray our location to the Iraqi Ministry of Defense. So, once again, we just pointed the camera forward, and every time we came to an overpass along this dual-lane highway, we shut down the camera so as not to provide the Iraqis with visible coordinates. We had to be particularly careful with road signs along the highway, which in Arabic and English told exactly how many kilometers we were from the next town.

Paul had to be especially careful navigating Old Betsy and trying to keep us alive. Again the gunfire was loud and unnerving, sounding as if hundreds of Iraqis were now shooting at us from every direction. We could not break ranks but had to ride in the convoy at a set twenty-five miles an hour, again like those tin ducks in the shooting gallery.

"A year later, it was still a totally surreal experience," Paul said. "There we were, driving along down a beautiful, four-lane freeway, with six tanks and Bradleys on either side of us, blasting away at both sides of the road."

And we were nestled in the middle of this rolling steel pocket.

"The stuff was flying everywhere," Sergeant Woodhall remembered about the huge stashes of RPGs the Iraqis had in those fields. "There were explosions in front of us, in back of us, everywhere."

In his mind's eye, Sergeant Woodhall still sees Iraqis shooting out of farmhouse windows on either side of the road.

"We saw the muzzle flashes, but it was hard to shoot back," he recalled, "because we didn't know what was in the houses."

The highway had to be cleared, however, because it was to be a major supply route for U.S. forces near the airport. So, the 7th poured forth thousands of rounds of ammunition, killing the Iraqis shouldering their RPGs, forcing other Iraqis to fire wildly rather than stick their heads up and be killed. Dead Iraqi soldiers lay in the passing fields around the caches of RPGs that the soldiers couldn't get to before they were killed.

The Iraqi fire became more intense rather than abating, and we were broadcasting the entire length of the gauntlet, which extended for miles. What was a ferocious hour-long firefight for us translated into boring little blue dots, icons on the commanders' electronic battlefield board down in a bunker hundreds of miles distant in Qatar. After the war, Knight-Ridder's senior military-affairs correspondent Joseph L. Galloway interviewed Centcom Commander Tommy Franks at his headquarters there.

"I noticed that there was a blue dot eight to ten miles in front of a big bunch of blue dots," Franks told Galloway. "This blue dot seemed to be moving up Highway 8 in the southern part of Baghdad, headed for Saddam Airport."

The general said he started channel-surfing on his TV monitors "until I found the embedded reporter [CNN's Walter Rodgers] who happened to be with this troop of the 3/7. He was reporting a live thunder-run down Highway 8, talking as they were shooting. Within five minutes of this event, David McKiernan called me on the red switch phone and said, 'Are you aware of this unit moving on the airport? They will be at the airport in an hour.'"

Soldiers of the 7th Cavalry later proudly reported their relatively small unit had been cutting such a swath through Iraq that they had an icon of their own on General Franks's who-is-where electronic warboard. These same cavalry troopers also were gleeful upon learning some very senior generals became envious of the 7th both for having the icon and for the media attention they were receiving via their embedded correspondent.

What General Franks found amusing was Apache Troop in a hair-raising running battle, with CNN in the middle of it, and we couldn't shoot back. The only shred of armor we had was our Kevlar vests and helmets. Paul maneuvered Old Betsy through the thick of it.

We all sensed the worst fire was coming from the right, my side of the road, so Paul kept trying to creep up on the left side of Captain Lyle's tank, using it as shield, except Captain Lyle was swinging his 120 mm cannon to that side, and if we were anywhere close when it went "bang," which it did several times, we would all be deaf, dumb, and maybe dead, especially if Captain Lyle was using the armor-piercing projectiles that spewed out lethal steel shards when the projectile came out of the barrel.

All of Apache Troop's guns were blazing: machine guns, 120 mm cannon, 25 mm cannon, the whole shebang. It was an ear-shattering fight, and there was no place to hide. Seeking shelter in the lee of Captain Lyle's tank was out of the question for yet another reason. Everyone was maneuvering and shooting and rolling at upwards of thirty miles an hour in a blizzard of lead, and we risked getting run over by the very tank beside which we were seeking shelter. It was, in Paul's words, "just incredible," and we could see no end to it.

Somewhere ahead lay a cloverleaf and Highway 1, which was where we were supposed to turn north. The generals at Centcom had an erroneous impression of our destination. The 7th Cavalry was not supposed to take the airport. The unit had no "dismounts," no infantry required for such an assault. The airport already belonged to the 3rd ID. What General Franks was watching with his blue dots was a cavalry pincer movement west of the airport, a flanking maneuver to protect U.S. troops at the airport from an assault by whatever divisions Saddam had north of the city that might still be brought to bear. The 7th was assigned to clear Iraqi Route 1, which ran on a more north-south axis. Somewhere above the airport Route 1 intersected with Route 10, another east-west road just north of us. But there was a devil of a fight immediately facing the 7th cavalry before that flank was secure. No sooner did we roll through one infestation of Iraqi fighters than more of them leapfrogged ahead as the 7th shot its way forward.

At the intersections of Routes 8 and 1, the Cavalry turned north on 1, and the shooting intensified. Ahead, American tanks were now dueling with Iraqi tanks, the beginnings of the first real force-on-force engagement of the war. From the sides of the road, from Iraqi farms and fields, from foxholes and makeshift bunkers, the Iraqis were shooting at us. There was no cover. Our best hope was that the U.S. forces were firing back so furiously it was spoiling the Iraqi soldiers' aim. In another two days, Apache Troop alone would have spent 1.7 million rounds of 7.62 ammunition from its tanks and Bradleys. That firepower sprayed out over the Iraqi foxholes and trenches did indeed degrade the enemy's aim and kept them at bay and perhaps off-balance.

None of us knew how far north on Highway 1 Captain Lyle intended to push that night, but the sun was lowering now. The unit's forward progress slowed and then halted. We sat there, no longer moving targets. Paul had the best view of the situation. The Iraqis had dug an RPG emplacement in the middle of the dirt berm separating the north-south lanes, in the median. The U.S. armor took it out without a problem but many rounds of rockets and small-arms fire were ablaze and exploding intermittently, checking Apache Troop's forward progress. We stayed in place, now a sitting target, waiting until the fires of the explosives from that emplacement died down.

As we sat there in our unarmored Humvee, I scrunched down again trying to make myself as small a target as possible. Charlie and I were on the right side of the vehicle, and there was nothing between the Iraqi bunkers and foxholes and us but the Humvee's thin, plastic doors. In the dirt along the shoulder beside the road, I could see the dust being kicked up by the bullets hitting three feet away. For some bizarre reason, I was only worried about the incoming bullets giving us a flat tire, so that we couldn't go forward. But, we couldn't go forward anyway because Captain Lyle's tank, designed to survive a nuclear battlefield, squatted in front of us. While the tank was largely impregnable to the incoming fusillade peppering the dirt shoulder a yard away from me, we were not.

Such moments are frozen in time and thought. None of us in our Hummer will ever forget Charlie Miller that afternoon, and we still laugh about it. Sitting in the front seat just ahead of me, he lowered his camera and noticed the same incoming bullets splattering beside me that I had been silently watching. Charlie was not silent, however. Paul remembers him as "quivering."

"Could you move forward just a little," Charlie said, his voice definitely quavering as he looked down at the bullets dancing all about us. "Get up there beside Captain Lyle's tank."

I don't know why I thought that was funny. Charlie was pretty fearless. But it was funny to see his reaction to all those bullets slamming beside us on our side of the car. I should have been equally nervous except by now, after all we'd experienced, I was beginning to feel as if none of those bullets would touch me. Ten to twelve miles outside Baghdad, I was beginning to feel I had on an invisible suit of armor, that the Iraqis simply couldn't see me to hit me. It was dreamlike. We were in the battle, in the thick of it day after day, and yet the damned Iraqis couldn't hit us.

Captain Lyle apparently did not share that opinion. After leading us about a mile and a half or so more up the road, for some reason he waved to us that he was turning his tank around. He never said anything, but it may have been at this point in the war that Apache Troop began to feel very protective of its embeds. I sensed Captain Lyle thought it was time to pull us out, fearing his embeds were about to be killed. Having come this far, I had a growing sense everyone in Apache Troop was determined to keep its embeds alive for the duration. He signaled he was going to lead us out of there, and no one in Old Betsy demurred. The lead elements of Apache Troop continued to slug it out on Highway 1, banging away with their big guns. But with an M1A1 tank as our special escort, we hightailed it out of there, back to the cloverleaf interchange where we would overnight and close to where Colonel Ferrell had set up his command post.

Ahead of us, about two miles to the west by the intersection, an ugly column of black smoke was rising, a pillar of cloud, leading us back to our night encampment. Given what we just emerged from, we had never heard this shooting, but we saw that the cloverleaf interchange was filled with more U.S. armor from a unit I didn't recognize. It was the "mighty army" that was converging on Baghdad, filling in the blanks in the road behind us. There were more tracked vehicles, M-113s, some with big mortars aboard, and others with .50-caliber machine guns still hot and smoking. About fifty yards away, in a field beside an irrigation canal, what had been a white Toyota was still ablaze, pouring that great cloud of black smoke fueled by burning tires, oil, and dead Iraqis.

All those American soldiers parked along Route 8 had been just too inviting a target for small bands of Iraqi diehards. Three young Fedayeen, Saddam's most fanatical foot soldiers, took a Toyota and started driving along an earthen dyke beside the irrigation canal that ran perpendicular to Route 8. The U.S. soldiers watched in disbelief as the Fedayeen drove toward them but did not fire. When the Iraqis came to within half a football field of the massed American armor, they stopped their Toyota, got out, and walked back to the trunk of their car. American machine guns were trained on them the entire time. The Fedayeen opened the trunk and grabbed three AK-47 semi-automatic rifles as if they believed they, too, were invulnerable. It was the last thing they ever did. If they wanted martyrdom, they got it, in bone-smashing .50-caliber bullets that ripped their bodies apart and set the Toyota ablaze for several hours afterward.

"Stupid assholes," I muttered under my breath.

Many of the Fedayeen fighters we were seeing were youngsters spilling their guts in the green spring fields. After the war, I asked Iraqi army captain Hamdi al Keshali why so many of the fighters we had seen were such youngsters.

"We sent out the kids because we knew they had small brains," he replied.

The Ba'athists promised them anything, promised them they would become privileged members of the Ba'ath political party, promised them positions in the ranks of the elite Fedayeen.

"They were told to be wild and reckless," Hamdi went on. "No one can stand up to you."

Perhaps the Iraqi captain had it right; perhaps they did have small brains.

With the sun having set somewhere five hundred miles away, Charlie, Jeff, Paul, and I decided we would bed down amid the relative safety of all this armor. The fighting immediately about us was tapering off a little, although up Route 1, from which we had just come, sporadic battles would rage much of the night and all the following day. Up Highway 1, the Iraqi fighters were taking cover in civilian homes in suburbs west of the airport. Somewhere in the distance, there was still a loud battle, up where the forward platoons of Apache Company were. The most inviting place to sleep appeared to be in a depression between the dual lanes of the highway. It was low enough that any incoming Iraqi fire on a horizontal trajectory would go over us, and the only thing that would really threaten us would be incoming mortars. The mind makes allowances for all those possibilities after daily combat. But all the mortars that night were outgoing, and they came from the Cavalry's own mortar position in the field immediately behind us. Their irregular booming throughout the night attested to the fact that sergeants like Wheatley, Gerry Gilmore, and Chase were fighting off night attacks on their platoons. The sergeants and their platoons did not enjoy the luxury we had of sleeping in a ditch serenaded by the rolling thunder of outgoing mortars. Only the stars were quiet that night.

9

Force on Force

Taking advantage of the darkness, the Iraqis attempted to reinforce their defenses along Route 1 west of the airport. They believed night afforded them a modicum of security and freedom of movement. It was a mistaken and for many a fatal assumption. Standing in the turret of his tank, using night-vision goggles, Sgt. Matthew Chase watched Saddam's soldiers filling the gaps in their lines thinned the previous afternoon during Apache Troop's foray. For Sergeant Chase and the other Americans, the coming battle unfolded in a greenish-white tableau illuminated by starlight. It was not unlike the way in which a tiger stalks and hunts at night. The helpless prey's every movement is watched. Without night-vision goggles, Iraqi soldiers and Fedayeen moved unaware they were observed in the gunsights of the U.S. soldiers until the shock of a high velocity M-16 or 7.62 mm bullet slammed into their bodies. The first thing they would feel was a numbing shock. The pain would come more gradually as they lay there dying under the same starlit canopy beneath which I was sleeping two and a half miles distant.

The Iraqis could shoot only at shapes and shadows, sounds and ghosts while U.S. soldiers targeted their every movement, slaughtering them. Efficient killing is what soldiers are trained and paid to do. Worse for the Iraqis, they were generally on foot attacking American armor, blind to the hopelessness of their assault. Their pluck and willingness to attack blindly at night only hastened their deaths. When the muzzle flashes of the Iraqis' rifles glowed in the greenish-white illumination of the Americans' night-vision goggles, it was as if the Iraqis were saying to the soldiers of the 7th Cavalry, "Shoot me! I am here." The Iraqis' only advantage was raw numbers, but overwhelming American firepower erased that. The ground that Apache

Troop had gained the previous afternoon would be held throughout the night at a frightful cost to Iraqi families.

"They were bringing reinforcements in dump trucks," Sergeant Chase remembers. "It was a hornet's nest of fire. We destroyed three of the dump trucks [with his tank's main gun] and destroyed over four hundred dismounts [Iraqi infantrymen]. Sergeant Gilmore's Bradley hit a number, too. Then we called in artillery."

Sergeant Paul Wheatley remembers his tank was taking small-arms fire and rockets "off and on all night," but again, the Iraqis were technologically handicapped in night combat. Every time they fired, they died. Other tanks and Bradleys recorded similar enemy-body counts. Estimates ran to over a thousand Iraqi dead in this engagement alone although confirmation was not really possible, and the numbers of American kills may have been exaggerated. One Iraqi soldier who went AWOL just before the beginning of the fighting said he believed the actual number of Iraqi war dead was in the neighborhood of five thousand, far fewer than in the First Gulf War where estimates ran to sixty thousand. The continuing evaporation of whole Iraqi divisions, soldiers just going home rather than standing and fighting, contributed to the rather low Iraqi body counts.

While Sergeant Chase and others had been assigned to guard Highway 1 from Iraqi reinforcement, another platoon was diverted to guard and block a spur road that ran west toward Fallujah. With the Coalition forces under building pressure to end this fight quickly, much of the countryside seemed at times clogged with Iraqis trying to flee Americans coming up from the rear. One Iraqi family with three adults and two children in a car on the Fallujah road accidentally collided with a tank, one with the big cow-catcher–like plow on the front. The tank had fired warning shots at the oncoming car, but seeing the women and children inside, the crew decided not to shoot to kill. A passenger car smashing into a sixty-nine-ton tank is not a normal fender bender, and this one was no exception. The Iraqi occupants were pretty shaken up. The U.S. soldiers called up some medics to treat them for bruises and scrapes. The man who was driving, however, disappeared in the confusion. He walked away. First a man, then a specter, then nothing. A search of the car later located a uniform and documents revealing him to be a fleeing Iraqi general. It was quite impossible to keep track of everything in the middle of an engagement. An Iraqi general gets away. Embedded journalists get separated from their unit. An American general sees us on an electronic map and thinks we are headed to the airport when we are going somewhere else. War is the ultimate catalogue of snafus.

The following morning, Captain Lyle came looking to retrieve his CNN charges. The captain knew where all his soldiers were but his CNN embeds must have seemed at times like errant puppies that had to be periodically rounded up. We had become separated for the night, but it seemed unwise if not utterly stupid to go charging around a battlefield after dark, unable to use headlights and having no radio communication. We went to ground. With more and more armored vehicles coming up from the rear and clogging the roads, getting separated seemed a matter of course.

That morning, Captain Lyle did not have to look far. We were only a quarter of a mile from him when darkness had fallen. With a wave from him in his turret, we knew we were to follow him as he plowed across the median strip crushing guardrails into twisted steel ribbons. But, while his tank could force its way through such obstacles, our trailing Humvee had to be navigated as if we were moving through a minefield. The guardrails he rolled over could rip the bottom out of our vehicle. We could not follow too closely because after relieved of the weight of the tank, the guardrails would spring back as lethal spears. A year later in Iraq, the major highways would still have these twisted steel spikes bent threateningly toward oncoming traffic. At war's end, my friend Elizabeth Nueffer of the *Boston Globe* would die violently on a twisted guardrail like these in Samarra. Her Iraqi driver was speeding. The car went out of control, crashing into one of the guardrails outside Baghdad. Elizabeth was impaled on a beam of steel that pierced through the automobile. Her body could later be identified only by the clothes she had been wearing. Paul knew the risks as he gingerly drove Old Betsy over the twisted steel.

Captain Lyle's tank pulled off the road at the cloverleaf where Highways 8 and 1 intersected. There, in the shelter of several highway entrance and exit ramps, next to a lone palm tree, most of the officers of the 7th Cavalry had gathered to plot what would be the final days of the war. The threat was still perceived to be the Hammurabi division, believed to be positioned somewhere north of Baghdad. The fear remained that the division would swing south and challenge either the 7th Cavalry or launch a counterattack against the airport, which was still firmly in American control despite what the BBC had reported. After the war, the Iraqi captain Hamdi al Keshali said U.S. intelligence again erred. It was his understanding the Hammurabi division was at that time east, not north of Baghdad, on standby, ready to do battle with U.S. Marines advancing northward from Nasiriyah.

For the officers of the 7th Cavalry, it mattered little whether it was the advanced elements of the phantom Hammurabi Division or an incorporation of other Iraqi units. Apache Troop had fought most of the night, and they had encountered stubborn Iraqi opposition in the kind of no-man's land in front of them. This morning, it was good to see all of them gathered around the back ramp of Colonel Ferrell's Bradley. They were dirty and weary, but they were alive, and astonishingly, they reported no casualties. It was always interesting to me to see the easy mixing of junior officers, senior officers, and NCOs. Sergeants would venture an unsolicited opinion to a light colonel. Often it was just good-natured bantering. But there seemed a high comfort level among everyone in this unit. This morning, they were joking about reports over the SCO's radio that Ba'athist Party members were fleeing Baghdad with suitcases filled with money, headed west to Al Fallujah, Tikrit, and Ramadi in the so-called Sunni Triangle.

"You gotta wonder what makes them want to flee so badly," someone in our midst observed.

Most of the soldiers knew that Saddam and the high-level Ba'athists had fled or were in the process of fleeing, and the soldiers' laughter was a kind of safety valve after days of tension. Less humorous were reports that Saddam's Republican Guard units were joining the battle for Baghdad outside the city.

Despite the media's inclination to call these Republican Guard units elite, the term applied only in comparison to other Arab armies and was otherwise meaningless. Most of Saddam's army including the Guard, had never really been resupplied after the First Gulf War. Additionally, the Republican Guard's ranks were now brimming with regular army soldiers and conscripts. In 1994, on the road between Basra and Baghdad, I had observed a Republican Guard unit whose soldiers' boots were literally falling apart. Their loyalty to Saddam had already become questionable, and it appeared he thought them sufficiently untrustworthy to keep them outside of Baghdad as less than loyal guardians of the city. Important Guard elements attempted to overthrow Saddam on various occasions. What may have made them "elite" was that the Republican Guard was a volunteer rather than a conscription force. By that token, the entire U.S. Army was elite.

Listening to reports of a mass exodus from Baghdad, it would have been tempting to think the war was over, but that judgment would have been premature.

"We've got them rocking on their heels," Colonel Ferrell told the assembled soldiers and us. "We need to keep the pressure on for the next couple of days."

I asked the colonel about the previous night's slaughter and the Iraqis' inclination to launch suicide attacks.

"It's sad when you have an overmatch like this, but you don't have a choice in war," he replied.

Captain Lyle was becoming impatient with the early-morning small talk.

"Last night was the first night in a while I haven't shot at somebody," he declared.

His sergeants were up Highway 1 on the line, and he was anxious to get back into the fray.

The captain turned to me. "You guys want to go with us?"

"Sure, why not," we shrugged.

It was not that we really wanted to go back up that road where the bullets were landing all around us yesterday and where Sergeants Wheatley, Chase, and Gilmore had been shot at all the previous night. It's just that there is no precedent in Miss Manner's Guide to say "No" to an invitation like that, especially after all we had been through together.

Captain Lyle was proud of the devastation his soldiers had wrought upon the attacking Iraqis. Along the southbound oncoming lanes were burned-out buses and dump trucks. These were Arab kamikazes, boys, many of them from Saddam's hometown of Tikrit, given an AK-47 rifle and driven south to try to stop oncoming American tanks while shooting from open dump trucks or school buses. Most of these kamikazes had been dispatched by machine guns aboard the tanks or by the Bradleys' 25 mm guns. At dawn, about two hours before we arrived on the scene, the Iraqis had attempted a counterattack with a tank company.

"Another four hundred Iraqi soldiers made a very bad decision," Captain Lyle observed without emotion.

Several of the attacking Iraqi tanks had been taken out by aircraft circling in the skies overhead, just waiting to be called in to help out ground units like the 7th. The road itself was awash in .50-caliber and 7.62 mm shell casings.

As we followed Captain Lyle's main battle tank up Route 1, he stood in his turret and pointed at the carnage. The road was littered with the bodies of dead Iraqis, charred corpses in burned-out pickup trucks and buses, uniformed bodies sprawled in the road, soon to become food for feral dogs and cats. It would be several days before villagers from either side of Route 1 would get up the confidence to come claim the dead to give them a proper Muslim funeral. There was no point in trying to reckon the numbers of dead Iraqis lying about us there. They were everywhere: on the shoulders, in the median strip, and off in the fields. They had enlisted in these suicide charges for the promise of a promotion, the honor of service in an elite unit, and entrance into the privileged ranks of Ba'ath Party membership. Instead most died, cheated out of the promise of a mellow Mesopotamian spring. The only thing anyone could do for them now was to bury their bullet-riddled corpses before the warm April sun made them smell any worse.

We had not gone far, perhaps three miles, before Captain Lyle decided to forge on up the road alone to check on the positions of his advance units. He signalled for us to stay behind at an interchange that had some graded ramps onto the highway from an overpass. There was still some shooting here, and killing continued from the previous evening. One of Apache Troop's M1A1 Abrams tanks was stationed up the ramp on the highway cloverleaf, and a Bradley was on the other side of the highway on another entrance ramp. Once again, Old Betsy was nestled between belching dragons. Even though there was still a lot of shooting going on about us, we were somewhat protected by the highway's entrance and exit ramps. Shielded from the Sunni suburbs to the east by those entrance ramps, we decided to try a live broadcast using the videophone for transmission. It took fewer than five minutes to set up and establish a connection to Atlanta, and there was still plenty of "bang-bang" about us. Off to the east, about an eighth of a mile, was a low, flat line of Iraqi homes, a Sunni neighborhood that lay between where we were and the airport, which was now in the hands of the 3rd Infantry Division. Units of the 101st Airborne were already pushing the perimeter of the airport farther back so as to make the runways safe for night landings. As a consequence, some of the Iraqis retreating from the vicinity of the airport were now banging up against Apache Troop along Route 1.

It would have been comforting to have had some of the helicopters assigned to the 7th Cavalry escorting us that morning. They could have flown protective cover with their rocket pods and Hellfire missiles and cleared out some of the remaining Iraqis who were still shooting at us from over to the east. But at some point earlier, a decision had been made higher up the chain of command that there were to be no more helicopter casualties after the Apache fiasco earlier in the war around Karbala. Dead and disembowelled helicopter crews did not play well for the folks back home, and we all knew it. Additionally, in an urban environment where U.S. forces were loathe to cause civilian casualties and where Iraqis could run back and forth between houses using shoulder-fired missiles, the "bad news" quotient would have been too high if more U.S. helicopters were brought down. Thus, the soldiers of the 7th were left to slug it out on the ground by themselves the old-fashioned way.

There still was more than a little slugging about us. Rocket-propelled grenades were whooshing over our heads, and there was plenty of small-arms fire where we parked. It came from Iraqi soldiers who did not choose to be mopped up that morning. Their RPGs would fall beyond us and explode over to the left in the raw earth. It was reassuring to see them exploding forty to fifty yards distant, because it told us that those firing them couldn't draw a direct bead on us and were firing more or less blindly in our general direction. Apparently, they knew we were on the highway just below the entrance ramp. We would have been much the worse for it if they had had mortars they could have lobbed down on us, but fortunately, mortars were not in the inventory of these particular Iraqis. Occasionally, heaven would thunder and earth shake when the main battle tank would let fly back at the Iraqis with its 120 mm gun, but as long as that tank was positioned up to our left and the Bradley off to the West on the other side of the interchange, we were sandwiched nicely.

More troublesome, however, was the Iraqis' use of Soviet-vintage 23 mm anti-aircraft guns as antipersonnel weapons. They were firing the damned guns right over our heads, banging away at us. The only thing that shielded us from a more depressed and therefore more threatening trajectory was the graded highway ramp to our right. Still there existed the nasty threat of those airbursts directly over our heads. It was just like the movies, exploding puffs of black smoke above us and shrapnel designed to bring down airplanes raining down about us. I tried to calculate just how high above us the 23 mm shells were exploding and guessed that they were only about forty to fifty yards up in the air. In my mind's eye, I can still see the pompoms of black smoke bursting up there. They had our range perfectly. We foolishly did not put on our helmets.

Charlie set up the tripod and began a broadcast of the engagement, which had enough action to please the folks back home—whooshing and banging and the rattle of small-arms fire. It was the closest any TV crew had come to the airport at that point, and it documented that some Iraqis still had fight left in them.

Jeff and Paul were not needed for the videophone broadcast so they decided to hike back down the road in the direction of a bridge over Route 1. I did not share their curiosity for seeing the carnage more closely but was content to let the TV pictures tell it from a respectable distance. Not much earlier, the 7th Cavalry had taken out one fairly new T-72 tank and a Soviet-era BMP armored personnel carrier just about where we were now to set up the camera. There were still flames licking about outside the hatches from smoldering fires within fed by burning oil, ammunition, and human flesh. Slumped over the T-72 turret hatch was a dead Iraqi soldier. His uniform was charred as black as his corpse, which was cooked from the feet up. This tank had made history a few hours earlier because it was knocked out of action, not by another tank but by the 25 mm gun on the turret of a Bradley fighting vehicle. Using uranium-depleted shells, the Bradley's much-smaller gun was able to punch holes in what was once the top-of-the-line tank for the Warsaw Pact. It was a small but phenomenal event in the history of armored warfare, I was told later, because there was no precedent for a Bradley's taking out a tank the size of a T-72. For me, it was but another indication the Warsaw Pact armies' numbers were overrated by Western military analysts. In the First Gulf War, as well as the Second, it was always assumed an equal fight among tanks was four enemy tanks up against one American M1A1 Abrams. Accompanied by Bradleys in an engagement, the odds for U.S. forces increased even further.

A few yards behind the T-72 was yet another burning vehicle, the Soviet BMP, with more corpses lying on the road. The Iraqis had escaped their burning vehicle only to die beside it. Someone from the 7th Cavalry evidently had stacked the dead soldiers' rifles in the middle of the road to be retrieved later. Paul and Jeff walked among the bodies while Charlie and I were broadcasting under fire farther back down the road.

"There were body parts all over the road," Jeff remembers. "Blood and guts were smeared and splattered along the steel guardrails."

He was dutifully taking pictures with his digital camera, recording the corpses strewn about the tank. One Iraqi was sprawled in a pose of death with a shiny silver watch gleaming on his wrist in the morning sun, his forearm pointing skyward into nothingness. Soldiers' contortions in death are, in one respect, like snowflakes. No two are ever quite the same. Perhaps the most grisly of sights that morning was a scorched lower leg sticking out of a boot. The flesh had been stripped from the shattered fibula and tibia, which were splintered three-fourths of the way up. Those bones and the guy's foot were still in a black boot neatly tied and laced. The rest of him was propped up against the steel guardrail where he had died, perhaps from shock or perhaps from bleeding to death.

As Paul and Jeff were turning around to leave, Jeff cried out louder than the shooting going on just over their heads.

"Holy shit, Paul!"

A dead Iraqi lying beside the road for several hours suddenly sat up, and Jeff caught it out of the corner of his eye. Paul grabbed a gun quickly because this resurrected Iraqi could have begun shooting at us at any moment. Jeff sprinted like a wild jackrabbit farther back up the road to where another Bradley was parked but not before picking up another of the AK-47s lying beside more dead Iraqis. Jeff was taking no chances on anyone else in the area coming to life and shooting at us. He eyed every dead Iraqi with considerably more suspicion from there on out.

Jeff, with some excitement, told the Bradley's crew we had a "live Iraqi" among the dead back down the road and asked if they would radio for a medic. These soldiers had been killing Iraqis for the past twelve hours and seemed more than a little disappointed that someone had been a poor shot. Jeff remembers these soldiers as "being totally disinterested" with the fact there was a wounded Iraqi about fifty yards away. They did, however, laconically radio back to the rear for some medics to come forward. The difficulty was that even when the Iraqi army saw a Red Cross vehicle trying to make its way up the road, they began blasting away at the U.S. medics. Jeff, meanwhile, returned to help Paul with the Iraqi who appeared to have serious but not necessarily life-threatening wounds. His worst affliction, and the most life threatening, may have been dehydration and shock.

Meanwhile, RPGs and 23 mm shells were still whizzing and banging over our heads. I was broadcasting, looking into the camera lens, worrying about the shooting that was quite close to us, and thus largely unaware of much of what was going on behind me where Jeff and Paul were. But beyond me, over my shoulder, Charlie could see our very own Lazarus, and it was his brilliant idea to terminate this live shot and just leave everything for the moment. He wanted to drive Old Betsy the half–football-field distance to where Paul had begun performing some very fine battlefield first aid again. Charlie smelled "good live TV" and persuaded me to hustle up there with him. He parked the Humvee beside "Lazarus," and we began transmitting some remarkable pictures of this wounded, if not resurrected, Iraqi lying on the side of the road and supported by Paul while Jeff held the IV bag. This guy had nine lives. He had lain beside the road in a scorching sun, unconscious and in shock for at least four or five hours. If he had so much as twitched when a tank or Bradley passed by him, a volley of 7.62 mm machine-gun bullets would have slashed into his body. Fortunately for this Iraqi officer, however, he came to when Jeff and Charlie were inspecting his dead comrades. The wounded man had fallen into the best of all available hands. Not only did the soldiers in the Bradley seem uninterested in redeeming him but later as Paul labored to resuscitate this Iraqi captain, I saw several other soldiers walk by with looks that seemed to ask, "What in the hell did you bother to help this guy for?" It was a natural question. At dawn, this Republican Guard captain had been trying to kill them, and now, he was at the least an annoyance and would be for days to come. But we were about to make him famous, and Paul was not about to let him die. It was part of the beautiful complexity of Paul Jordan's character to be able in one moment and without a second thought break another soldier's neck and a moment later to become a sensitive, caring human being who refused to abandon on the battlefield a wounded soldier of any stripe.

When this man first saw Paul standing over him with a rifle in his hands, he threw up his arms in a gesture of surrender and then fell backward, unconscious again. Paul set aside his rifle and took control, beginning an examination of him.

"He had lost a lot of blood and was in shock," Paul said.

The crimson on the ground about him was turning dark brown now as his blood seeped into his native earth where he was now sprawled. Cutting off the legs of the captain's trousers, Paul found badly cut up legs, riddled with shrapnel. Half of the soldier's right buttock had been shot away. It looked like a tiger had bitten a chunk out of his rear.

Fading in and out of consciousness, the soldier began vomiting. Paul rolled him on his side to prevent him from choking or aspirating vomit into his lungs. A young American soldier from the Bradley from which Jeff had earlier sought assistance wandered over and offered to help. Paul asked him if he knew how to put in an IV, but as he later recalled, "This kid was straight out of basic training and didn't have a clue." Paul handed Jeff the IV fluid bag with normal saline and tried to insert the needle into the back of the now semi-conscious Iraqi's left hand. He had lost so much blood Paul couldn't find a vein. Fortuitously, he located one in the soldier's left bicep, "and miraculously, it took."

It was an unreal moment. Paul had taken charge and young U.S. soldiers just stood around and gaped at his proficiency in combat medicine. I'm sure they privately envied his skills, and each of us quietly hoped that if we ever took a bullet, Paul Jordan, or someone from the Australian SAS, would be there. Charlie brought the guy a canteen of ice-tea mix, and Jeff was holding the IV bag. Bullets and RPGs were flying comfortingly high overhead. Paul had also given the Iraqi a shot of morphine, which transformed the wounded soldier's view on things considerably. A few minutes earlier, he was lying more dead than alive in a crusted pool of his own blood. Now, he was sitting up grinning and laughing, feeling no pain and grateful to be alive.

He grabbed Paul's hands and began kissing them. Paul also remembers the Iraqi trying to kiss his face.

"Oh Gawd," was Paul's reaction at the moment. "This guy was crying and slobbering and vomiting all over me at the same time."

Later, when I asked Paul how much morphine he gave this guy, he replied with an easy laugh, "Probably too much."

Throughout the entire episode, we were broadcasting live pictures around the world of the Iraqi soldier's rescue. The bright young video whiz kids, producers back at CNN Atlanta, just made a command decision: "Hey this is great stuff! Let's put it on the air." And they did. There were no rules in a situation like this. Sitting in the newsroom, Marianna Spicer from the standards and practices office was asked by a director how much of this we should air. She at that time had been with CNN for twelve years and had been fifteen years collectively at ABC and CBS News. Spicer, one of the best in the business, replied, "How would I know? This has never happened before!" All of us embeds, especially in TV, sometimes had to make it up as we went along. I was narrating the scene and the process while Paul Jordan brought this guy back from the dead. Charlie, having given the Iraqi something to drink, was shooting it, and Jeff was faithfully holding the IV bag.

In my ear, on the I.F.B. (interrupt fold back) circuit from Atlanta for return sound, someone kept saying to me, "Don't show his face, don't show his face." It was difficult not to. It meant telling the story from the neck down, and it also meant I had to address Charlie in an aside while on the air with the order not to show the Iraqi's face. The bullets were flying over our heads, and combat first aid was being rendered to a seriously wounded enemy soldier, and CNN was carrying it live. Pretty good stuff, if you ask me!

Still, if there was not precedent for live TV coverage of emergency medical aid to an enemy combatant in the middle of a war, there were several principles that came in to play. Foremost was the Pentagon's stricture that all embeds had signed mandating we were not to show the faces of Iraqi prisoners of war, although I confess with RPGs whooshing over our heads and exploding in farm fields across the road and the rattle of small-arms fire whizzing about over our heads, the farthest thing from my mind as we were tending a badly wounded Iraqi soldier was a piece of paper I signed a month earlier.

More pertinent at the time was the voice in my ear of a director or "minder" in Atlanta who kept repeating, "Don't show his face." In live TV broadcasts, that electronic voice in the ear is pretty much God.

If we had not been under fire at the time and given the opportunity for more sober reflection, there are additional issues of journalistic ethics that might enter the equation. If, for example, the individual had been an American civilian injured in an automobile accident, showing a victim's face might well have risked privacy claims. The principle in such a case is that the victim is not in a position to say "Yes" or "No" to being videotaped. And our wounded Iraqi was hardly in a position to be asked. The automobile-accident victim might well be unconscious. Our Iraqi soldier was on a morphine joy trip.

Neither individual is or was in a position to protest. The Iraqi soldier could hardly have walked away or put a hand to cover his face.

Ultimately, in a situation like this, even in a war, someone else has to make the decision for the wounded individual. The Pentagon's strictures aside, it seems to me the wounded Iraqi soldier's case could have been argued both pro and con. We had already shown images of the man's wounds including a buttock mauled by a large-caliber munition. Additionally, there was the comic aspect that is so often present in the worst of combat situations. The drugged and grateful Iraqi kept trying to kiss Paul who kept trying to restrain him.

From my vantage point, as opposed to that of a Pentagon legal expert eight thousand miles away, there seemed a more powerful humanitarian aspect that arguably comes into play during a war. I felt then and still do that showing the injured Iraqi soldier's face on a global television network like CNN that has a substantial Iraqi audience might at least have let the wounded soldier's family know he was still alive. In my live narration of Paul trying to save him, I kept saying on air, "I do not believe his injuries are life threatening." I did that deliberately in the hope somehow, somewhere, someone in Iraq would recognize the soldier and tell his family of his fate and more importantly the likelihood this guy would probably survive. So often in subsequent car bombings in Iraq and elsewhere, TV viewers did indeed recognize injured persons and telephone a family member to report the fate of a loved one. In this case, I had hoped we could have been a small force for good in a nasty little war.

There was no question however; our wounded Iraq was an exceptional case. No one can quite remember anything akin to that broadcast in the context of live-television war coverage. It may have simply been another case of hard cases making bad law. In the end, however, I was so delighted our Lazarus had been restored, I really wanted someone out there to see he was alive and would likely survive.

A year after the war, I made a considerable effort to discover the Iraqi captain's whereabouts, but I had no name, and I could not locate him.

After about fifteen minutes or so, when Paul had restored this man's life, an army medical M-113 pulled up, and a doctor came over to check out the Iraqi. The doctor took one look at the captain, now pleasantly stoned on morphine and juiced up with saline fluid, and perfunctorily asked if there was anything he could do. Paul reported his treatment, the army doctor nodded approvingly, had Lazarus loaded onto the vehicle and evacuated to the rear, where he lay about for about two days before he was taken to an Iraqi hospital. It disturbed me that the army had ordered up a Blackhawk helicopter in a futile effort to save a critically wounded Iraqi POW a week earlier near Al Samawah, but Paul's POW was left to lie on a cot beside a tracked vehicle for several days.

Paul, Jeff, Charlie, and I now had a vested interest in seeing Lazarus stay alive. The first night was critical. Communicating was nigh on impossible, and he kept pulling the IV out of his arm, endangering his chances of survival. The lesson of Lazarus was instructive in another way. I now began to doubt all of our assumptions that if we ever were wounded, we would be given excellent medical care and attention. The army was too busy fighting a war, too busy killing Iraqis, and too preoccupied trying to close in on Baghdad to put that high a priority on a wounded journalist, even an American. Ultimately, like Lazarus, wounded, we, too, would have been but another obstacle in the way of everyone's going home sooner. I had been hoping if any of us were wounded, a helicopter would have been sent in to evacuate us. But with the ban on helicopters being flown in combat over Baghdad, my assumption was now pretty much grounded in a different reality. And our Lazarus was going to live or die on his own for the next forty-eight hours until an Iraqi hospital could be found to take him.

Later that same day, Old Betsy and crew had another discussion with CNN's standards and practices folks. The day's fighting remained intense, erupting at uneven intervals. Unilaterally, Charlie, Jeff, Paul, and I decided to withdraw about a hundred yards to the south along Route 1 and resume our live broadcast from an even more protected location. The natural backdrop was the burned-out tank and the smoldering Soviet-vintage armored personnel carrier, a BMP. In truth, that was all the army would let us show because we were still forbidden to turn our camera to either side of the road for fear of giving away our location to the Iraqi military in Baghdad. "Dead bodies" was our only option. If we tilted the camera up, there was the commander slumped over the turret. If we tilted the camera down, there were more bodies sprawled on the ground. If we turned the camera right or left, we violated the Pentagon's rules about not betraying our location. If we left that relatively secure location sheltered by a superhighway ramp road, we would have been totally exposed to hostile Iraqi fire that was pouring in over our heads for the better part of that day.

Charlie set up the tripod, and we began broadcasting. In the background, thirty yards distant, there were half a dozen dead Iraqis visible. No faces. These had been burned beyond recognition. In the lens, they appeared like stuffed scarecrows knocked down in a windstorm. We hadn't been broadcasting five minutes when again, the word was passed through the I.F.B. circuit in my ear, "Stop showing dead bodies." We had to stop broadcasting there. Again, there were multiple concerns and principles to be addressed, among them that it might appear that we had used a burned-out tank and dead bodies as a convenient backdrop from which to do a live broadcast. In some circumstances, that might be a fair criticism. But at that moment, in the middle of a firefight in the middle of a war, I figured this was a reasonable exception. Standing behind the earthen shoulder of the highway interchange ramps was about the only shelter we had from snipers and incoming fire, something those back in Atlanta did not know.

I also learned viewers had been calling in and objecting to seeing dead bodies strewn thirty or forty yards in the distance. I went ballistic. How in hell could anyone cover a war without showing dead bodies? Every evening on American television, there are scads of fictional dead bodies shown to young children. Every Arnold Schwarzenegger movie has scores of villains blown sky-high. You need a calculator at a Sylvester Stallone movie to tally some of his body counts.

In retrospect, CNN showed more than a few dead bodies during the war, and these are never easy calls especially for correspondents under fire in the field. Ultimately, the rules ever seem to vary under the circumstances. My view, however, remains those horrors of war should be shown to TV viewers back home to disabuse them of the illusion that there is much glory in war beyond merely surviving. Just as important, it seems this same carnage should be thrice shown to the policy makers who send soldiers into combat at the risk of being killed as a check against committing the nation to dubious wars. Showing more of war's carnage might dampen the enthusiasm for war of some of the civilian leaders within the Pentagon: Paul Wolfowitz, Richard Pearle, and Doug Feith, as well as the president and vice president, who have never heard a shot fired in anger.

It turns out it would have been better not to have broadcast from there after all. The Iraqi tank burned all day as did the BMP, and when the breeze shifted, we inhaled the fumes. It was not until a little later that day, we learned the Iraqi armor had been taken out with uranium-depleted shells.

"You better get farther back from that tank," Captain Lyle yelled when he had returned from his sortie up Highway 1. "There might be some bad fumes from the uranium-depleted shells" that had incapacitated it. "Stay fifty yards back of it."

It was but another reason never to pick up souvenirs on a battlefield.

We had completed our transmission anyway and had been disconnected from any of the officers in our unit now for the better part of five hours, which is to say we were totally out of the information loop. So, when Captain Lyle signalled for us to return to the base camp by the lone palm tree, it seemed a capital idea because it was safer than the neighborhood in which we had been working most of that morning.

The 7th Cavalry's field headquarters was a few miles in back of us at that highway cloverleaf, the intersection of Routes 1 and 8 in the southwest suburbs of Baghdad. The encampment had two distinguishing features: that lone palm tree and a huge bulldozed pit in the ground filled with crude oil. It was one of those mindless innovations of the Iraqi Ministry of Defense that when set ablaze was supposed to obscure the vision of American pilots supporting troops on the ground. The Iraqi soldier charged with igniting this oil reservoir, however, was almost certainly lying dead somewhere back down the road on which we had come the previous day. These oil pits had but two real functions: They badly polluted the already badly polluted Iraqi landscape, and they were convenient urinals for most of the soldiers of Apache Troop.

Paul found a place to park our Humvee beside a tank, and we all sauntered over to Colonel Ferrell's Bradley where everyone was gathering. These were deceptively low-key gatherings. We had by now that easy access whereby we could just amble on up and join the conversation or ask questions and get some surprisingly straight answers.

"Hey what's happening?" was answered that morning with, "Well, we've got Baghdad surrounded on three sides now." There was an almost convivial mood. We all sensed that the end of the fighting was but a few days away. The celebratory mood was only slightly premature, for we would be up and down Highway 1 for several more days, and the snipers were still active. Fortunately, most of that sniping was attempted with AK-47s, the standard Iraqi soldiers' issue, and despite its much-vaunted reputation, at four hundred yards or more, it was not effective.

There was all sorts of gossip exchanged, laughs about, "Did you see that dump truck go up in flames when we hit it?" and some war news coming across the SCO's radio. The Baghdad elite had continued to flee along a highway that would ultimately take many of them to sanctuary in Syria. There was a rumor that Saddam's wife and daughters had fled taking that route just ahead of us. Because they were all leaving in civilian vehicles intermingled with trucks, there was no effort to intercede or intercept, and much of Baghdad's officialdom fled within just a few miles of the 7th Cavalry's guns. My assumption was confirmed after the war by Colonel Ferrell who said, "Our initial mission at the cloverleaf was to let people flee, especially if we could not ID them as soldiers." Given the numbers of Iraqis leaving Baghdad at that point and the relatively small numbers of soldiers Apache Troop had, it would have been impossible to have checked everyone, especially when so much of the Company was still taking sporadic fire and would continue to for the next thirty-six hours.

"Later," Colonel Ferrell added, "we started to run modified checkpoints looking for individuals on the most-wanted list."

I knew of the existence of the most-wanted list even this early in the war but could not persuade Colonel Ferrell to let us take pictures of the wanted flyers his soldiers had been given.

Over the short-wave, we also heard that the Russian ambassador's convoy fleeing Baghdad had allegedly been fired upon, and the Americans were accused of doing the shooting. Without any questioning, most of the media accepted this as fact. After all, the Russians claimed it was true, and there was a prejudicial inclination on the part of many reporters in this theater, especially Europeans and Arabs, to accept anything of a negative nature about U.S. forces. Because Colonel Ferrell had been candid with me during the combat operations, I began to question him about the allegation because we were fairly close to where the incident had reportedly occurred. From what little I could glean on the battlefield, the Russian envoy was fleeing west on Route 10 just north of where we had been earlier that day. It seemed at least plausible that it might have been the 7th Cavalry who fired on them although Colonel Ferrell denied it at the time. But it could just have easily been renegade units of Saddam's army or perhaps brigands shooting at the fleeing Russians, figuring they might acquire some booty to tide them over at war's end. That would have been a much less sensational news story than American troops shooting at the Russian envoy, a tale that took on a life of its own. The Russians eagerly seized the opportunity to blame the Americans.

After the war, a Russian TV journalist who claimed he was in the convoy assured me he was definitely fired at by the Americans. It struck me as odd, however, that of all the convoys of people leaving Baghdad on Route 10 west, including the absconding Ba'athists, the only one that U.S. forces stopped and turned around at this juncture in the war was the one with the Russian ambassador. Again I checked with Colonel Ferrell after the war, and he was categorical.

"The Russian convoy was not fired upon by any Squadron personnel," he said. "We were about two *k*s [kilometers or a mile and a quarter] from the location they reported receiving fire, heading west on Highway 10, and no American elements were closer than the Squadron [3/7th Cavalry]. Follow-on information suggested the attack was from a hostile Iraqi force firing at anything moving along the highway."

"I personally believe the Russian story is fake," the man in charge of that combat sector concluded. "It briefs better if the Americans are guilty!"

That's the way the BBC saw it and reported "an American attack on the Russian ambassador's convoy" for days, never letting the American denial get in the way of an otherwise good story.

Throughout the war, Colonel Ferrell's trust and generosity ever worked to CNN's benefit. Allowing near-total access to the information he was receiving from the generals above him enabled us to break story after story, sometimes two and three a day. (He did hide his intelligence officer throughout the campaign.) Still, it seemed a unique relationship of trust between a senior officer and a reporter. It saved my network's butt over and over because during much of the war, other CNN reporters, usually through circumstances beyond their control, seemed "out of position," especially as the fighting neared Baghdad. We had no one embedded with the 2nd Brigade of the 3rd ID when it began probing and driving into Baghdad. But Colonel Ferrell was keeping me posted on the relatively low-level street-fighting they encountered. From the southern suburbs of Baghdad, I was able to report on those probes when 2nd Brigade was flexing its muscle inside the Iraqi capital a few miles away. By allowing me to listen to the commanding general's daily radio briefings to his commanders in the field, the colonel kept CNN on top of the news. In Colonel Ferrell, I had the best source in the entire war. This unique vantage point also demonstrated the need for fluidity in news "calls" on network TV. At the outset of the war, I received an e-mail memo from the international desk, instructing me and other embeds to report only on tactical events that happened within our line of sight. I was specifically instructed not to endeavor any big-picture reporting. Fortunately, when the exigencies of the networks needs required bigger-picture reporting, the need for coverage superceded the earlier advisory that I considered confining. As in war so in television, the battle plans for coverage rarely survive more than a few days of combat. The network quickly recognized I had one fine source in this war, and my coverage of the assault of Baghdad exceeded my original marching orders.

While the 2nd Brigade of the 3rd ID was making one of those forays under fire into Baghdad, some Iraqis with a rocket got off a lucky shot at a field command post. When the word of the attack filtered out over the radio, I could see the grieving on several officers' faces. Word was there may have been as many as seven killed, including a senior officer. We were reporting this kind of information hours, even days before the Pentagon released it or before it came out of Centcom in Qatar. Later we learned there were also four foreign journalists killed in that single rocket blast. Theirs were perhaps some of the most ironic deaths of the war. The journalists had opted to stay behind at the field command post in the southern suburbs of Baghdad instead of taking the risky ride with 2nd Brigade along Baghdad streets and exposing themselves to rifle and RPG fire. Instead, they were killed in a freak accident when a lucky Iraqi rocket strike hit the military command post that they had decided would be safer than a convoy ride under fire into the Iraqi capital. In retrospect, one wonders if it was just their turn to die. Neither soldiers nor journalists died on the 2nd Brigade's sortie along the streets of the Iraqi capital that day. It was a reminder that the back of the Squadron commander's Bradley where we now stood was not that much safer than riding Old Betsy in a firefight when the shit hits the fan.

A little later, when we wandered off to set up camp for ourselves, I noticed a number of armored vehicles starting their engines again, among them Captain Lyle's. I asked what was up.

"Force on force," he replied gleefully from his turret, clasping his helmet's chin strap like a kid just being let out to play.

Force on force and with the biggest grin of the war, his driver engaged gears and ground out of the encampment. I deduced there was a bigger than usual engagement underway. This time he did not invite us.

He was off to the finale of the only force-on-force tank engagement of the war, Iraqi armor slamming up against American armor. Judging by the look on Clay Lyle's face, it was something he had lived for all his life. Intel was suddenly reporting that a substantial Iraqi tank force, sixteen to eighteen T-72s, some BMP armored personnel carriers, and, as they would later discover, more dump trucks carrying infantry were closing ahead of us on

Route 1. Initial reports had indicated the Iraqis had only ten or twelve tanks available. It was not the only miscalculation in the initial intelligence reports. At first, it was also reported the Iraqi tanks were coming from the west, but, Sergeant Chase said, the Intel folks got it wrong: "They were, to our surprise, along the east side of the road."

It was mid-afternoon when the two forces banged into each other. The Iraqis made some attempt to "feel us out," according to Sergeant Wheatley, but Sergeant Chase remembers that the majority of Iraqi tanks had been dug in on the east side of the road about a quarter of a mile back, with earthworks all around them shielding them from everything but an air strike or direct hit on the turret.

"They had great positions," Sergeant Chase remembers. "They couldn't have built a better defensive belt. They just couldn't hit anything. All their shots were high. The poor dumb bastards just couldn't hit anything."

By contrast, the 120 mm rounds from the 7th Cavalry's tanks hit home nearly every time. Close air support was called in to help root out the T-72s that were so deeply dug in they couldn't be destroyed by Captain Lyle's tanks. Sergeant Chase, who holds a master gunner's badge, claims he took out five Iraqi tanks that were behind their earthen breastworks, immobile.

"They couldn't engage," Sergeant Chase remembers. When our shells slammed home, "there was a shower of sparks and smoke from within the Iraqi tanks. Then came internal secondary explosions."

The T-72s' own rounds were blowing up inside.

"It was like a super-enhanced blow torch going off. There were flames shooting out every hatch in the tank, just like an acetylene torch burning," the sergeant said.

The Iraqi tanks fired back before they were ultimately dispatched. Sergeant Chase remembers a shell from an Iraqi tank went right over the back deck of his tank just behind the turret in which he was riding. Captain Lyle remembers the same shell passing just in front of his M1A1. Later, Sergeant Chase and Captain Lyle would argue good-naturedly over who came the closest to being hit with that incoming Iraqi round. The sergeant's loader, Ronald Murray, would recall "the poor dumb bastards," as his outgoing 120 mm shell slammed into one of the tanks. It did not miss its target.

"It was pretty exhilarating," Sergeant Wheatley remembered. "Another incoming shell just missed my tank and went through a steel guardrail along the highway. It hit the rail on the other side of the road and burst into flames."

He remembers eighteen Iraqi tanks getting knocked out that afternoon. The precise number of BMPs was less relevant. They just burned in the fields and in the facing lanes of highway, erasing forever the existence of hundreds of Iraq's soldiers whose fathers and mothers would never know where or how they died. None of us seemed to care at the time. I found that to be the true callousness of war, not the pictures of dead Iraqi soldiers we transmitted earlier. Callousness is the protective shell in which the winners encase themselves against what they have seen and done.

When Apache Troop rolled back into camp that night, the soldiers were exhausted and elated. They had performed brilliantly. They had met and destroyed the enemy by the hundreds. They had won the only tank battle of the war, force on force, without a single loss. They had stopped counting the numbers of Iraqis killed in tanks, BMPs, and kamikaze dump trucks. Not counting was part of that shell each of us built to shield ourselves from our own close calls and the bloodletting.

On a much smaller scale, another skirmish was brewing within the encampment itself between the translator Daoud and his senior officer Capt. Rick Cote. The Kurdish Jew had been a shadowy figure moving about the encampment throughout the campaign. He appeared a man who wanted to stay gray and in the shadows, someone who had grown up in a world where going unnoticed was a way to stay alive. Although he wore the standard army MOPP suit, he showed neither insignia nor rank. He never did disclose his surname. I knew him only casually, and in each of our brief conversations, he had been secretive if not furtive. He was not a happy camper. Daoud had been assigned to the security and stability operations (SASO) unit. He had great hopes of seeing Baghdad liberated and the attendant dream of reuniting with Kurdish relatives he had not seen for a quarter of a century—but it would not be with the 7th Cavalry.

Daoud and Captain Cote appeared to despise each other. Daoud tried to practice a little consciousness-raising with Cote, who was a fireman from Myrtle Beach, South Carolina, and did not think there was much about the world a Kurdish Jew could teach him. I suspect Daoud was also a rich man back in the Midwest and that, too, did not set well with Cote, who was openly derisive.

Finally, in desperation, Daoud buttonholed me and walked me away from the crowd to plead his case.

"You have lived in the Middle East," he began. "You know Muslims, and you know Arabs, and you know how it is when Muslim soldiers are left in the sun to rot along that highway. They are supposed to be buried within twenty-four hours."

Having seen Palestinians in their fratricidal wars with Israel, I understood well the Islamic way of death.

"Please," Daoud pleaded. "Nothing is going to do more to create a good impression with the Iraqis after this war than to show respect for their customs. You know they are to be buried quickly if they are to attain paradise. You know their bodies have to be washed, cleansed, and they have to have an *imam* perform a funeral service."

He was right, and I knew it. Daoud said he tried to persuade Captain Cote, as the civil affairs officer, to attend to the carnage and send the unit's SASO team and its Humvees up the road with loudspeakers to call out into the villages on either side of the road to come collect the dead. The worst thing the 7th Cavalry could have done along that highway, and there was contemplation of the idea, was to collect all the dead Iraqi soldiers and dump them in a mass grave or cremate them.

I was in a ticklish situation. I knew Daoud was right. I also knew if I stuck my nose into this and openly interceded on the side of an interpreter, I would alienate Captain Cote whom I knew and appreciated as a good old boy and who had been openly generous with us. It took about a New York minute to decide. I discreetly marched over to Colonel Ferrell and told him I needed a private word with him. He was that kind of officer. Any of his men could have requested the same audience. Without mentioning the personalities involved in this skirmish in his camp, I suggested that he might want to score some points with the locals by sending up the SASO unit trucks with their loudspeakers to broadcast to the surrounding villages that they were free to collect the bodies of dead Iraqi soldiers and that they would not be fired at.

Ferrell grasped the merit of the idea instantly and ordered Captain Cote to do just that first thing the next morning, assuming hostilities abated overnight. I don't know that the captain ever linked my suggestion to Colonel Ferrell to his much-despised translator whom he not long after had transferred to another unit. But Captain Cote seemed pleased when Iraqi villagers timorously emerged from nearby buildings to approach the American soldiers, telling tales of how awful life had been under Saddam.

In typical Iraqi fashion, the poorer Shiites lived on one side of the road and the Sunnis in the better homes on the other side of the road. At the first opportunity, the Shiias were asking the Americans when it would be okay to start killing the Sunnis. There were scores to be settled, Ba'athists to be killed, although I suspect the hated high-level Ba'athists were already well on their way to Damascus or the relative security of Tikrit or Fallujah. Meanwhile, over the next few days, the Iraqi soldiers' bodies were retrieved from the burned buses, the median strip, and the adjacent fields and given proper burials, albeit for a tardy entrance into the Islamic paradise. There the indigenous angels would question them on the kind of life they had led. As an infidel on the sidelines below, I could but wonder how Gabriel would receive a Muslim who had fought and died for Saddam Hussein.

I felt furtive but privately pleased with myself for helping facilitate the removal of those bodies on Route 1. I sensed that most of the American soldiers, as they rolled back and forth up and down that highway, were indifferent to the dead Iraqis. I, too, was indifferent, figuring they were beyond my help, but I could not ignore the Kurdish Jew's unspoken reminder of another more familiar stricture, "Blessed are the merciful."

Facilitating those burials was a small act, ultimately carried out by some good and decent U.S. soldiers and officers. In war, any manifestation of goodness or gesture of kindness, however small it seems at the time, takes on greater weight. It is the leaven of humanity in the grinding wheels of war that may ultimately separate the good guys from the bad guys. I suspect old Lazarus would have agreed. He lay over against another tracked vehicle, a few yards away. He was still not certain at this point whether he had a rendezvous with the angel Uzra or with a terrestrial Iraqi physician who might yet patch up his bloody ass. Most of his Republican Guard and Fedayeen comrades had indeed found a hundred ways to die earlier that day. But with the innate goodness and gentle care of Paul Jordan, our Lazarus had found a way to live.

10

Into Baghdad

> Where are your monuments, your battles, martyrs?
> Where is your tribal memory? Sirs,
> in that gray vault. The sea. The sea
> has locked them up. The sea is History.
> —Derek Walcott, "The Sea Is History"

In the deserts of Arabia, the Bedouins imagine the trackless sands to be the sea. They see themselves as sailors, Iraqis included. It is said there are two hundred different words or phrases to describe camels in the Arabic language. One definition of camels translates into "ships of the desert." Nomadic tent encampments in the desert and even small cities are in the Arab mind islands. Small wonder that amid the frequently foul weather in the military campaign of March and April of 2003, the unusual dust storms and vile winds blowing at night when normally they would have risen during the day were interpreted by many Iraqis as Allah's wrath visited upon the infidel Americans. The people of the desert, including many Iraqis, believed, hoped, that the sea of sand might yet rise up and drown the invaders.

At our encampment at the lone palm tree, there was a force-nine gale build-up that night. The sea of sand again rolled, roiled, and raged. We, the infidels, were battening down. The desert wind had arisen not long after dark and was sweeping overboard much of our camp that was not lashed or bolted down. Jeff was, once again, climbing the rigging of Old Betsy in a gale to make sure his satellite dish was reefed, folded, and secure. Having moments earlier spread my sleeping bag and insulated mattress pad on a newly acquired cot, I was now in the rigging of Old Betsy helping him.

In a matter of seconds, as the blow stiffened, I looked down and saw my sleeping bag fill and billow like a newly unfurled sail. The blue foam-insulation pad, like a blown hatch cover, lifted vertically, flying upward and disappearing into the greenish-black night. It levitated like a magic carpet and embarked after my white sock that had earlier taken up residence somewhere in Saudi Arabia. It joined the rest of the flotsam and jetsam of the armada of the 7th Cavalry in the late winter and spring of 2003. Fortunately, my down sleeping bag snagged on a thorn bush twenty yards away and was snapping like a top gallant ripped off a yardarm in a hurricane in rounding Cape Horn. After Jeff and I secured the sat dish, I bedded down in this blow and debated whether it would have been better to have been lashed with the cold salt spray of the South Atlantic or drowned in dust and grit again.

When the wind dropped later that night, the stars again became visible and grand. Lying in my sleeping bag, I reflected on those that bore Arabic names: Algol, Betelgeuse, Spica, Aldebaran, and I thought of an earlier era when the Arabs were on the cutting rather than the trailing edge of science and technology. There was a time when the Arabs did indeed navigate and rule their desert seas—but no longer. The children of European primitives who once wrapped themselves in skins while the Arab world was in its ascendance now ruled the Iraqi sea with tracked ships of steel.

The stars were beautiful. With my insulated pad spending the night elsewhere in the desert, I did not sleep warmly and awakened often to look up and delight in the cold stars above. The heavens were all that had kept me from aesthetic starvation in the previous weeks. Everything earthly was dirty, diseased, despairing, or dead. As I lay there on that hard cot, uncomfortably cold, only the heavens seemed unpolluted, exquisite, and eternal. Dawn would surely bring more killing. Another few hours, another few nights of tranquillity under the desert stars would have to last me until summer vacation when I could once again see the Milky Way. It is the same delicious solitude savored by the night watch at sea. The stars above the ocean's swells and over the rolling desert are timeless and humbling. By now, I was confident I would survive this war, and I began to realize how much I would miss the unpolluted night sky above the land of Nebuchadnezzar, Belshazzar, Daniel, and the Bedouins.

At age sixty-two, I also suspected this would be my last war, my last campaign. The stars would forever sweep across these deserts at night but I would be gone as surely as were the Babylonians and Chaldeans. I had grown accustomed to being up at 0430 every day now. It was camp life in the army. I knew I would come to miss drinking tea with one boot on the bumper of Old Betsy watching the sun rise over Persia to the east. Many times afterward, I would be asked, given the harrowing experiences we had, "Would you want to do it again?" My reply was always the same: "Only with the same crew—Jeff, Charlie, and Paul." And I would quickly add, "Only with the same soldiers and only in the 7th Cavalry." It was a safe answer. After the war, we would all go our own ways, and many of the soldiers with whom we served, albeit with different masters, would be transferred to other units. I enjoyed this kind of soldiering, but I knew this unit would not stay together, and we could not do this again. Something teaches us that all is flux.

So at dawn, when Captain Lyle once again approached us as we were having our tea on Old Betsy's hood and announced, "We're going out for a ride, want to go?" of course we replied, "Yes." He told us he suspected that after the previous day's force-on-force engagement, the Iraqis might try to send some more tanks down that road. If they did, he would get yet another chance to "punch them out." His delight was barely concealed. For us, it meant we would get to see the remnants of the previous day's "smash-up" along Highway 1 just west of the airport. If we were lucky, the Iraqis would have learned their lesson and headed for Tikrit or Fallujah. If we were very lucky, they were all dead.

Once again, Old Betsy bounced out of the encampment, and while I would continue to curse the discomfort of the Humvee with sandbags piled under my feet driving my knees up under my chin, I was becoming hardened to the throbbing in my butt. Rolling out on to Highway 8 and then 1, I kicked open the back door to see what Custer's heirs had wrought. The burned-out kamikaze Toyota with the three Fedayeen was still there, charred now, no longer white, and no sign of the dead Iraqis. As we rolled north up Highway 1, I began looking in the dirt shoulder beside the road trying to remember exactly where I had seen the Kalashnikov's bullets dancing in the dust a few feet from Charlie and me. Ahead lay the bridge, the overpass with the burned-out BMP and the T-72. I wondered if the internal fires had burned out and if it was safe to breathe near the tank's carcass now.

Ahead of the CNN Humvee, Captain Lyle stood within but not too far out of the turret of his tank. Nobody was convinced we could relax yet. Everyone else in Apache Troop ahead of us and to the rear kept their hands on their machine guns, just in case, ready to fire. None of the body armor issued by the U.S. Army that I saw would have been much good at stopping an incoming machine-gun round. As I have noted, the army's body armor was antiflack vests: better than nothing but not much. It lacked the Kevlar plates necessary to protect the chest's vital organs.

On the right side of the divided highway in the oncoming lanes were dozens of burned-out vehicles, mostly trucks along with school buses, pickup trucks, and the occasional car, the kinds of vehicles Iraqi soldiers had commandeered to go to war in the previous two days. The vehicles were now less than scrap, unredeemable. Not all the dead Iraqis' bodies had been collected yet, and in the warming day, they were becoming rank. On the right side of the road to the east toward the Saddam Airport, the side on which I was sitting, I could see villages of low, flat, rectangular mud or cinderblock houses. A few may have had second or third floors; they sat back from the road three hundred to four hundred yards. I wondered and worried how many Iraqi soldiers were lying out of sight within them, watching us and crouching with RPGs or rifles. They were little threat to Apache Troop's armored column out scouting that morning, with one exception. Old Betsy was once again the only soft-skinned, wheeled vehicle in the convoy. It remained a soft target, once again a sitting duck. The threat, or my imaginings, surely explained why I watched those adobe villages more closely than the soldiers in front of or behind us.

Several miles ahead, we would come upon the evidence of the previous afternoon's force-on-force engagement. Five hundred to six hundred yards back from the road, on the far side of an irrigation ditch, there were bulldozed escarpments enclosing at least a dozen burned-out tanks. The earth about them was as charred as what was left of the tanks themselves. It was "the perfect defensive belt" Sergeant Chase had described to me except that the Iraqis had shot high. I mulled the advantages and disadvantages of burrowing a tank into the ground as opposed to maneuverability to run and shoot. I think I would have opted for the latter if I had been one of those Iraqis. Captain Lyle later speculated some of the men the Iraqis had thrown into those tanks had had precious little training. But in the end, it didn't matter. The M1A1 Abrams main battle tank was so much better than the T-72s, and the U.S. soldiers were so better trained that it didn't matter what tactics the Iraqis employed or how brave their soldiers were, the outcome was inevitable disaster and death for them.

A little farther up the road, we dipped into what should have been an underpass or a tunnel, but there was nothing overhead but blue sky. It was as if the Iraqi highway-construction engineers intended to dig a tunnel. They built a road that went down into the ground, but they couldn't figure out how to put a top over it, so they left it open. Perhaps, in this ancient land of wars through the millennia, they were building a hidey-hole from enemy aircraft overhead. It was only later that we, too, came to appreciate the protection this thirty-foot-deep depression in the road was to afford. When we emerged on the other side, we were nearing the area where Captain Lyle believed the Iraqis had planned to reinforce at the intersection of Highway 10. All of us anticipated an ambush at any moment, especially when we emerged from the two-hundred-yard-long depression. The Iraqis' defensive positions were always embarrassingly predictable. They inevitably dug in and fortified a major intersection at a cloverleaf on a highway but rarely showed any defensive imagination. Even the dirt berms behind which they hid their tanks were classic armored defensive tactics. And they always got clobbered.

As Apache Troop's forward tanks and Bradleys rolled farther on approaching the intersection, the lead element encountered two Iraqi tanks that looked spanking new. In the instant decisions that soldier make in combat, it was assumed these tanks had taken up positions late that night and were waiting for us. Sergeant Wheatley took one look at them and let fly with two 120 mm shells, each slamming home. The two, Iraqi T-72s shook in their tracks, exploded, and burned on the right side of the road. The death rattle came from deep within: exploding magazines followed by the acetylene-torch effect of everything and everyone within burning in a white-hot flame that shot upward. Burning fuel tanks blew up next sending horrible columns of black smoke into the sky. In a subsequent assessment, it was determined these tanks had been "killed" the day before in the force-on-force engagement. But because they had been hit with sabot armor-piercing rounds that had merely punched clean holes in them, these T-72s looked clean and ready to attack us. So, they were killed twice, and this time, they burned furiously when hit with high-explosive shells. Sergeant Wheatley then had to turn his attention to an armored vehicle semiconcealed on the left side of the intersection, a BMP that was shooting like hell at us with machine guns. With great foolhardiness, the Iraqi commander tried to attack an American tank with a machine gun and twenty infantrymen. Sergeant Wheatley swung his turret about, and this time, his 120 mm gun claimed a fresh kill, including more hapless, unthinking young Iraqi men who impaled themselves on the tip of the tip of the spear perhaps believing those American tanks were really made of plywood as some had earlier been told. These Iraqis were now being cremated, ascending to paradise in ash and a Biblical column of fire and black smoke. The burning armored vehicle seared the new green buds in the copse in which the BMP had been concealed.

Other Iraqis in the area, however, were not so easily intimidated or eliminated. From concealed positions on the west side of the road, they began shooting at the platoon, using mortars, rocket-propelled grenades, and machine-gun fire. We were in a hot zone again and not entirely certain where the Iraqis were. The engagement was loud. The crushing decibels are the most unnerving thing about combat. Loud noise is disorienting. You can't see the incoming bullets in a daylight firefight. But the noise wounds your ears. The worst of the shooting seemed about a hundred yards in front of us. We had been trying to get the videophone working again to transmit and broadcast the engagement, but the vexing thing now only seemed to be working half the time. In the last weeks of the war, we suspected the U.S. military had been doing a fair amount of electronic jamming, knocking out our ability to report via satellite phone. A week or so earlier, all journalists had been asked not to use their personal Thuraya sat phones. No reason was ever given, except the standard army reply, "It's classified."

But we were pretty certain the order came down because the Iraqi senior commanders were using the same phones to communicate with their field commanders. And five hundred reporters in theater with the same phones made it that much more difficult for intelligence agencies to monitor and sift through the phone calls from Iraqi command. We never did get our satellite telephone working again to report live on this last engagement. But it was pretty exciting regardless of whether the rest of the world got to see it. There was a lot of shit in the air flying about us, plenty of booms, and shooting and billowing black smoke from burning Iraqi armor.

At the head of the column, Sergeant Wheatley's tank was still in the thick of it, and there were more than a few explosions about him as he conned from the turret. The shooting and explosions all seemed to be up by him and the Bradleys about him. Captain Lyle's tank was closer to us, and he was now uneasy about his embeds being in it again. Having brought us this far, Apache Troop's commander wanted us to survive the war. So did most of the NCOs.

"You can not even imagine how much you meant to us by just being there with us," Sergeant Wheatley would later write. "You were a true hero for sticking with us through it all. I want you to know that I always had an eye out for you and your crew. Your truck was the first thing I looked for after every encounter."

Sergeant Wheatley had more to worry about in that engagement than the CNN crew, however. We were a hundred yards back or so, and the bullets were not splattering in the earth about us or punching through our Humvee but they were bouncing off the lead armored vehicles. Hot lead may have been going over our heads. I was never sure. Night fire and tracers are easier to gauge. Charlie was trying unsuccessfully to send out pictures of the exploding T-72 tanks. Paul was wheeling the Hummer about trying to anticipate where Captain Lyle's tank would go next. Jeff and I had become quite skilled at making ourselves smaller targets in the back seats, cringing and wondering if the shooting would get worse. For Sergeant Wheatley it did. A piece of hot shrapnel, the size and shape of a slightly curled little finger cut like a spinning scythe through the lead laden air and hit the sergeant in the back. It was like a sharp jab, a punch that raised an ugly painful bruise but did not penetrate his body armor. Instead, it sliced into it and lodged there. "It hurt like hell," Sergeant Wheatley later grumbled, rotating his shoulder as if he had merely been tackled hard from behind in a football game rather than having had another narrow escape from death.

Later, after the war, the sergeant took the flack jacket home with him to Georgia and hung it in his closet. The grimy thing hung there for months. Finally, his wife asked him why he wanted that big old heavy thing in the closet.

"I finally broke down and told her about some of the things that went down and about the piece of 'schrap' that was in the middle of my vest," he wrote. "When I showed her the piece of shrapnel and the vest together, we both clung to each other and cried. I cannot tell you how that felt so long after the fact, but I can tell you that we went through hell together and what a great group of guys to do that with. I would not change a thing in the way that every day and every mission went down. We, you included, Walt, built a tie that will be with us until we die."

Throughout the Iraqi campaign, I kept asking myself if I were sufficiently detached to report objectively on this story, and the answer was always a qualified "Yes." There is no question but that when your life depends upon the soldiers about you, a certain partiality is inevitable. They are keeping you alive.

I first noticed that phenomenon with the Soviet forces in Afghanistan in 1986 and 1987. I found myself pulling for the Russians and against the Islamic mujahideen. Flying in an Antonov 26 just after the siege at Khost, with the Afghan resistance trying to shoot us out of the air with anti-aircraft missiles, I acquired a genuine partiality for the Soviets and still have that. I was especially bitter that the stinger missiles the Reagan Administration supplied the mujahideen had been paid for with my tax dollars.

Ultimately, there is no denying that men in combat bond under fire, whether they have a rifle in hand or not. I remembered Olivier Rafowicz, an Israeli army lieutenant colonel, who, as I did, escaped the same brush with death from an Iranian-supplied roadside bomb in South Lebanon that killed an Israeli general and an Israel radio reporter. That day, I was supposed to be in the general's car. No one survived the blast, which was well documented by a Hezbollah combat cameraman. Rafowicz was supposed to be in that convoy, too. Both of us, by sheer fate, are alive today. Several years later, in the spring of 2002, when Olivier was the Israeli defense forces spokesman during the siege at the Church of the Nativity in Bethlehem, several of my colleagues were critical of his "spin" on the confrontation between Israel and the Palestinian Liberation Organization fighters. I recognized the spin but found myself reluctant to join in the carping. Upon seeing each other again, Lieutenant Colonel Rafowicz and I had exchanged a knowing look, without words, that said "that day the Lord God of Abraham, Isaac, Jacob, and the prophets delivered us out of the hands of the enemy in his mercy." People who share the same profound near-death experiences, such as soldiers and journalists, can see it in the eyes of the others who were there.

None of us died this day in Iraq although more Iraqis did. Captain Lyle was determined to get his embeds out of there. He turned his sixty-nine-ton tank around and with a hand signal indicated we were to pull back while the shooting continued. He led us back to the relative safety of the underpass. Paul parked Old Betsy, and we got out and stretched our legs in what amounted to a sunken stretch of highway. We were in the safety of the depression while some RPGs and mortars exploded harmlessly above and about us. There was plenty of spent shrapnel lying about in the highway and a surfeit of 7.62 mm casings. Back up the road at the beginning of the grade, from which we had just come, I noticed a civilian car started to approach Apache Troop's forward units. How it got on to the highway without someone shooting it before this, God alone knows. But here came these two civilians in yet another white Japanese car, creeping up the highway toward us. There were enough machine guns pointed at them to instantly reduce their car to a sieve. Given the numbers of Iraqi suicide vehicles the unit had stopped in a hail of fire in the last forty-eight hours, I figured the life expectancy of these two Iraqi civilians would be about five more seconds. I could see the driver's face, and he seemed more bewildered than ready to die. A soldier in the unit very decently fired a warning shot. The Iraqi driver slammed on his brakes and commenced serious deliberation about whether he was prepared to begin his ascension to the promised paradise of Islam. The world about them and us seemed to freeze. Almost imperceptibly from a hundred yards away, I still imagine seeing him reaching down to shift his car into reverse, and he began slowly backing out of the grave into which he had driven himself and his companion seconds earlier. Quietly, I cheered to myself. I suspect the American soldier who opted to fire the warning shot was also grateful he didn't have to dispatch an Iraqi whose only crime was to get lost in the middle of a firefight.

We did not know it, but the war was now effectively over for us after that incident. Captain Lyle would lead us back to the lone palm tree where Colonel Ferrell relayed the news. We would be breaking camp at map coordinate

Objective Montgomery west of Saddam airport and moving to a new location south of Baghdad, again on the perimeter of the city. Until that moment, we were under the impression we might be arcing farther north and then east around Baghdad taking up yet another blocking position north of the airport and northwest of the Iraqi capital. Yet, we had come to learn nothing was predictable during the campaign, even at the very end. The Troop's orders were fluid. With a four-hundred-thousand-person army at the outset of the war, the U.S. military still had to anticipate the possibility of an Iraqi division coming down from the north although that seemed increasingly remote now.

"There is no longer an organized military threat out there," Colonel Ferrell later announced in one of the chats on the back of his Bradley.

There were, however, more than a few Iraqis who still wanted a dead American on their trophy shelves, and the Iraqi countryside was loaded now with sullen, deserting soldiers with guns; freebooters, soldiers of fortune, and opportunists under neither discipline nor moral constraint. A later intelligence report I overheard suggested AWOL Iraqi soldiers were now "trying to get into the city to loot."

Increasingly, Iraqis were deserting en masse. The fleeing Iraqis continued to park their tanks and armored vehicles in date palm groves or copses and simply abandon them, leaving their uniforms behind as well. It brought derisive laughter from the U.S. soldiers. The abandoned Iraqi vehicles were reported to be in "pristine condition." According to one incoming radio report, soldiers in the Medina division had parked and walked away from "a couple of hundred tanks." Initially, the U.S. soldiers would shoot them up to put them out of commission until Gen. Louis Weber gently reproached his boys over the radio and reminded them that the Iraqis would need an army of their own after the war. Thus, minor vandalism was employed to disable the Iraqi armor rather than destroy it; simple things like removing firing pins.

In 1991 and now, it was the blitzkrieg attack of the American assault on Iraq, penetrating it on several fronts simultaneously, that caused the rapid and near-total dissolution of this once feared and formidable Arab army. Despite the wistful BBC and French reports on short-wave radio of the American advance bogging down along the Iraqis' Euphrates River defense line, the Iraqi army knew the dam had burst. And if the advance of the American fighting force slowed at one point as in Nasiriyah, the flood of American forces would engulf the Iraqis elsewhere. It could not be checked, and it moved and inexorably toward Baghdad. Saddam's army voted with its feet, and it was a vote of no confidence in the Ba'athist regime. It was a statement of no confidence in the leadership of Qusay Hussein, Saddam's son charged with the defense of the Iraqi capital. At the division level, the Iraqi army simply opted not to stand and fight before brigades of the 3rd Infantry Division launched their audacious convoys through Baghdad. Before the advancing columns of U.S. forces, even the fear of punishment from Saddam's lieutenants for desertion was swept away.

We could not see the fleeing Iraqi soldiers that day. They simply evaporated—stopped fighting, kept their rifles, and by and large went home. There would be exceptions, such as the bloody skirmish with some remaining Iraqi diehards like the special Republican Guard forces inside Baghdad who ambushed a major resupply column. The trains of the 3/15th Infantry, 2nd Brigade were badly mauled as they tried to resupply brigades of the 3rd ID already in the city. The Iraqis were learning in defeat. Those leading the ambush let the leading tanks with their overwhelming firepower advance into Baghdad, and the Iraqis lay in wait for the supply train that was following. What ensued was an ambush and firefight that saw ordinary truck drivers and army chaplains alike fighting for their lives under murderous fire in the city's southern suburbs. It was the same road Jeff, Charlie, Paul, and I would have to use shortly after this ambush to go into the city. But generally, the countryside about us simply went quiet as the Iraqi army went to ground. It reflected a decision made individually and collectively by the vast majority of Iraqi soldiers that "Saddam was simply not worth dying for" in the words of Lieutenant Colonel Ferris al Bakry. Every officer in the Iraqi army knew that Saddam had paid high salaries to his friends in the army—the Ba'athists and senior officers—and even Sunnis like al Bakry, a lieutenant colonel, were expected to live on $35 a month. Morale had dropped abysmally low. The Iraqi army had never really recovered, nor was it resupplied, after the disastrous First Gulf War in 1991. Training had become haphazard, and even so-called elite units and Fedayeen irregulars relied more on brute force and terror than on military skill. When it became clear that the second Bush administration was determined to redeem the honor of the first and that it was not going to stop south of Baghdad this time, reports filtered down into the ranks that senior Iraqi officers were packing suitcases full of money and fleeing. The ordinary Iraqi soldier knew he had been betrayed and spoke freely of it after the war.

"I decided I did not want to die for Saddam," al Bakry said. "In the end it was not just the Shiias who were going to desert," the Sunnis went AWOL just as quickly when U.S. forces were banging on the gates of Baghdad. "This was just another war to protect Saddam."

Into Baghdad

Al Bakry deserted ten days before Baghdad fell.

Capt. Hamdi al Keshali later told me, "The Ba'athists betrayed us." He, too, went AWOL even though he knew the punishment was public execution. One desertion in the Iraqi army meant an entire unit would be punished. Iraqi soldiers, ever resourceful, deserted in entire units figuring if punishment was going to be collective, so would their crime.

"The U.S. was too afraid of us," al Kheshali concluded in retrospect after the war. "They didn't need that much force to defeat us. When the Iraqis saw this huge American army, it was all bullshit, and we went home. Saddam threw his army up against impossible odds. We loved our country more than they [the Ba'athists] did."

It was true. They did not blow the bridges across the Tigris River, slowing the American advance into Baghdad. And they did not engage in house-to-house city fighting, which would have greatly destroyed the Iraqi capital.

If the U.S. Army succeeded so well in that military campaign because of superior officers and leadership, the Iraqis knew they were destined to fail because of an absence of the same.

"The best officers were lost in Saddam's First Gulf War," al Kheshali recounted later. "Many of those pressed into service this time had no more than six months' training. They pinned stars on them and sent them off to fight."

His lip curled with contempt beneath his black moustache when he spoke of the Iraqi command.

The Iraqi collapse was, in the eyes of the humiliated Arab soldiers, a consequence of the stupidity of Saddam and even more so of his son Qusay, a military amateur.

"He [Qusay] was too young to have had that responsibility," al Bakry later said. "I am glad Qusay was killed. He killed so many people. In the end, Saddam lost the war because he did not trust the army. He should have put Sultan Hashim Ahmed, the Minister of Defense, in charge of the fighting. Saddam trusted no one but himself, and that is why the defense fell apart."

In truth, Saddam was even afraid of the Republican Guard because they, too, had earlier attempted to overthrow his regime. The Guard was kept out of Baghdad as were other army units because in the end, Saddam could not trust his own army.

In the Iraqi army command was an element of *Dolchstosslegende*, the old German stab-in-the-back theory, which had swept the Imperial German Army after the First World War. It is the feeling a group isn't really defeated by the enemy but is sold out and betrayed by the politicians. The Iraqis felt this in their army's defeat. Conspiracy in the Arab world is the mother of all failures and defeat. In Iraq after the war, one could hear *Dolchstosslegende* grumblings as the rationale for why the Iraqi army was so soundly thrashed. Some defeated Iraqi officers later claimed that the day the airport fell to the Americans, Qusay had changed the units guarding the airport, pulling out the regular Iraqi army forces and replacing them with Fedayeen and special-forces units.

"They lost the airport, not the army," one Iraqi soldier lamented after the war.

"We were surprised they changed troops at the outset of the battle for the airport. They were not soldiers, they were little girls," another Iraqi said.

True to the predilection for conspiracies, al Kheshali still refused to believe Qusay was dead months after American forces had killed him.

"They [the two brothers Qusay and Uday] would never have been stupid enough to have been caught together," he argued.

This disintegration of Iraqi defenses across a wide front was not immediately apparent to soldiers who had been shot at nearly every day for nearly three weeks straight. The morning of 8 April, the 7th Cavalry was still killing Iraqis up at the juncture of Highways 1 and 10, and by that afternoon, we had begun to feel comfortable sticking our heads up again as we rolled back east southeast along Highway 8. In the difference between morning and afternoon, the same U.S. soldiers were expected to become "fixers" and ombudsmen for Iraqi civilians trying to make sense out of their lives. It was a mental downshifting of the gears that was not as easily accomplished in the minds of soldiers as it was in the planners back in Washington. For the men of 7th Cavalry, the idea of having an RPG slam at them from a concealed enemy lingered in their minds for some time after the threat had diminished. They had been through too much in the previous three weeks. Besides, intel was now reporting that the Fedayeen units were using ambulances and other emergency vehicles to approach convoys like ours to carry out suicide attacks.

Our convoy now retraced its march through fire of a few days earlier. The squat mud farmhouses from which the ambushes had come were still brooding about us on either side of the road. The foxholes in the fields were still there, presumably with corpses still slumped in them. To this scenario was suddenly added the emergence of a civilian population from outlying towns, Arabs babbling incomprehensibly to American soldiers who were never really quite sure which of the men who approached them had been shooting at them the day before. Ultimately, this cautious outreach by Iraqi civilians was perhaps the most persuasive element in convincing U.S. soldiers the Iraqi army was no longer in the field. Some of those Iraqi soldiers may be the men with hostile, sullen faces who were now milling about in civilian clothes.

These approaches to their "liberators" by Iraqi civilians were never more than tentative. Cultural differences, Muslims versus Christians, or the concept of *Dar al-Islam* versus *Dar al-Harb* (the house of Islam versus the house of war) were obvious to anyone who had ever worked in the Middle East. This bipolar world is indigenous to the Muslim faith. No matter how charitably U.S. soldiers would perform during the coming occupation, they seemed doomed to fail because of this dichotomy in the minds of the occupied. Freshly liberated Iraqis in these hamlets did not celebrate. They just came out of their homes and their hidey-holes. It was insular Islam as much as any cultural insensitivity on the part of the Americans that checked any genuine people-to-people embrace between the American soldiers and their newly freed charges. Despite what these U.S. soldiers had been promised about being liberators, they never saw anything even faintly confirming that myth dished out by the Pentagon and the Bush administration. Unlike their grandfathers who had liberated Rome and Paris from the Germans two generations earlier during the Second World War, the soldiers I was with met no Iraqis who danced in the streets, no Iraqi women throwing flowers. The Americans may have freed them from the tyranny of an Asiatic despot, but they were still perceived as invading and occupying infidels by many Iraqis. Infidels were momentarily the lesser of two evils, but they were in the eyes of an Arab Muslim people still evil.

I stood off to the side watching it all. Having been in a hundred such impoverished Arab towns, I chuckled at the attempts at interaction between young American soldiers and Iraqis with their *souk* mentality. The Iraqis I encountered seemed far less interested in freedom, liberation, or democracy than they were in trying to inveigle favors out of their new conquerors. Something deep inside was telling me even then that the deep cultural differences between the West and an Islamic society only highlight the absence of any successful precedent for what the Americans wanted to do. This was not Europe; this was the Muslim world in which I had worked for the better part of twenty years.

Still, that was the last thing anyone back home wanted to hear from a reporter at the end of a brilliant military campaign. I should have kicked myself then and there for not telling the world the new Middle East was going to be the same old Middle East—bloody, fractious, and chaotic and inclined toward another strong leader even if he turned out to be another despot. Like most of the soldiers I had accompanied, however, I just wanted to get the hell out of there and go home. Unlike George W. Bush, Dick Cheney, and Paul Wolfowitz, I had been shot at a few times over the years in the Arab world. I had lived and worked with Arabs, and I was convinced that no amount of wishful thinking was going turn the people we were seeing that day into aspirants for a liberal democratic society, at least not in my lifetime.

The Iraqis crowding around Apache Troop now as it rested along the road were obsequious and sullen. I did not delude myself. They would have torn anyone of us apart and danced on our corpses if we were wounded and left alone in their midst. Fortunately, it was now they who were weak and outgunned. Having been historically weak for centuries now, however, these Arab peasants recognized their new conquerors were not above being exploited. War is ever the great multiplier of human misery, and everyone in Iraq that day had a problem that needed solving. As a crowd gathered along a railroad track, a mob began besieging Captain Lyle. Many wanted a piece of paper, written permission to travel somewhere else or authority to retrieve some property. It had been the way of Ba'athist bureaucracy so why shouldn't it be the same now? There were scores of questions from civilians wanting to know if it would be all right now to kill Saddam's Fedayeen forces. Someone brought forward a boy aged nine or ten with a piece of shrapnel still in his back. The wound was raw and ugly. I had the feeling Captain Lyle wanted to throw up his hands in despair. Soldiers became referees, judges, jurors, and social workers within half a day of fighting their last engagement. An Iraqi woman approached and explained that her daughter and husband were last seen in Ramadi, sixty-three miles west of Baghdad. Could Captain Lyle help her locate them? The crowd from the village town alongside a railroad track south of Baghdad multiplied and became several hundred, each with a personal problem to be solved.

Without any warning or preparation, the army found itself in a total transfer of roles, from an attacking force to an instrument of humanitarian assistance. The unit set up a checkpoint for the villagers to cross the highway so they would not be milling about the armored column. Almost invisibly, another elderly Iraqi man, gaunt, with brown, leathery skin approached and whispered to the translator that he had a personal problem he needed to discuss. His manner suggested privacy was required. It was not available as Iraqis tried to out-shout each other. Yet, the old man persisted, and Captain Lyle and the translator cut him out of the herd to have him whisper, "I know where an American soldier is buried ten kilometers [six miles] from here. The Iraqis wanted to burn his body. I saw where he was buried. I know the location of the grave."

No one knew whether to believe the old man or not. My impression was he was telling the truth. At first, Captain Lyle thought so, too, and appeared to be considering sending a search party out with the old Arab. But Captain Lyle then, using the interpreter, brutally warned the old codger if there was one shot fired by anyone when the soldiers were out there looking for that body, "I am going to blow your brains out. You will be the first to die." I had no doubt Captain Lyle was not bluffing, and apparently neither did the old man. Another mendicant approached the captain, temporarily distracting him with another request. Before anyone noticed, the old man had melted into the crowd. The old fellow was overheard to say he needed to go buy some tobacco, and as silently as he had appeared, he seemed to evaporate. Captain Lyle and his men decided he was out to lead them into a trap. I was not so sure. I thought I later saw him timorously hovering on the edge of the crowd as if waiting for the Americans to seek him out. Meanwhile, Captain Lyle called in an initial radio check and got a response that indicated no U.S. soldiers had been reported missing in that area. It was probably just as well. The unit was short on translators, and this was still uncharted and hostile territory. The following day, however, my initial gut instincts were confirmed. Someone higher up the chain of command had gotten back to Captain Lyle and confirmed that indeed an American soldier was definitely missing in action in this area.

All I could think was "Some poor kid from Illinois, Florida, California, met a horrible death in Iraq, executed brutally and may have been lost forever." The Iraqis have a barbaric tradition of murdering helpless prisoners of war. I felt sick. We never went looking for the dead kid. It was just too risky. Overwhelmed with petitioners and·with the sun seeking the western horizon off to Ramadi where the woeful woman's daughter and husband were thought to be, Captain Lyle decided to pull out of the village by the railroad tracks and make for our assigned campsite. It would be dark before we got there. Increasingly, the highways south of Baghdad were clogging with hundreds if not thousands of military vehicles, fuelers, supply trucks, Humvees, tanks, Bradleys, M-113s, all dust-coated from their desert passage north from Kuwait. In victory, the U.S. Army looked shop-worn and in need of a bath.

Somewhere ahead in the darkness, the lead tank pulled off on a dirt road, abandoning a fine Iraqi superhighway south of Baghdad. It was black night, the dark of the moon. Straining to see in the darkness because there were still no headlights allowed in these convoys, it appeared as if we would be camping out on the verge of a farm field beside another irrigation ditch. As we bounced along on a side road, we were assaulted by the revolting odor of men too long left unburied. I kicked open the back door of the Hummer and gasped for cleaner air. There they lay on the edge of the dirt road. Visually, they were merely dark shapes; at night, they could have been manikins. Anyone who has been on a battlefield in warmer months knows the smell. By way of comparison, the closest thing I could think of was fresh pig feces. But the smell could not have been pigs, in a Muslim culture in which swine are forbidden. It was men who were rotting. The stench was overwhelming.

Continuing along in the dark another quarter mile or so, we seemed to outreach the smell of death. The unit parked in darkness amid several large mounds shaped like beehives that must have risen upward thirty feet or more. Iraq is rich in archaeological treasures; the countryside abounds in them, and these resembled the burial mounds of an ancient civilization. By morning, we would see that Saddam's defenders had shaved off the tops and used them as elevated anti-aircraft emplacements. That explained the clusters of bomblets, unexploded American CBU 97 WCMD munitions we saw lying about when with flashlights we probed the area that had been selected for a campsite. In the morning, the engineers would mark the munitions' locations with bright-orange tape. But, presently we were too tired to care, and we all bedded down amid the ancient tombs and modern munitions.

It was another beautiful spring night in ancient Mesopotamia with the entire blanket of the heavens above. More than a few of us were feeling homesick, Sergeant Chase especially. I loaned him my telephone to call home. In the darkness, I overheard him calling his wife. Other soldiers climbed the burial mounds for privacy. Sergeant Chase was simply too exhausted to climb an unnecessary hill.

"I want you to know, Honey," we overheard him plaintively say. "I'm thinking about you every day. I love you. Don't worry. I've seen enough killing for five life times. I want to come home . . . and please don't worry. I don't know when I am coming home. But I am coming home."

On the edge of a darkened bean field, these sentiments resonated in each of us.

I decided to sleep on the hood of Old Betsy again, staying as far off the ground with its litter of bomblets as I could. It was a quiet night and should have resulted in a sound sleep. But at 0200, I was suddenly awakened. A newly risen east wind brought the smell of the dead Iraqi soldiers again, filling my nostrils and jarring me awake as uncomfortably as if someone had shaken me. Being awakened by the stench of death was a new experience for me. I could only fall back asleep with a sweat-soaked t-shirt over my face to filter out the smell of decomposing Iraqis. I cannot recall any smell ever as odious, and I pray I never do again.

At dawn, we saw just how precarious our encampment was. The antipersonnel bomblets were everywhere, and we had been sleeping amid dozens of them. About every ten yards or so were explosive devices lying on the ground, delivered I was told, by 155 mm shells that had targeted the Iraqi anti-aircraft batteries atop the earthen mounds. With flashlights at night, we were careful not to step on the bomblets. Even being able to see them in daylight, the bomblets were so numerous that a soldier accidentally kicked one. It exploded giving him a nasty gash in his leg.

We were now fully aware that American troops had taken up permanent positions inside Baghdad. The 1st Brigade of the 3rd ID owned the airport, and the 101st Airborne was on its way up from Al Hillah and An Najaf. Lacking "dismounts," the 7th Cavalry increasingly appeared at a loss for something to do. Charlie, Jeff, Paul, and I were still embedded with Apache Troop, and if the soldiers we lived with were becoming unemployed, so were we, and the story was rapidly shifting to downtown Baghdad. I had been in the city in earlier years and had no desire to go into the media melee. We had fought our war and had survived, as Charlie and I agreed we would do when we started back at Embed U. in Kuwait. But, there was no precedent for detaching from a military unit to which we had been assigned. Could we just walk away? Where would we go with armed, roving deserters roaming the countryside all about us? None of us was keen to say good-bye to our protectors and strike out on our own in that hostile territory. Western ideals about the sanctity of the news media were not recognized in the world of Dar al-Islam. Events of the coming day would signal pretty clearly that there wasn't going to be much news coming out of where we were, and our raison d'etre was collapsing as quickly as Saddam's army had collapsed. The combat phase of the war was over for the 7th Cavalry and for us, and we needed new marching orders. It was too early in the morning for anyone in Atlanta to make a decision on our fate, so we went on a hike with Apache Company up the road because a weapons cache had been found and needed investigating.

I was also procrastinating. We were all exhausted. We had covered our war, we needed a bath, and we needed a break after living at the tip of the tip of the spear. Thousands of journalists from around the world would soon be descending on Baghdad, scores of them from CNN alone, and I wanted nothing to do with that story. Neither did the rest of my crew. We had reported our war truthfully and honorably with fine soldiers. We had been shot at nearly daily. The fighting would soon fall to network TV stars battling for airtime in the liberated Iraqi capital. I have always preferred working alone, even if it meant a secondary, nonstarring role. So, once again when Captain Lyle, said, "Hey, do you want to go for a ride with us?" our answer was, "Sure, why not?" Saying good-bye to friends in the 7th Cavalry could wait for another day.

There was almost a good reason to go gallivanting about the countryside. One of the chemical-biological-warfare-weapons units had heard a report of a possible weapons site south of us, and the 7th Cavalry was to be their escort. The parallel between this search for elusive caches of chemical and biological weapons and the quest for the dubious Holy Grail did not escape me. Still, our last ride with Apache Troop looking for Saddam's weapons of mass destruction offered yet another view of the Iraqi countryside, which in hindsight revealed more signs that the American occupation would not go smoothly. Travelling down country roads, we saw Iraqis dragging or pushing carts laden with desks, chairs, anything that could be stolen from government installations. "They stole from us, why shouldn't we steal from them?" The matter of stealing being inherently wrong was not a factor for these devout Muslims: Steal from your oppressors, and kill your enemies were the rules in the Iraqi countryside long before and long after Saddam had disappeared.

When our convoy turned into what was supposed to be a water-treatment plant, we all nosed around like kids on an Easter egg hunt. In a back rear corner of the installation were several Abalil missiles, twenty-seven feet long, lying harmlessly on racks. They were designed to carry a three-hundred-kilogram (six-hundred-pound-plus) warhead, but there was no evidence of any chemical or biological weapons about, according to the various sensors employed. I still selfishly held hope we would find some of these weapons, for it would justify my avoiding Baghdad's media circus. We found plenty of missile instruction books in Arabic and Russian, and several men from an adjacent hamlet approached and asked the army to remove the rockets.

"We just want to live in peace in our houses. We're still afraid those rockets will explode," they said through a translator.

Actually, there was a more serious threat to their homes than some aging surface-to-surface missiles lying about, and that was a huge unexploded American JDAM bomb deeply implanted in the ground within twenty yards of their houses just the other side of the "water-purification" plant's perimeter fence. Children were playing around the small crater with the unexploded bomb still sticking out. If it went off, there would be no village, no water-purification plant, nothing. Someone made a note of it, and we left. No one in our party was qualified to defuse a piece of ordnance of that magnitude.

On our return to the burial-mound campsite, we passed through other villages largely unchanged for a hundred years except perhaps for the occasional strand of electric wire and some battered Japanese cars badly in need of washing. Again, there was no welcome from the populace. Instead, there were just more glowering Arab faces who clearly did not want an American army there. The soldiers atop their Bradleys and tanks saw this, too, because they kept their hands on their machine guns in the event someone took a shot at us.

On the return to our base camp, we went on a hike through another Iraqi training facility, and we found graphic instructions on how to use gas masks and how to survive a chemical or biological battlefield. The mystery of why these WMDs were never employed lingers. Some intelligence people concluded that Saddam sent them all to Syria to be hidden. Most of us figured Saddam was afraid of the unknown, the effects a large unconventional-weapons' release would have on his own civilian population and how they would react and also afraid of American retaliation. Ultimately, use of chemical or biological weapons would not have affected the outcome of the war. That was a given before the first U.S. forces crossed into Kuwait. Colonel Ferrell had said we were prepared to "fight on through." In the end, one U.S. soldier dismissed the CBW threat with a grunt. "A lot of people talk big," he said. The only weapons we found that afternoon were huge caches of 23 mm anti-aircraft shells. The engineers were called up to blow them. There was so much surplus Iraqi ammunition to be detonated that the engineers ran out of C-4 to blow it up that day. None of us found any weapons of mass destruction on our sorties, and we looked diligently.

A return to our base camp and a telephone call that same afternoon signalled the military campaign was nearly over for Charlie, Jeff, Paul, and me. We discovered Atlanta was apparently pretty concerned because downtown Baghdad had fallen, and no CNN correspondent had made it into the city yet at a time when the good citizens of Baghdad were looting and tearing down monuments and statues of Saddam Hussein. Then came the questions: "Where are you? How far outside the city are you, and can you get into Baghdad?"

I had previously been in no hurry to get into the heart of the city, first, because I was with an army unit that was not going into downtown

Baghdad. Secondly, I assumed that Christiane Amanpour, Nic Robertson, Martin Savidge, Rym Brahimi, and Jim Clancy had already taken Baghdad by storm with cameras. It was apparently not so. Some of my CNN colleagues were still stuck in Kuwait, and others were en route scrambling to claim limited seats on a military charter that would take them to Baghdad. Savidge, tied down with the marines farther outside Baghdad than I was, was still being towed toward Baghdad behind a marine vehicle. He was unable to get his Humvee repaired on the battlefield in the midst of a war. CNN clearly needed a presence in the just-liberated Iraqi capital, and Jeff, Charlie, Paul, and I were the closest to ground zero.

We had to convince CNN headquarters that despite our proximity, making a dead run for the Iraqi capital despite the competitive pressure they were feeling was not exactly feasible. At first blush, theirs seemed a reasonable request for us to dis-embed and make our way into the city. But from our vantage point, it was extraordinarily unwise to leave the security bubble of the 7th Cavalry and try to make it into Baghdad on our own with no military escort and no armor. Paul gave away the AK-47s when we left the 7th Cavalry. Even with weapons, it would have been damned dangerous. The last American I knew of to wander about the Iraqi countryside alone was that poor American soldier whose grave the old Iraqi man tried to lead us to. For reasons of safety, even the U.S. Army was still moving in large convoys with tanks as escorts. Even large convoys were not safe. At about that same time, a large resupply convoy got badly ambushed and whacked on the same road. For Charlie, Jeff, Paul, and me to get into downtown Baghdad the day that it fell would have required us to drive off on our own and drive in a lone military vehicle, a Humvee with desert-brown military paint, unescorted up a road where a few hours earlier an entire supply convoy had been ambushed and nearly wiped out.

"We might just as well have hung a banner in Arabic along the side of Old Betsy which read, 'Shoot me,'" Charlie said later.

Worse, we would have to run a final gauntlet with hostile Iraqis skulking on each side of the road, making a hell-bent-for-leather dash into Baghdad on a road we never had been on before and with dusk falling. I had a bad feeling about this.

I knew the decision ultimately was mine to make. Again, I called Atlanta and said, "We just can't do this." It was excruciatingly difficult having survived all we survived having to tell headquarters, "No. This request cannot be fulfilled. Not today. Not this afternoon." Additionally, I had already consulted with Colonel Ferrell, and he warned any attempt to get into Baghdad alone with dusk falling would be "suicide." In truth, I believe if I had to try to force Paul, Jeff, or Charlie to make a run for Baghdad alone that afternoon, there would have been a mutiny. Colonel Ferrell warned us there had been a lot of shooting farther up the road. Baghdad had only fallen completely that very morning. Paul, our security advisor there to keep us alive, also advised me, "Don't do it." To me that was pretty definitive. He and I decided to revisit the issue early the next morning. I remember thinking that for a soldier who had never worked with a television crew before, Paul had grown immensely and quickly in the understanding of our craft and what was expected of us.

None of us slept very well that night. Those dead bodies had had another day to rot in the sun. At about 0430 in the nacreous dawn, when Apache Troop's encampment began to stir, and I was feeling pressure to break with my embed and get into Baghdad, Paul and I talked briefly between ourselves and then walked over to chat with Colonel Ferrell. The squadron commander was already sipping coffee with some junior officers on the ramp of his Bradley. He was in a good mood. I excused myself for interrupting and explained to him that I thought it was time for us to dis-embed and head for the city. I asked him what he thought our chances were of trying to make an unescorted early-morning mad dash through Baghdad's southern suburbs and into the city, which was still seeing more than a little shooting, and plumes of smoke were still rising over the skyline. We chatted for a few minutes. I noted the colonel no longer used the word *suicidal* as he had when I asked the same question the day before.

By now, Jeff and Charlie had walked over to the colonel's Bradley and joined us. After a few moments, I turned to them and said, "Fuck it! Let's go." I was fully mindful this was potentially a life-and-death decision, calculating in my head we probably had a fifty-fifty or even a sixty-forty chance of getting into the city alive. Those seemed outstanding odds compared to what we had been playing with over the past two weeks. In truth, those were pretty good odds for war correspondents in the midst of a shooting war that would heat up again violently in the year to come. Before departing, we all turned in our chemical-weapons suits to Captain Lyle and Sergeant Woodhall although for months afterwards, we received letters from the army asking us to return whatever property and equipment of theirs we might still possess. I was indignant every time they suggested any of us might filch something belonging to them.

Our farewell to Apache Troop might have been a much more emotional parting except we four of CNN were already preoccupied with what lay ahead: driving alone up the highway through the hostile neighborhoods of southern Baghdad and crossing a Tigris River bridge under fire.

The early morning quiet was ominous and unsettling when I stop to think about it. Paul was driving up a strange highway in a country at war where none of us spoke the local language. As we drove deeper and deeper into built-up areas, the next sound we expected to hear was an AK-47 shooting at us or an RPG homing in on Old Betsy. All along the road on both sides, there were still-smoking American vehicles, burned out after having been ambushed, interspersed with dead Iraqi armor and trucks. On either side of the road, low strands of black smoke also hung over the buildings still burning from the previous night's fighting. There were no women or children about, and that, too, tends to be an usually bad sign.

I noticed Paul seemed taut as he steered our Hummer northward into Baghdad. Charlie sat across from him studying a road map written in German and trying to navigate us into a city he had never visited. I leaned forward from the back seat, studying the map and assuring Paul that once we got deeper into the city, I would recognize landmarks, and we would be OK. I was the only one who had ever been to Baghdad before. Jeff was ever laconic, reflecting on what he had survived.

The evidence of fighting along the road was conspicuous. We would still hear the occasional AK-47 being fired off to our right that morning and were certain we were within range of the shooters.

Ahead, blocking a highway ramp to another road, sat a U.S. Army Bradley with its machine gun now pointed directly at us. Paul stopped two hundred yards away, and everyone knew we had just as real a chance of being killed by anxious American soldiers that morning as by freelance Iraqi deserters. We knew to keep our hands up and visible inside the Humvee. I suggested to Paul that I would be the one to get out and approach the Bradley.

I held my hands high in the air and on foot and alone approached the Bradley's machine gunner. My press pass was fluttering in the breeze in my left hand. Although I was now wearing full Kevlar body armor and a helmet, I was Swiss cheese if a soldier in the Bradley decided to pull the trigger or the machine gunner let loose. I walked the two hundred yards forward to the Bradley, surrendering to my fellow Americans. It was comical then but in retrospect seems as dangerous as death itself.

About thirty yards in front of the machine gun now pointed at my groin, I stopped and shouted, "My name is Rodgers. I am with CNN. We're trying to get into the city."

Off to my right back, in one of a few squat houses, someone was still banging away with a Kalashnikov, and the smell of burning tires and fuel was pungent in the air.

"Go ahead," the soldier replied, flagging us through. I had to surrender in the same way—hands held high, press pass fluttering in the breeze—two more times that morning, working our way through U.S. Army checkpoints. I wish Charlie had shot that on video but his better sense argued against it. Some soldier surely would have seen something pointed at him from the Humvee, assumed it was a rocket launcher instead of a camera, and we would have all been killed. It has happened to other cameramen in the Middle East over the years. I think the overwhelming fear of most journalists during the war was that the American forces would shoot them. The physical proximity between journalists and Coalition forces increased that likelihood. Embeds were the exception. We were inside, not outside the bubble. Having been embedded, getting shot by my own side was the farthest thing from my mind until that morning when we suddenly became free agents moving around the battlefield on our own.

A little farther up the road, I saw the crossed swords of the Victory Monument in Saddam's Parade Square.

"Hot damn! I know where we are, I know where we are," I said. "Go straight, Paul."

We faced yet another military checkpoint, but I knew we were close to the Tigris. There off to our left was the al Rashid Hotel, all shot up now. It was once the government's VIP guesthouse, reputed to even have had listening devices in the lovely hotel garden. After another interminable delay at that army checkpoint, we finally joined three or four other journalists who had worked their way into the city and were waiting for permission to cross the Jumariya Bridge, which now had a couple of U.S. Army tanks parked smack in the middle. Small-arms fire from the Rusafa neighborhood on the north bank of the river was still coming toward the bridge. Over the city, significant plumes of black smoke were rising, but it was small potatoes compared to what we had survived.

When there was a lull in the shooting, we determined we would make a dash with the other journalists across the bridge over the Tigris to get to the Palestine Hotel. By unanimous consent, we from CNN determined we would let the other civilian four-by-fours go ahead of us. To all outward appearances, Old Betsy was a military vehicle, albeit festooned with a satellite dish, and we did not want to appear to be leading a convoy of civilian cars across the Jumariya Bridge in the middle of another shoot-out between remnants of the Special Republican Guard and some 3rd ID soldiers who had taken up positions on the bridge.

Fully braced to be shot at again, we made the daylight dash across the Tigris, and with the other journalists' cars, we turned right, Paul driving a few more blocks east and parking on the sidewalk adjacent to the Palestine Hotel. It was to become the media ghetto. Associated Press and Reuters News Service had their satellite dishes on a lower roof. I looked up to see if I could spot the rooms where a week earlier, at least two journalists were killed when the 3rd ID opened fire on the building. The army claimed Iraqis were using the seventeen-story hotel to fire on them so they shot back killing the journalists. Truth in war zones is ever murky. Anyone is a fool to stand in a hotel window when there is shooting going on about him.

As Jeff threw up our satellite dish, my colleague Jason Bellini strode up and welcomed us to Baghdad. He had a huge grin on his face. Jason had beat us into downtown by forty-five minutes, under full armored escort with the 15th U.S. Marine Expeditionary Unit. We had dashed into the city alone after having been in the Baghdad suburbs for a week. Still, I was glad to see Bellini's familiar and cherubic face. We were both grateful to have survived. Later, that same sensation of survival would grow. It would become like a cleansing, warm wave, engulfing me with the overpowering realization that I had indeed survived. I was unspeakably happy to be alive. It was a feeling I have never quite experienced before. After leaving the theater of operations, I would tell anyone who would listen—CNN management, the Pentagon, and people in seminars—that embedding was extraordinarily dangerous, and in the next war, they should expect many, many more journalists to die. It was foolish of me to expect anyone to fully understand the gravity of my warning at that point without having been there. The war was still too heady in the weeks shortly afterward.

Behind me, as we set up for our first live shot in Baghdad, was Furdose "Paradise" Square, which was really a traffic circle. Circular squares made as much sense as anything else in Iraq did. Until the day before we arrived, a superheroic statue of Saddam had stood there. Now toppled, the despot's bronze head was lying a hundred yards away in the middle of the road. Half a dozen young Iraqi boys were alternately kicking it and trying to roll it off somewhere else. War's end brought a kaleidoscope of similar images in Baghdad. There remains the troubling mental snapshot I have of another TV crew, including the correspondent, who arrived at the Palestine Hotel not long after we did. They all stood there gaily posing for pictures of themselves after they said they just had looted the home of Iraq's Deputy Prime Minister Tareq Aziz. Proudly they were sporting a couple of his fedoras and chewing on some of Aziz's Cuban cigars, which they had liberated and called their "spoils of war." Included in their stash was one of the former Iraqi official's oriental carpets. A block away, another Iraqi strode past leading a fine Arabian stallion he had just liberated from someone better off before the war. Dan Rather, the CBS evening news anchor, walked by with some colonel or general in tow, and Dan graciously congratulated me on my war coverage.

Everything made sense. Nothing made sense. About me swirled hordes of newly liberated Iraqis looting—stealing—rolling hospital beds with sheets on them and stainless-steel operating-room equipment past me as I stood in my "live shot" position. The world was already blaming exhausted young American soldiers and marines for permitting the looting, which seemed patently unfair. They had no orders or authority to shoot looters at that point, and shooting them would have been the only way to stop them. Many of those U.S. soldiers lounging in their tank turrets hadn't slept in a week and had just taken up positions at strategic intersections inside the city. Technically, under international law, the Americans were responsible for preventing the looting. But I remember shaking my head and asking, "Why are you blaming disciplined professional American soldiers when it's the Iraqis who are stealing?" Again it was another of those questions people did not want to hear. Once again, it was easier for the world's media to blame the Americans than to point out that it was Iraqis who were the thieves. The international media ranted about the Iraqis as "poor victims" without electricity, without jobs, etc., absent any journalistic indictment of Saddam. Blame the Liberators became the instant theme of the international media. Everything wrong in the world was to become the fault of the Americans after the 9/11 attacks. Blame the victims. The "truth-telling" business was becoming increasingly discouraging. I needed to get away, go home.

I took a stroll down a side street to try to get a feel for the mood of these newly liberated people, those Iraqis not engaged in looting and thieving. Unabashedly, Iraqis would walk up to me and ask to borrow my satellite telephone so they could call their brother in Los Angeles or uncle in Detroit to let them know they were alive. Someone always wanted something from someone else in Iraq. Feeling magnanimous, I was happy to help them out and placed the calls for them and then handed them the phone when my Thuraya began ringing through on the other side of the planet. It seemed the American infidels were ever to be exploited by the Iraqi faithful. Within a few weeks or months, these same Iraqis would be derisively mocking the freedom bestowed by their occupiers. In less than a year, more than a few of those Iraqis would be openly recounting the good old days when Saddam was in power.

A girl of about fourteen with some younger siblings in tow approached me and in fine English asked me if she, too, could use my phone to call a relative in Chicago. She said her name was Saria Horia, and she explained she had attended the Clinton school in the Chicago area. In Saria's case, there was a price to be paid for using my Thuraya. Because her English was excellent, she could tell me what it was like to be a teenager in Baghdad the past several weeks. Any inhibition had earlier been bred out of her in an American junior high school.

"The bombing really hurt my ears," she began. "It was weird. The Americans have such power."

I urged her to tell me more as I scribbled furiously.

"Every night I would lie in bed crying listening to the bombing," she said. "I saw a lot of people dead in front of my eyes. Cats would come up and eat the corpses as they lay in the street."

As an aside, I wrote into my note pad, "Children should not have to see such things."

Afterward, when I walked back to the Palestine Hotel, more newly arrived CNN correspondents were eager to put down a footprint and take over the TV live shots in the newly liberated city. Jeff, Charlie, Paul, and I had risked our lives on that solo dash into Baghdad earlier, passing through sporadic AK-47 fire in the suburbs. We wanted to go home. Paul and I looked at each other, and I told Atlanta we wanted to be out of "Dodge" the next day. I needed an evening to begin to wash the dirt and grime out of my gear in the cold-water flat that was my hotel room. It was my first night in a bed on a mattress in nearly a month, and it was singularly uncomfortable sleeping on a mattress again. I slept better under the stars.

Our war was over. Forty-eight hours later, Charlie, Paul, and I would be in Kuwait. Jeff had to stay in Baghdad because the network needed more field engineers. Apache Troop of the 7th Cavalry would be stuck in Iraq for several more months. They never had a single soldier killed during the race to Baghdad. But they never got to march in the victory parade they thought they deserved. So many of them were so quickly ordered to other assignments and units on their return to Fort Stewart, Georgia, that, sadly, they never even got to throw a private party for themselves.

The soldiers of the 7th Cavalry just came home largely unthanked. It very much reminded me of the poignant old military adage that goes:

God and the soldier we adore,
in time of danger and not before.
The danger gone and all things righted,
God is forgotten and the soldier slighted.

Several months later, the following August, up in Iraq's Nineveh province, a colonel with the 101st Airborne would say to me, "You guys had it the worst of anyone in the war." He said the 101st was close behind the 7th Cavalry during much of the campaign, and he really was excited following in our tracks. I was more grateful to him than I knew how to express. A mere four months after the campaign, my recollections of the battles we survived were losing their sharpness and credibility. I needed the colonel's validation of what we had been through to again persuade myself that none of what I was remembering was imagined or exaggerated.

Shortly before we had said good-bye to the 7th Cavalry in the last days of the campaign, Colonel Ferrell and I had chatted about the absence of combat fatalities or serious casualties within Apache Troop.

"There has been something very special about this unit," he agreed.

I sensed he was implying something preternatural although he was at a loss to explain what it was, and there was no time to press him on it.

Charlie, the cameraman, took no souvenirs from the campaign. True to his word, he was only determined to survive the war. Jeff, the satellite engineer, took three hundred digital photographs compiling one of the best frontline photo records of the campaign. I knew that Paul, the only warrior in our TV crew, had a collection of combat soldiers' berets back home in Australia, so two days earlier on the approach to Baghdad's Jumariya Bridge over the Tigris River, I had shouted, "Paul, stop the car. Stop the car!" With gunfire crackling not too far away, I dashed out of Old Betsy and scooped up off the sidewalk an Iraqi soldier's lost or abandoned black beret. It was one of the few foolish things I did in the war. The beret could have been booby-trapped with a hand grenade rigged to go off when I picked it up. Climbing back into the Humvee, I handed the Iraqi beret to Paul and said, "Here, for your collection." It was the only way I could properly thank Paul, who would soon be returning to Australia.

I wanted but one souvenir for myself: a "brass" from the 7th Cavalry, one of those fabric lapel patches the soldiers wear on their collars, something from "Custer's unit." The 7th's brass was two crossed, black cavalry sabers with an embossed 7 over a 3. I had asked several cavalrymen if they would send me one of those brasses, hoping at least one might remember my request after the war. The following autumn, a manila envelope arrived in the mail. It was from the commander of the 3rd Squadron of the 7th Cavalry. Colonel Ferrell had enclosed a handwritten note along with the brass he remembered to send. The note read, "I wore this all through the war." That brass now hangs in a small frame above my desk in London along with the autographed pictures of Presidents Gerald Ford, Jimmy Carter, and Ronald Reagan whom I covered earlier in my career. The soldiers of Apache Troop of the 3/7th collected souvenirs of a different sort. Captain Lyle collected a Silver Star for valor. Sergeants Wheatley and Lonnie Parsons were also awarded Silver Stars. Among the rest of the company, there were awarded forty Bronze Stars, many of those for valor. They richly deserved the honors.

I was most fortunate to have been along for the ride.

Epilogue

We are not the first
Who with the best meaning have incurr'd the worst.
—King Lear, in Shakespeare's *King Lear*

A year later, in March of 2004, riding eastward across the Iraqi desert, I reflected on the groundswell of skepticism and scorn over the war I had covered at serious risk to my own life the previous year. At the outset of the invasion, it seemed the war had a certain plausibility, if indeed Saddam Hussein had the chemical and biological weapons the U.S. administration insisted he had. I had volunteered to report on the Second Gulf War at this point in my career as an embedded reporter with all the attendant risks because I felt the issues involved were of no small consequence. By way of example and in addition to the unconventional-weapons question, there was the perceived threat from Saddam to Western oil sources in the Persian Gulf and the implicit threat to the survival of the Jewish state. Despite considerable global suspicion about the U.S. motives in launching a war in Iraq, I genuinely believed the British Prime Minister Tony Blair when with near-religious fervor, he cited Iraq's quest for nuclear weapons and Iraq's suspected arsenal of chemical and biological weaponry as a casus belli.

In March of 2004, with miles of desert rolling past my car window and with no unconventional weapons found, it seemed the preponderant balance of evidence in the international debate over the war had clearly shifted to the skeptics and critics. In writing this book, as this shift even in U.S. public opinion intensified, I nonetheless detected little or no disillusionment among the soldiers of the 7th Cavalry with whom I had ridden into battle a year earlier. A soldier does not publicly question his Commander in Chief's motives to a reporter. As they are fond of saying, "That is a decision way above my pay grade." Still, several soldiers who participated in the military assault in the spring of 2003 had become extraordinarily critical of Washington's immediate post-war policy that allowed the Sunni Triangle, especially the city of Fallujah, to become a festering wound that would not be cauterized. Officers and noncommissioned officers, now second-guessing their commanders, say, "We should have gone into Fallujah right after we took Baghdad, instead of leaving it to become the center of the revolt against the occupation." Over and over, these dissenters were saying, "What the Sunnis needed was a whiff of grapeshot and some cold steel to show them who was boss." To the man, they said, "We should have occupied Fallujah" immediately after the war.

"Tactically," one soldier said, "that is one place we should not have bypassed. We should have chased all those disgruntled Sunnis up into Turkey or over into Jordan."

When I pointed out that if the Turks had not refused the U.S. the right of passage for the 4th Infantry Division, an occupation in force of the Sunni Triangle would have been much more feasible, any soldier I spoke with replied bitterly, "Yeah, that's right." Thus, they held the Turks as responsible for Coalition problems during the occupation as they did the French for their perceived mischief-making. Still, these same soldiers, who at this point wish to remain anonymous, agreed, "There are now a lot of dead American soldiers because someone f—— up." It seemed a damning criticism from soldiers who had risked their own lives to make the policy makers in Washington look good.

As the various reasons for the United States going to war on Iraq again lost currency—weapons of mass destruction, links to the 9/11 terror attacks on the United States—other writers on this same subject have often cited one casus belli, to wit, the seeming Bush family obsession to get Saddam. And it has been argued that the war was in no small way about catching the fish the first President Bush had let get away. Perhaps a latter-day historian will be able to expand more thoroughly on this theme given that several key figures in the first Bush administration were given a second chance to get Saddam during the presidency of the son.

Musing about all this in March of 2004, I noted the only weapons I could see littering the Iraqi landscape were conventional. Most of them were rusting Iraqi armored personnel carriers. And with U.S. combat deaths climbing daily and more than fifteen hundred as of this writing, I wondered if the parents who lost sons and daughters in Iraq still accepted the Bush administration's much-touted goals of establishing freedom and democracy as a legitimate rationale for this war.

Instead of riding in a soft-skinned Humvee as I did a year earlier, I was now going into Iraq in a heavily armored, bullet-proof BMW nicknamed

"the Shark." With me were two friends, Andy Kain, the president of AKE Security Company, based in Britain, and John MacGaffin, former associate deputy director for operations of the U.S. Central Intelligence Agency, now working for Andy. Both men were becoming wealthy from the growing instability and continued killing in Iraq. A year after the end of the war, Iraq was not only not safe but was much less safe than at war's end in April of that previous year.

Several hours earlier, we had left the relative security of Jordan and were now travelling in a two-car caravan approaching Fallujah, the volcano of Sunni resistance to the American occupation. There was a hopeful sign on the other side of the highway, the new Iraqi police force, four cars and a machine gun, setting up a checkpoint to intercept insurgents. The question was, were they a deterrent to brigandage and violence or simply window-dressing for the American experiment in Iraq? Five weeks later, that same road would be closed because that stretch had by then become extremely dangerous. Andy observed, "Every day, two or three roadside bombs are discovered along this stretch of highway." Will Scully, the AKE guard in the other vehicle several hundred yards ahead, had just warned on the radio, "We are entering the most ambushed stretch of road" in the next few miles south of Fallujah.

A few minutes later, Andy, riding in the front passenger seat, became anxious about a big white Lexus with two men in the front seat that had overtaken us on the right and was now maneuvering to pull alongside what I perceived to be their target—Scully's big Chevy Suburban with darkened windows, up ahead. What was most unnerving was that the Lexus was a right-side-drive British style—Iraq is a left-side-drive country. The right-side configuration was gaining favor with insurgents and highwaymen because the shooter, the gunman, could sit on the left front seat and blast away at whichever cars were on the main highway or the left lane. Those right-side-drive vehicles had become a threat, and security people were always on the alert for them.

The two men in the Lexus had substantial black beards and were riding with the left front seat window fully open on this cool March day, I noticed as they swept past, virtually ignoring us. The Shark looked like any other stolen Iraqi BMW with stolen license plates. The Chevy Suburban model was frequently used by contractors or American government officials entering Iraq from Jordan.

The bearded men managed to pull up alongside Scully's car, paralleling it as if trying to decide whether to open fire. A few weeks earlier, another

CNN vehicle had been attacked in a similar ambush with a similar method of operation, and two Iraqi employees of CNN had been murdered. By now the passenger in the Lexus could have pulled an AK-47 and opened fire in a trice. Andy used the walkie-talkie to radio ahead that the threat was now on Scully's right side. He ordered our driver to step on it.

In seconds, the Shark was again sitting off the Lexus's left rear fender, all of us cruising along at about seventy miles an hour. If there had been the slightest evidence of a gun being brought to bear in the Lexus, the Shark was ready to nudge the Lexus with its Osama look-a-likes and send it spinning out of control.

"We'll knock the legs off him," Andy said.

The bearded Iraqi driver, who looked like a recruiting poster on an Al Qaeda Web site, realized he was now dealing with two vehicles, not one, and he correctly assumed his lone shooter was badly outgunned so he peeled off and fell back.

A year after the war, everywhere in Iraq was now hostile. The situation had deteriorated badly from when I was last there in December of 2003.

"The bad guys are now 'taking on' anything that resembles Westerners," "Blue" Harding, another AKE security guard, had warned me. "All your movements on any story you travel to will be in an armored vehicle, and you will take your Kevlar vest in the car."

"It simply isn't safe to move about the city [Baghdad] now with all the kidnappings and roadside bombs," grumbled MacGaffin, who had spent much of his career in the Middle East working for the CIA.

As an old "spook," he was as depressed as the rest of us were with what had become of the Bush administration's great experiment in Iraq. This new crowd, MacGaffin said, "lacks a basic understanding." He later lamented to me about one senior U.S. official on Administrator Paul Bremer's staff in Baghdad who boasted to him, "I am not an Arabist, and history doesn't matter here. We are rewriting history." MacGaffin groaned about putting neoconservative ideologues and Texas extremists in charge of U.S. foreign policy. To him, they seemed intellectual bedfellows with the old Soviet ideologues who thought human nature could be made to conform to Marxist or evangelical Christian assumptions: Draft your paradigm, and force it on a reluctant world.

Our experience with the Lexus seemed to argue against the myth that security and democracy were taking root in American-occupied Iraq. In my reporter's notebook, I scribbled, "Without security there is little democracy." The idea was not profound but it contradicted the platitudes spewed

out of the daily press briefing in Baghdad that were sadly reported with too little questioning.

> We increasingly make progress, and we increasingly move along to handing over sovereignty and handing over a democratic Iraq at peace with itself, at peace with its own citizens. . . . And that is just around the corner.
>
> —Dan Senor, Coalition spokesman
> 31 March 2004

The signs were at best conflicting in the spring of 2004. In one breath, "civil war" was on nearly everyone's lips. Yet, there was a real-estate boom, and Iraqis were rushing about to purchase new television sets and refrigerators on Baghdad streets. They were cursing their American occupiers under their breaths and at the same moment openly admitting that the American presence was needed to forestall a bloodbath between Shiites and Sunnis. The only thing I could conclude was that Iraqis are not long-term planners or perhaps they only believed in the quick-profit motive.

The American administrator in Iraq, Paul Bremer, was spending that March flitting about the country praising the progress of reconstruction. But wherever he went, he travelled with a phalanx of security people wearing bullet-proof vests and carrying automatic rifles, even in closed and secure rooms filled with American-appointed Iraqi council members. Perhaps more revealing, the American-led Coalition was importing security personnel from around the world: Ghurkhas and Filipinos, Brits, anybody but Iraqis because they could not be trusted with security responsibilities under American occupation. This alone spoke powerfully of the rapidly deteriorating security situation. One night during that month in Baghdad in the so-called green zone, a supersecure American military compound, a U.S. soldier was savagely stabbed by an Iraqi assailant, who apparently had security clearance to be inside the compound and who then escaped. Even more telling, the most respected Muslim cleric in all Iraq, Shiite spiritual leader Ali al Sistani, still refused to meet with Ambassador Bremer. No journalist I knew in Iraq believed the American experiment was working very well a year after the war had supposedly ended, despite the platitudes about progress.

One of the most questionable assumptions made by the United States administration was that the "hearts and minds" of the Iraqis, a conquered people, were for sale, or up for grabs after the war. It was naïve at best and

smacked of ignorance. Iraqis have seen what the United States has done in the Middle East under half a dozen U.S. presidents, and they recognize the gap between the democratic values Washington espouses and its support for what the Arab street sees as corrupt, secular Arab governments in Egypt, Jordan, Saudi Arabia, and elsewhere.

With the aid of Arabic TV like al Jazeera, Osama bin Laden has been brilliant at exploiting this gap between America's stated values and its actions.

"It is why he has been so successful," according to an Egyptian journalist who asked not to be named. "The U.S. has failed to win the hearts and minds of the Iraqi people because of its indifference, hypocrisy, and ill treatment of the Arab Muslim world. It imposes military bases on soil Muslims consider as sacred as Jews believe in Israel. Bin Laden's offering Arabs a violent alternative."

"Who do you think will win the hearts and minds of the Iraqis?" the American-educated Egyptian journalist asked. "If you cannot establish democracy for the Palestinians in their quest for independence with Israel, how can you ask Arabs to trust you with their hearts and minds in Iraq?"

Sadly, the Americans believed they could secure their goals of freedom and democracy in Iraq with good deeds and money, overlooking that the mosque remains at the core of Muslim society and dominates the popular thought. Slapping paint on an Iraqi school classroom barely merits gratitude. It does not disguise the ugly reality that Washington has long been less interested in promoting democratic values in the Middle East than in ingratiating itself with totally undemocratic Arab regimes, usually those with oil or a strategic canal.

I was sent back to Iraq for the first anniversary of the war to revisit many of the places through which I travelled with the 7th Cavalry. That was now quite unrealistic. Iraq was a much more dangerous country a year after the U.S.-led invasion than it was before Coalition forces entered the country. Few in the outside world realized how absolutely dangerous Iraq had become. Towns and villages in south central Iraq could not be visited without the same tanks and Bradleys that accompanied us the previous spring. Outside Baghdad, much of southern Iraq was hostile and lawless, and it would have taken another column of tanks and Bradleys to revisit the towns that the 7th Cavalry had fought its way through. Baghdad cab drivers were now openly telling passengers how much better things were under Saddam. "There was discipline and order then," they lamented. A week later and about an hour's drive south of Baghdad, an Iraqi policeman warned us to be off the road by 3:00 in the afternoon, saying, "Otherwise you are likely

to be kidnapped or murdered." Without a tank to escort my camera crew, retracing our steps with the 7th Cavalry was out of the question. As an alternative, I proposed to CNN perhaps we could revisit several select places where our experiences were most harrowing, that in this way we might still be able to turn a story or two about Iraq a year later. A return to the bridge at An Najaf seemed doable.

The collection of sleepy farms at that bridgehead was a natural story because surely the Iraqi civilians who had fled during the war would have returned by now. Our British AKE security guards decided that with an early start, we might be able to visit the farm if we travelled on several back roads, avoiding the main highway south from Baghdad where there had been a spate of drive-by shootings of Westerners in recent weeks.

We arrived at the farm at about 8:30 in the morning, figuring most of the "bad guys" start late and sleep late. It has always proved an accurate assumption in Middle East trouble spots over the years. My Iraqi interpreter, Ferris Qasira, explained to the peasants we were with CNN, a global television network, and had camped at their farm during the worst of the fighting. He asked if they would object if we took some pictures.

Karin Kitab seemed the family patriarch, and he was anxious to help. He was lank, perhaps in his late-forties, and seriously disabled with an immobile arm injured during Saddam's war with Iran nearly two decades ago. He was badly scarred.

I began by asking, "Would you show me the haymow where I had spent the night with U.S. artillery rockets going out over my head?"

I had been so numb and exhausted at the time, this would be another reality check for me.

Kitab remembered that night well. "I sent the family away, all six children and my wife. We left everything behind. We fled for our lives, and we drove the cows off into the woods along the river so they would not be killed."

He spoke also of the Iraqi soldiers, five or six of them, who died in his front yard. They had been assigned to the South African surface-to-surface missile battery.

"The Americans first bombed an Iraqi armored personnel carrier," Kitab said. "Then they hit the missile launcher. The officer and the soldiers were all killed. Some of the soldiers had their heads blown off, others lost their legs and hands."

I had seen the body parts that the ambulance had not taken away.

He also insisted on showing me the window in his house that he said had been shattered in the bombing. A facing wall still had a serious scissure.

"Do you remember the little black and white puppy that was here then? What became of him?" I asked.

"We have so many animals about here," he said, shaking his head. "Perhaps the dog is across the highway."

This was another collection of farmhouses. It was not the answer I wanted. There were more than a few mongrels milling about but not our black and white puppy who had frolicked with us amid the sandstorm and the fighting.

Soon, other members of Karin's extended family joined us on our stroll about the little farm.

"I remember your chickens," I told him, reminding him pointedly, "the Americans didn't take any of them."

"We were glad it was the Americans," the gathering crowd chattered. If it had been the Iraqi army that night, anyone who stuck his head out of the door would have been shot. "When we came out of the woods, we felt more secure with the Americans here."

Another voice in the crowd said, "We saw the Americans who told us, 'You are safe, but don't harm us.'"

I had seen adrenalin-pumped soldiers and knew their concerns about an Iraqi taking pot shots at them.

The American soldiers were "good," one Iraqi told me.

"Very good ethics. We hid our gold, jewelry, and money in the woods," Sattar Hadi Obeid told me. He still seemed shocked the U.S. soldiers, both in the 7th Cavalry and those units that followed afterward, did not loot their homes or go digging for the buried treasure.

Because these were the much-oppressed Iraqi Shiites, I got the impression they were neither exaggerating nor insincere. I noticed women discreetly moving about the farming compound that was home to several generations of the family. There seemed no longer any fears for their women or young girls, who were washing the family clothing in a small watercourse. Privately, several of the Iraqi men told me in the days of Saddam, his soldiers would go through Shiia farm communities like this one kidnapping and raping the halfway-decent-looking women.

"They treated us like animals," they said. "The Americans did not do that."

I noticed several prepubescent Iraqi girls running about barefoot not far from where we chatted. They were pretty, about ten or eleven, and I shuddered at their fate had Saddam's Sunni mafia not been deposed. In the Arab world, a raped and despoiled woman might as well be executed and sometimes was. She would have lost her currency as a wife or mother. There is no reasoning with most Arab men on this subject. Everything about an Arab woman must belong to the man, including her virginity, for her to have honor or worth.

At every juncture on my tour of the farming hamlet, I asked about the small black and white puppy that we had found when we arrived one year before. They seemed dumbfounded anyone would ask or care about a dog, the lowest of creatures in the Islamic bestiary.

There was the inevitable invitation to tea inside one of the houses, which I accepted and instantly regretted when I recalled seeing this hamlet's water supply. It was the small stream in which the Shiite women had been scrubbing their laundry. I fear I winced visibly, and I prayed the water was well boiled.

Sitting cross-legged with five Iraqi men from the family, on a bare floor in a room without furniture, each of the men agreed that life was certainly better now with Saddam gone.

"It will be even much better if we can get passports and go to Lebanon or Europe," one said. "The Jordanians don't recognize our travel papers. We are trapped in our own country."

If everyone wanted to leave, I wondered, what was Iraq's future?

There was overwhelming joy that Saddam was gone, one of my tea-sipping Iraqis said. He hoped Saddam and his rapists would be "chopped up into pieces and thrown into the air." Without inquiring further, I got the impression someone dear to him, a sister, a wife, a mother had been kidnapped and raped. The young man's rage was barely under control a year after Saddam had been ousted from power. Another young man told of an older brother who had been dragged from his home by Saddam's press gangs and sent off to war in Iran never to return. More than once, I heard the word *murderer* used synonymously for Saddam amongst these Shiites. Except for the one angry man who wanted Saddam butchered, literally carved up like a carcass in an abattoir, everyone else preferred Saddam tried in Iraqi court of law. They wanted justice.

And they wanted jobs. The problem with employment, they told me, was that when they went to the mayor's office in An Najaf, the mayor's deputies would demand bribes for a man even to be considered for work. That clearly had not changed after the war. In Iraq as in much of the Arab world that the Americans hope to democratize, bribery represents business as usual.

"If you don't pay, you don't get a job. If you have connections, you can get a job. Democracy doesn't exist here, or if it does, it exists in name only. There are no human rights here. Judge for yourself," I was told.

If these farmers wanted to truck their cattle to market to sell them, another bribe was requisite. Again, I noted, corruption of this magnitude did not bode well for the Bush administration's plan to turn the Fertile Crescent into a garden of political rectitude. This remained a society corrupt to the very core, at least by Western standards. Without a legal culture to protect the weak and disenfranchised, there was at best marginal hope for the democracy that the ranking members of the Bush administration had been preaching about for much of the previous year.

Offhandedly, I again inquired, "Are you sure no one remembers that little black and white puppy that was on this farm a year ago, the one with the rope around his neck?"

Suddenly, the face of one of the boys who had joined lighted with recognition.

"Kootchie, we called him Kootchie," he said.

"Where is he?" I asked hoping to see my furry friend from the sandstorm the previous year.

"Dead. Someone poisoned him."

I don't know how I would have fitted the dog into my story of a year later, but I wanted to. In truth, I cared as much about that mongrel pup as I did half the Iraqis the Bush administration was out to democratize. Damn! I had saved the puppy's life, freeing him from that tether on which he might have choked that night during the sandstorm and shooting. We fed him our best MREs, but ultimately, we could not save him. Perhaps his fate prefigured the fate of all Iraq. Eighteen months after the 3rd ID slammed into Baghdad, everyone from the American CIA to the British Royal Institute for International Affairs was forecasting civil war in Iraq.

Thanking Kitab for the tea, we excused ourselves and went outside again. He followed us, fully expecting to be thanked in cash as did the mayor's deputies in An Najaf from whom Kitab had been seeking work. Shaking hands, I discreetly transferred a U.S. twenty-dollar bill from my palm to his. It was a month's salary for him. Whether it was enough to secure a job from what they perceived to be a corrupt local official was beyond my ken.

"*Allah Kareem.*" "God is generous."

Despite all the violence and uncertainty caused by the enemies of a free Iraq, it is clear that Iraqis sense dramatic improvement in their everyday lives and anticipate much more.

Epilogue

—Deputy Secretary of Defense Paul Wolfowitz
Testimony before the Senate Armed Services Committee
20 April 2004

I wanted very much to revisit machine-gun alley farther down the road. We drove past green wheat fields with camels grazing in them. A dozen small girls crossed the highway on their way home from school. The only threat to them now was crossing a superhighway on foot with traffic speeding past.

We came upon a startling moment of déjà vu when we saw large columns of black smoke rising from adjacent fields as we retraced the drive down machine-gun alley. A year earlier, it might have been burning Iraqi armor, "killed" by the attacking Americans. These, however, were merely squat brick kilns, fueled by heavy crude oil. I was watching Iraqi peasants baking bricks the same way their Sumerian and Babylonian ancestors had several millennia earlier. Only the fuel was different. Adjacent to the kilns, Iraqi peasants had pitched their tents and parked their burros.

We stopped and got out because I was curious to see if the American rhetoric about freedom and democracy resonated beyond Baghdad's Arab intelligentsia. One brickworker appeared so dehydrated as to have just emerged from an ancient Babylonian tomb, having cast off his mummy's shroud. I might as well have launched into a discussion with him about Italian opera. He was not in the least interested in alien cultural concepts like freedom and democracy.

"Tell Mr. Bremer to come here," he insisted. "We have no jobs, no schools. The smoke from the kilns kills our children."

Another wizened brickworker standing off to the side said, "We have only this soil from which to make bricks. And we have God."

The first Iraqi resumed his grumbling, "What have the Americans done for us? Our drinking water has salt in it."

A dry, white rime on the surface of the land seemed to confirm his complaint.

Retreating from their anger, which had made me angry, I walked across the road to a drainage ditch hoping to catch sight of a returning rail or green sandpiper. Bird watching has ever relieved my anger. The new spring greens and reeds were coming up, reborn amid the gurgling of frogs. The amphibian chorus seemed the only joyous note in the Iraqi countryside that spring. Beyond the drainage ditch and the frogs, a lone, gray, wool Bedouin tent stood out. This was a free-fire zone a year earlier. Now another Bedouin greeted me with another grouse.

Epilogue

"This tent is all I have; this and five sheep," he said.

Apparently, he did not assign much value to the three little girls peeking out from within the tent. Having survived a ferocious firefight there a year earlier, I was grateful just to be alive. The Iraqis, by contrast, seemed to thrive on carping.

A few miles farther down the road, we stopped by a palm grove from which the Iraqis had been shooting at us in the dust storm a year earlier. It seemed odd now to be walking in the enemy's trenches. Between the roots of the rows of regal date palms, the Iraqis had dug ditches less than a yard deep. It was from these positions they were firing at us in the sandstorm during the 7th Cavalry's run up machine-gun alley. I looked out across a fallow field at the road about 130 yards away. In retrospect it seemed that what most of the Iraqis had done was merely stick their arms and rifles out of the trenches without ever sticking up their heads to aim. My guess was that if they dared show more than an arm or a hand, they would have been targeted by the U.S. soldiers' thermal-imaging and killed. So they held their rifles over the rim of the trench while not elevating their heads and pulled the triggers, emptying the magazines in the direction of the noise of the passing convoy of the 7th Cavalry.

On this warm day, a slight chill passed over me. The Iraqis had been firing at us point-blank. The 7th Cavalry's tanks and Bradleys may have passed through that maelstrom of lead protected by their heavy armor, but Charlie, Jeff, Paul, and I had travelled naked down that same road with less metal about us than the average Honda. Just ahead of us on that and nearly every other day had been Captain Lyle's sixty-nine-ton tank. Standing now where the Iraqis had been shooting that day, I chuckled bitterly. Then that warm wave of overwhelming gratitude for being alive swept over me again.

> There is no dividing line—there is a dividing line in our world, not between nations, and not between religions and cultures, but a dividing line separating two visions of justice and the value of life.
> —President George W. Bush
> The East Room
> 19 March 2004

Any halfway-decent Middle East reporter will tell you that one of the best barometers of the public temper in a Muslim country is the sermon during Friday prayers at the mosque. Seven days after President George W. Bush was assuring the public "there is no dividing line" between religions and cultures, I decided to attend the Abu Hanifa mosque in a Sunni neighborhood in Baghdad. The neighborhood still bristled when foreigners passed through a sea of sullen and often malevolent faces. Across the street from the mosque, there was a bombed-out building. Other nearby buildings remained scorched reminders of the fighting in the Iraqi capital a year earlier. Atop the mosque a year later, now, some Iraqis had set up a machine gun on the roof. They seemed to be a kind of local militia, theoretically outlawed during the American occupation. The newly hatched, American-sponsored Iraqi police were timidly standing outside the mosque gates as the faithful were entering. The cops wore smart new uniforms, and the one nearest me had dressed his up a little with a Tommy Hilfiger belt buckle. This policeman was but a boy.

He eyed me, although I never imagined that trouble might erupt from the Iraqi crowds who were gathering for prayers. After all, this was his Iraq. I was the foreigner, an infidel, a non-Muslim. For the Bush administration in Washington, the enemy was Saddam's holdouts, Sunni Muslim insurgents and Islamist extremists. But on Baghdad streets, even to the American-trained Iraqi cop like the one eyeing me suspiciously at that moment, the enemy remained the foreigner, the American standing in front of him. Abu Moussab al Zarqawi, the nemesis of the U.S.-led occupation, could have freely walked into that mosque for Friday prayers, but this tenderfoot Iraqi cop intuitively saw a foreign journalist, an alien, as the greater threat to his country than whatever Arab extremists may have been lurking about.

The American authorities are widely believed to monitor Friday sermons in Baghdad mosques, and the Abu Hanifa mosque was a prime candidate for watching. It was the last place Saddam had been seen publicly before he went to ground with American troops close on his heels the previous April. Yet, despite the threat of censorship and the occupying power listening to that Friday sermon, one did not have be a classical Arab scholar to fathom the cultural chasm separating the Muslim world from George W. Bush's evangelical Christian vision of a planet devoid of fractious religious divisions.

The censored and thus tame mosque sermon began with, "Do not be humble, and do not submit to the Infidel [the American occupiers]. We are better than they are. We are the righteous. When God is with you, you will be on top. Your enemy does not believe this."

The *imam* could not rail at the American president by name, but he did not need to. Nor could he be indicted for incitement, because there was sufficient religious ambiguity for those unlettered in Islam. The *imam* could have argued he was speaking only in a theological context, not political. His obfuscation was aided by the fact that most of the American occupiers maintained the Western assumption that there is a difference between theology and politics in the Arab world. Yet, in the realm of the mosque and minaret, that line is ever blurred, despite the ignorance or wishful thinking that emanates from the Bush White House.

The Abu Hanifa *imam* was only beginning to wind up. "We are the righteous. They are on our land. They are transients, but we the believers are armed with mighty power. We may feel helpless now, but remember the early Muslims also faced difficult times. We are defending Islamic virtue and fighting the people of vice."

I rather wished the president and his then National Security Advisor Condoleezza Rice could have been standing outside the mosque, hearing what I was hearing. Someone should remind the U.S. policy makers that in the Islamic world, Muslims revel in a history in which eighty percent of their prophets died violently in battle. From where I was standing outside that mosque, it seemed me the Iraqis were once again a defeated people licking their wounds, demanding Islamic retribution and justice.

"Patience, patience, patience!" the *imam*'s voice lectured over the loudspeaker to the faithful who were so plentiful they now spilled out on to the courtyard of the mosque.

I wondered how far up the intelligence chain the tone and temper of these sermons made it before someone decided the boss, either Paul Bremer or the president, did not want to hear what was being said.

"God says all force must be brought against our enemies. Never be humiliated [by the Americans]. Pray God we are not defeated by the Infidels. Allah give us victory over the Infidels."

As I stood there scribbling down my notes under the watchful eye of that Iraqi policeman with the Tommy Hilfiger belt buckle, it seemed to me incitement was spilling out of the loudspeakers of the mosque, and the Americans supposed to be monitoring it either couldn't recognize it or were powerless to do anything about it.

My thoughts drifted back to a few days earlier. A young Iraqi woman named Mazhda, who was the supervisor of maids on my floor at the Palestine Hotel in Baghdad, shyly engaged me in a conversation in broken English. She wore a Christian cross around her neck and said she had a brother in New York or Detroit.

"I am a Catholic," she said nervously. "Don't trust the Muslims."

I suppose she had reason to be fearful. My experience has been that many Christians clinging to an existence in the Arab world often share similar paranoia. Then she disappeared.

Four months later on 1 August 2004, Mazhda's fears were borne out. Bombs detonated by Islamist militants at five Iraqi Christian churches, four in Baghdad and one in Mosul, killed eleven people. On 27 September 2004, seven other Christians were killed in Baghdad. Quietly, the Iraqi Christian community, protected under Saddam, is beginning to look for places to immigrate to, usually Australia via Syria. The Iraqi Christians are acutely aware that the destabilization of their country unleashed by the U.S. invasion has left them almost entirely without protection. Inadvertently, U.S. policy is contributing to the further Islamization of Iraq.

I wanted to question the believers as they emerged from the mosque; I wanted to again try to take the temperature of the street in Baghdad a year after the American army had driven into the city. The anti-Semitism, more properly the Judaphobia, was malevolent. The entire Gulf War II was a Jewish plot in the eyes of many Iraqis, I was repeatedly told.

"America has fought not to advance its own interests but to advance the interest of the Jews. The Jews have been the enemies of our religion for a long time," an Iraqi with a *kafia* on his head pronounced.

A man who would identify himself only as "Mustafa" said of the war, "This is a Jewish conspiracy hatched against Iraq. From old times, the Jews have had an eye on our lands. Always there has been the slogan, 'from the Nile to the Euphrates.' It's an American-Jewish conspiracy hatched since the prophets' time."

It had become an Arab catechism throughout much of the Middle East, "The American invasion is to protect Israel and its people." This sentiment was not just on the Arab street but permeated the educated classes. An Iraqi physician who had studied in the United States, Dr. Omar al Rawi, said, "They [the Jews] must kill. It is written in their Bible. From the Euphrates to the Nile, they believe this is their land."

Everyone in Baghdad knew someone who knew someone who knew of a Jew buying up the best properties, especially the prime real estate along the Euphrates River. "They" were coming back. One Iraqi newspaper claimed that hundreds of Israeli spies were now in Iraq, having been given U.S. Army uniforms to disguise themselves.

Saad Jawad is a British-educated Iraqi with a PhD in political science. Chatting with him in his garden, I was told that there is a universal belief in Iraq that what happened during the war was not in the Americans' interest.

"This chaos and instability is only in the interest of Israel," he lectured me. "It is not in the interest of the Israelis to have a big or strong Arab state like Iraq. . . . Ninety-five percent of the Arab people were glad to see Saddam go. Even the Ba'athists wanted rid of Saddam. But then chaos and indecision followed. The Americans frittered away so much good will. They foolishly dissolved the Iraqi army, the police forces, and created a group of one and a half million disgruntled men, unemployed with no hope at all."

Jawad claimed he personally had warned the first American administrator in Iraq, retired Gen. Jay Garner, telling him, "Your losses in peacetime will be more than your losses in the war." Months later they talked again. Jawad told me, "General Garner remembered my warning." Outside his security cocoon in Iraq, I was discovering, Bremer was viewed with contempt by large numbers of Iraqis. For all his attempts to make better the lives of the Iraqi people, I sensed that if the Arab mob could have slipped a noose around his neck, they would have dragged his body through Baghdad's streets with glee.

Jawad was now quite animated and furious over the disbanding of Iraqi police forces and the army. Had they not as a group largely refused to fight for Saddam and instead deserted him?

"This was a stupid decision," he said. "None of this needed to happen. When the Americans foolishly regarded a traffic cop as a threat and sent him home with no pension, what did they expect him to behave like? If I were a policeman in America, I would arrest Bremer and put him on trial for the deaths of every American soldier since the end of the war."

In a Baghdad coffee shop dating back to Ottoman times, I begged anyone to cite something constructive Ambassador Bremer had accomplished in his tenure.

"When he came, he found ruins and this is still what we have, ruins," Hassan Mohammed said. "If power is given to the Iraqis . . . if Bremer leaves, we will have Iraqi leadership."

Despite Saddam's brutality, I constantly tripped over a deep craving within the Iraqi soul for yet another strongman. There remains a palpable longing for iron-fisted leadership, a trait antithetical to decentralized power vital to genuine democracy. Iraqis seem to share this same penchant with the Russians to the north, ever desirous of a tsar figure. One wonders if the penchant for a strongman also explained the ties between Moscow and Baghdad at least as much as business dealings in oil. Iraqis and Russians understood each other. It was not difficult to imagine a Russian peasant wringing his hands during the Great Terror and moaning, "It is our fate," just as Iraqis were to lament several generations later. Saddam may well have understood this better than the American establishment bent on building an Arab democracy. It may also explain why Saddam was keen on patterning himself and his regime after Joseph Stalin. In my coffee-shop discussions, I gently pointed out that in living memory, Iraqis had never done a good job of governing themselves, that all they had produced was thuggery, assassinations, and violence. My skepticism was met with more Muslim fatalism.

"Ah, but we hope for the best," I was repeatedly told.

> It's going to take fifty years to straighten this place out.
>
> —Lt. April Bennett
> 1457th Battalion
> Utah National Guard
> Summer 2003

Hikmat Mahmoud was in his eighties when I met him. He has been cutting men's hair in Baghdad since Iraq was occupied by the British. He would also cut hair at the British Officers' Club.

"They used to wear gloves so they would never have to touch an Arab," he remembered.

The "best of times" Hikmat said was when Iraq was a monarchy.

"And the worst of times?" I asked sitting in his barber's chair getting a rather good shave.

"These days," he said. "Politics, tricks. I cannot mention names. These are not good times."

A climate of fear had outlasted Saddam. Hikmat intimated that Saddam's agents were still out there, still watching and listening.

Another customer awaiting a haircut said, "They killed a doctor the other day. His only crime was that he worked with the new government."

Hikmat remained cautious, reminding everyone, just in case, that Saddam did good things like kicking out the oil companies and nationalizing oil production.

"That was good," he added as a kind of insurance policy.

"Under Saddam all sense of ethics was destroyed," someone countered. "Young people lost their way."

Few agreed on much of anything in Iraq a year later except that the American authorities seemed to have bungled the occupation.

Epilogue

One of the most frequent laments was that the streets of Baghdad were no longer safe at night. The glass door to the barbershop had a clean bullet hole through it.

"Every day there are explosions," Dr. Chazal, a friend of the barber, said. "America is weak. It can't solve our problems. Hotels are shelled, and still the Americans don't know what to do. Don't they know who is doing this with their intelligence services? Weak," he concluded contemptuously.

The Iraqis were clearly covering their bets, saying bad things about Saddam, saying unflattering things about the Americans: a pox on both your houses.

"We are Arabs and Muslims," I was told while paying for my shave. "Anyone who occupies us against our will is not loved. You might love someone against your will, but inside your heart, you know you don't."

Hikmat Mahmoud, my octogenarian barber, died a few weeks later, killed in a car-bomb blast outside his shop.

Walking back out onto Rashid Street, reputed to be the oldest thoroughfare in Baghdad, I searched for just one friendly face among the glowering sea of Iraqi Arabs. There was none. The words "Anyone who occupies us against our will is not loved" vaulted about in my head as if just preached by another seething *imam* at the Hader Khana mosque a hundred yards down the street.

> It's very discouraging. A lot of times you wonder if you're making a difference. This process is going to take a long, long time, and people back home need to realize that, need to understand that.
> —1st Lt. Joe Bessing
> 101st Airborne Division

Just before finishing my spring 2004 tour of Iraq in April, I decided to do a story on some Baghdad high school students, hoping that by talking with the next generation, I might discern the future of the country. The school was Baghdad College, which Saddam's two sons Uday and Qusay had attended and graduated with the highest honors. The children of all Ba'athist party officials always received the highest grades, I was told. But Baghdad College was the institution where Iraq's best and brightest were educated in a society that has always put an extraordinarily high premium on education. Over the centuries, Iraqis have prided themselves in having produced the best scholars in the Islamic empire.

212

Epilogue

Outside the main gate, parents drove up in Mercedes and BMWs and deposited their young men who seemed oblivious to the plainclothes guard standing there with an AK-47. If an Iraqi father could afford a top-of-the-line automobile, he could also afford to pay a handsome ransom to kidnappers. This school was taking no chances. Inside the compound, a short man was marching about like a martinet blowing a whistle. I was not so long out of high school as to not remember his doppelganger in some of the teachers we had a half-century earlier in the Washington, D.C., area. The electricity was again down so the bell could not sound for the junior high and high school boys to be called to class.

My crew, translator, and I were met by Ghazwan Majid, a gangly, teenage science student. Both his parents spoke English. He also had a cousin in Florida. All of this helped explain his excellent colloquial American English. Majid was almost too good. He reminded me again of my own high school, which seemed to have a surfeit of teenagers blessed with such brains that no one ever doubted they had fine careers ahead of them. Majid, if he survived, had a bright future no matter who was in authority in Iraq.

At first, he assured me "nothing changed" in his life since the abdication of Saddam. Reacting to his pretense of rectitude, I became American blunt and told him, I did not enjoy being bullshitted, whereupon he confessed that "everything changed" since Saddam fell.

I reminded him that pictures of Saddam used to hang in every school classroom, and I noticed those were all gone now.

"Only the nails in the wall remain," I observed.

Majid became increasingly forthcoming. "We were never blind about Saddam."

"At what point in a young Iraqi's life," I asked, "did you realize it was best not to open your mouth and speak critically of the regime?"

"I was about ten when my father said to me, 'Never, never say anything critical about the regime. Keep your mouth shut,'" Majid said. "He told me of the regime's crimes. I understood what my father told me. I grew up with the fear the police would punish not just me but my family. We learned early."

In between classes, I chatted with more than a few boys who seemed not at all fearful of an American television crew from CNN. Several told similar stories of growing up in Saddam's reign of terror.

"I will never forget the time they shot somebody," another Iraqi boy said. "They shot him in the forehead. He was my friend, but they killed him."

Iraqi children have grown up knowing incalculable violence.

"We've seen people, neighbors killed, assassinations," one young man said.

"At any moment, without an excuse, they could shoot you," the boy at the back of the gathering crowd offered.

Another boy named Leith had a mother who was a teacher. He said she was disciplining the child of a prominent Ba'athist party official and "The boy looked my mother straight in the eye and said, 'My father is deputy head of the Muhabarat [the secret police], and I will kill you.'"

"Well, at least that kid and his Ba'athist father aren't around any more," I said, trying to be philosophical.

"Yeah they are living the high life in exile in Britain now," Leith replied.

I continued to wonder if the concept of justice would ever come to have any meaning in Iraq at all. I was highly skeptical.

Half a century after the death of Stalin, Saddam had done a fine job of recreating the terror of Stalin's Russia, and it will leave its scar on Iraqis as it has on generations of Russians unto today. Chatting further on the playground, Leith told me about one of those bad days all students seemed to have.

"I was sitting in the classroom, cross and tired, and I looked up at the picture of Saddam above the chalkboard, and I said, 'Damn you, Saddam. I hate what you did to make my life so miserable.' The son of a Ba'athist party official overheard me, and when I realized it, I knew if they came, they wouldn't hesitate to kill me."

A teacher overhearing the exchange acted as referee and tamped down the outburst quickly.

These young Iraqis attended classes in citizenship now, but there were still no textbooks for political science or history courses. Previously, those books had all been paeans to Saddam and his Tikrit mob, and the boys remembered a big book burning in the schoolyard.

Eavesdropping on an English-language class, I overheard an Iraqi teacher ask, "What about democracy? Can we speak about democracy in Iraq?"

The answer seemed born more of rote than conviction.

"Democracy means the opportunity to share ideas and thoughts, how to respect people's ideas and thoughts, how to respect their manners," Majid replied.

I might have been more convinced had not another student approached me an hour earlier on the playground and asked, "Are you a Jew?"

In Arabic I replied with one of the most useful Arabic phrases I know, "*La, Ana Messehee*," "I am a Christian."

"Good," he said. "We prevent Jewish people from coming here. Islam teaches we must respect other religions, but Jews are bad."

He assured me without ever having met a Jew in his life.

The American soldiers occupying these students' country now seemed held in only slightly higher esteem than Jews. As we were taking pictures on the high school grounds, an American army Humvee drove through the school gates with an escort vehicle with a soldier manning a machine gun. An almost courtly young army officer got out and went to visit the headmaster to discuss travel credentials.

The Iraqi boys assured me they knew all these American soldiers arrested Iraqi girls, "put them in prison, and made them pregnant." I tried reasoning with them and assured them American soldiers were schooled enough in the ways of Islam that I really thought that story most implausible. It was a "hard sell" to these testosterone-laden, teenage Iraqi boys. I am not sure after the prisoner-abuse scandals at Abu Ghraib I would even try now.

Watching these youngsters go through lessons in nuclear chemistry, physics, and mathematics, I was easily persuaded they were brighter than any American high school senior I had ever met except in the area of critical thinking. In that discipline, they were unthinking automatons.

"American motherfuckers" was what young Iraqi boys from this elite high school called the U.S. occupying forces. Each of the boys assured me he had seen an American soldier smash down the door of an Iraqi home or had seen the Americans beat old Arab men into the ground. When a pair of U.S. Army helicopters flew low over the campus, the Iraqi boys assured me the Americans were deliberately trying to frighten them. Most of the student body still believed the Americans invaded their country to get their hands on Iraqi oil.

There was no question but this was a generation of children terrified by war. In their brief lifetimes, Iraq had fought two wars with the United States and its allies. The children were still traumatized. This Iraqi high school had been under suspicion all during the occupation. It had a nuclear-bomb shelter on campus, which was built during Saddam's war with Iran two decades earlier. Classrooms had computers that had been sufficiently troubling that the American army took all the hard drives from them and never returned them, according to one teacher. Worse for the school, Saddam's missile corps parked some of its mobile Scud-missile launchers next to the campus.

Working deep within the bowels of Iraqi society, moving as stealthily as the worst computer virus, there remains a species of anti-Americanism in Iraqis and is twinned with indigenous xenophobia. At times, this evil marriage seems to make the situation as hopeless as the foregoing quotes from

U.S. military personnel suggest it to be. Turning my back on Baghdad College, I thought there wasn't a prayer the Americans could win the hearts and minds of even the most enlightened Iraqi youth. If the climate was this dark at a school where many of the classes are taught in English, one could only imagine how much worse it was in the provinces where teachers had no access to second opinions other than what emanated from the mosque on Fridays. And if the best and brightest are unpersuaded of the worthiness of the American endeavor, who in Iraqi society does believe in it? More militant Muslims openly reject democracy and freedom as products of the infidel and inferior Western culture. They argue forcefully that the Islamic legal code, the Sharia, is perfect in its inception and affords all the democracy and freedom Muslims want or need.

> When America came, it was supposed to protect us,
> wasn't it? Such a big army, strongest in the world.
> They can't even protect themselves.
> —Abu Yasub, Baghdad,
> whose house collapsed on his family
> after a car bomb detonated
> Spring 2004

The foremost success of the American campaign in Iraq seems, in retrospect, to have been the removal of Saddam Hussein. But even that seemed at times ephemeral. In April 2004, I openly heard taxicab drivers in Baghdad speak of the "good old days" under Saddam when "there were no traffic jams," and the only violent crime was committed by the regime itself. Hoshyar Zebari, the foreign minister of Iraq, observed, "It will take quite some time for the Iraqi people to realize the damage Saddam did to society." The plain truth is, however, that the vast majority of the Iraqi people alive today were born under Saddam's lodestar. He ruled for a quarter century or more, and tyranny aside, the Iraqis were not totally uncomfortable with the certainty of Saddam. Oppressed peoples generally learn to manipulate tyrannical systems to their own ends and make the best of a bad bargain. The madness of Saddam became the norm. In the vacuum left by the collapse of the Ba'athist regime, Iraqis were left awash in a sea of insecurity. During the American military occupation, even on the eve of the much-vaunted Iraqi democratic elections, car bombs were detonated almost daily leaving the average Baghdad pedestrian far more vulnerable than when Saddam and his Ba'athists were in power.

Despite the fig leaf the elections provided, a major miscalculation by the Bush administration remained: There never was a blueprint for shifting from a war of liberation to an occupation in force. As more than a few Iraqis told me eighteen months after the end of "major combat operations," the Coalition forces, especially the Americans, seemed to be making it up on a daily basis as they went along. Americans tend to be good at improvisation, but it is hardly a process that inspires the confidence of an occupied people, and without the confidence of the occupied people, the outcome of the experiment remains uncertain.

In retrospect, it was naïve of many to think the Iraqi people would welcome an American military operation or that a foreign presence would be long tolerated with any pleasure by a Muslim populace. More than a few analysts have concluded that while winning the war, the American military has lost the occupation. And while that judgment may be premature, it would now seem the only way to redeem the occupation will be with the help of America's European allies, whose counsel was initially shunned by the Bush administration. Indeed, the best hope for Iraq may still lie with other NATO partners helping train indigenous Iraqi security forces to fight their own Muslim brothers. It has been rather credibly demonstrated American unilateralism did not serve Washington's interests well, the earlier Pentagon bravado to the contrary.

> By now, it must be clear one nation cannot defeat the extremists alone.
> —U.S. Defense Secretary Donald Rumsfeld
> 12 February 2005

Weighing the post-war balances, Iraq inflicted huge damage done to the image of the United States. In Europe, the "Iraq generation" of America haters has grown up as the "Vietnam generation" sprouted there thirty-five years earlier. Throughout the Middle East and the Muslim world, rather than being hailed for deposing an Arab despot and liberating an Arab Muslim people, the Americans have become to be seen as foreign oppressors. However cynical it may sound, Arabs generally seem to prefer to be tyrannized by a despot of their own making than being occupied by a well-intentioned Western military force. Compounding America's problem, the Bush administration has been seen as too closely tied to the government of the hated Israeli Prime Minister Ariel Sharon. The overwhelming majority of Iraqis I met invariably believed the war of 2003 was America doing Israel's bidding.

Western-educated Iraqis constructed grand arguments to back up their contention that Americans had little to gain from the war. Instead, they believed the principal beneficiaries were the Israelis, whose security was greatly enhanced with the removal of Saddam. Very few in the Arab world will accept the oft-stated Christian altruism of George W. Bush until this American president radically changes what is perceived as his indifference to the suffering and deprivation of three million Palestinians under Israeli domination.

Consistently, even friendly Iraqi officials blamed the failings of the first eighteen months of U.S. military occupation of their country on what they saw as the ham-handedness of Bremer, who in cultural ignorance, they complained, treated Arab Muslims as if they were Eastern Europeans.

"The Americans thought they could reconstruct Iraq with little more than a sudden infusion of large amounts of capital," Zebari has said quite dispassionately."

There is ever this unwillingness in the Arab world to accept responsibility for one's own failings because it is always so much easier to blame someone else.

The results of the 2003 war still remain highly arguable. The much-heralded January elections of 2005 could never have been held without the protection of over a hundred thousand U.S. and British soldiers. Even with that protection, there were attacks on Iraqi civilians outside mosques and bakeries in the run-up to those elections. Iraqi tribes continue to quarrel among themselves, sometimes murderously. Public goodwill, a vital constituent of the democratic process, remains in terribly short supply. The old Iraqi mindset of "keep your head down" nurtured under Saddam lingers—even with a fifty-eight-percent voter turnout in the interim parliamentary elections, many stayed away.

Lawlessness still is rampant. Car theft has become an Iraqi national pastime. One commonly heard analogy in Iraq is that the Coalition forces are the doctor, and Iraq is the patient, and Iraq is still too sick for the doctor to leave. Now it would seem, the cure in Iraq will not be exclusively the American prescription. Rather, if the patient survives, the solution will be Arabic: messy, chaotic, and predictably corrupt. And that could be the optimistic view.

The brief euphoria after a moderately successful election in Iraq constitutes the best of the "good news" for the Bush administration after twenty-four months in Iraq. There it is instructive to note the Sunni presence in the new government is sparse, even though Sunni Muslims constitute nearly a third of the Iraqi population. Only two percent of Sunnis even voted. Whether the first-round election results translate into a stable Iraq would at this point seem to hinge on whether the embryonic Iraqi security forces, including the police, demonstrate a willingness to die for a new Iraq and for a system designed in no small way by the United States, which is perceived by many Arabs as yet another reincarnation of the ancient Crusades. The success of the new Iraq will also depend on whether its sometimes-anxious neighbors—Turkey, Iran, and Saudi Arabia—are tired of regional instability and whether they now want the American experiment in Iraq to succeed. Any one of them could spoil it if they decided it was in their interest, especially Iran.

> Democracy has become an excuse for unilateralism by the United States.
>
> —Dr. Hanan Ashrawi,
> Palestinian legislator
> Dubai
> 13 December 2004

Two years after the 7th Cavalry's great ride to Baghdad, the payback in terms of the effort exerted by some fine American soldiers seems at times disappointing. The Coalition forces fought bravely to liberate the Iraqi people who, even today, no more understand the Americans than the Americans understand them. One of the more bittersweet remarks heard in diplomatic circles two years after the war is "the Americans cannot be allowed to fail in Iraq because of the consequences of such failure." That falls considerably short of a resounding military victory, and worse, it recognizes that the success of the Bush administration's experiment in Iraq is far from guaranteed.

Fortunately, most of the soldiers of the 7th Cavalry got to go home before many Iraqis learned to loathe the occupation. One can greatly sympathize with the replacement troops, those of the American occupation force in Iraq who garnered none of the glory of the military campaign. Every American should feel deep anguish over the dangers U.S. soldiers have faced over the past two years, the lethal roadside bombs, the increasingly skilled insurgent snipers, and the animosity of an Arab people whom the U.S. soldiers are still trying to help.

Two years after the American military campaign to free Iraq and with one national election under its belt, no one can predict what will become of that country or its people, rich in oil but poor in democratic tradition. At this writing, with the insurgency still going strong and ordinary Iraqi citizens dying in frequent car bombings, not to mention the psychological ravages of personal insecurity, it is not too much to say Iraq is still a tragedy today for the Iraqis albeit for very different reasons than it was under Saddam. Iraq has also become a serious disappointment for the fine U.S. and British soldiers because they were sent to help a people many of whom really did not want very much of what Coalition forces had to offer culturally or politically.

First and foremost, Iraqis wanted personal security, and that has proved elusive. In the end, Iraqis traded the insecurity of the "terrifying knock on the door" by Saddam's security forces for the insecurity of possibly being injured or killed in the ongoing violence.

That U.S.-led Coalition forces now face not only attacks by insurgents but protests by Iraqi citizens calling for the Coalition's departure suggests the United States has not won the battle for the affection of the Iraqi people. One could debate endlessly how much U.S. forces are liked or disliked by the Iraqis or for that matter how much they dislike the Iraqis. The American taxpayer paid a huge price for the war with a burgeoning budget deficit and a badly tarnished image in the world four years after the sympathy inspired by the terror attacks of 9/11 on New York and Washington. Thus, the cold truth remains that despite the successful military campaign to overthrow Saddam, the United States has as a consequence of this war fallen into widespread international disfavor. And outside the United States, George W. Bush is perceived in many quarters as the singularly most unpopular U.S. president in the history of the American republic.

But the election in late January 2005 may have changed that, as a key Coalition goal was realized. U.S. and Coalition forces were deployed across the country to provide protective cover as eight million brave Iraqis voted in their first free and fair election.

Appendix: DOD Embed Ground Rules

GROUND RULES. For the safety and security of U.S. Forces and embedded media, media will adhere to established ground rules. Ground rules will be agreed to in advance and signed by media prior to embedding. Violation of the ground rules may result in the immediate termination of the embed and removal from the AOR. These ground rules recognize the right of the media to cover military operations and are in no way intended to prevent release of derogatory, embarrassing, negative, or uncomplimentary information. Any modification to the standard ground rules will be forwarded through the PA channels to CENTCOM/PA for approval.

Standard ground rules are:

All interviews with service members will be on the record. Security at the source is the policy. Interviews with pilots and aircrew members are authorized upon completion of missions; however, release of information must conform to these media ground rules.

Print or broadcast stories will be datelined according to local ground rules. Local ground rules will be coordinated through command channels with CENTCOM.

Media embedded with U.S. Forces are not permitted to carry personal firearms.

Light discipline restrictions will be followed. Visible light sources, including flash or television lights, flash cameras will not be used when operating with forces at night unless specifically approved in advance by the on-scene commander. Embargoes may be imposed to protect operational security. Embargoes will only be used for operational security and will be lifted as soon as the operational security issue has passed.

The following categories of information are releasable.
— Approximate friendly force strength figures.
— Approximate friendly casualty figures by service.
— Embedded media may, within OPSEC limits, confirm casualties they have witnessed.
— Confirmed figures of enemy personnel detained or captured.

Appendix: DOD Embed Ground Rules

- Size of friendly force participating in an action or operation can be disclosed using approximate terms. Specific force or unit identification may be released when it no longer warrants security protection.
- Information and location of military targets and objectives previously under attack.
- Generic description of origin of air operation, such as "land-based."
- Date, time, or location of previous conventional military missions and actions as well as mission results are releasable only if described in general terms.
- Types of ordnance expended in general terms.
- Number of aerial combats or reconnaissance missions or sorties flown in CENTCOM's area of operation.
- Type of forces involved (e.g., air defense, infantry, armor, Marines).
- Allied participation by type operation (ships, aircraft, ground units, etc.) after approval of the allied unit commander.
- Operation code names.
- Names and hometowns of U.S. Military units.
- Service members' names and hometowns with the individuals' consent.

The following categories of information are not releasable since their publication or broadcast could jeopardize operations and endanger lives.

- Specific number of troops in units below CORPS/MEF level.
- Specific number of aircraft in units at or below the air expeditionary wing level.
- Specific numbers regarding other equipment or critical supplies (e.g. artillery, tanks, landing craft, radars, trucks, water, etc.).
- Specific numbers of ships in units below the carrier battle group level.
- Names of military installations or specific geographic locations of military units in the CENTCOM area of responsibility, unless specifically released by the Department of Defense or authorized by the CENTCOM commander. News and imagery products that identify or include identifiable features of these locations are not authorized for release.
- Information regarding future operations.
- Information regarding force protection measures at military installations or encampments (except those which are visible or readily apparent).
- ̤graphy showing levels of security at military installations or encamp-

̤ment.

—Information in intelligence collection activities compromising tactics, techniques, or procedures.

—Extra precautions in reporting will be required at the commencement of hostilities to maximize operational surprise. Live broadcasts from airfields, on the ground or afloat, by embedded media are prohibited until the safe return of the initial strike package or until authorized the by unit commander.

—During an operation, specific information of friendly force troop movements, tactical deployments, and dispositions that would jeopardize operational security or lives. Information on on-going engagements will not be released unless authorized for release by on-scene commander.

—Information on special operations units, unique operations methodology or tactics, for example, air operations, angles of attack and speeds; naval tactical or evasive maneuvers, etc. General terms such as "low" or "fast" may be used.

—Information on effectiveness of enemy electronic warfare.

—Information identifying postponed or cancelled operations.

—Information on missing or downed aircraft or missing vessels while search and rescue and recovery operations are being planned or underway.

—Information on effectiveness of enemy camouflage, cover, deception, targeting, direct and indirect fire, intelligence collection, or security measures.

—No photographs or other visual media showing an enemy prisoner of war or detainee's recognizable face, nametag, or other identifying feature or item may be taken.

—Still or video imagery of custody operations or interviews with persons under custody.

The following procedures and policies apply to coverage of wounded, injured, and ill personnel.

Media representatives will be reminded of the sensitivity of using names of individual casualties or photographs they may have taken which clearly identify casualties until after notification of the NOC and release by the OASD (PA).

Battlefield casualties may be covered by embedded media as long as the service member's identity is protected from disclosure for seventy-two hours or upon verification of next-of-kin notification, whichever is first.

Media visits to medical facilities will be in accordance with applicable regulations, standard operating procedures, operations orders, and instructions by attending physicians. If approved, facility personnel must escort media at all times.

Appendix: DOD Embed Ground Rules

Patient welfare, patient privacy, and next of kin/family considerations are the governing concerns about news media coverage of wounded, injured, and ill personnel in medical treatment facilities or other casualty collection and treatment locations.

Media visits are authorized to medical care facilities but must be approved by the medical facility commander and attending physician and must not interfere with medical treatment. Requests to visit medical care facilities outside the continental United States will be coordinated by the unified command PA.

Reporters may visit those areas designated by the facility commander but will not be allowed in operating rooms during operating procedures.

Permission to interview or photograph a patient will be granted only with the consent of the attending physician or facility commander and with the patient's informed consent, witnessed by the escort.

Informed consent means the patient understands his or her picture and comments are being collected for news media purposes, and they may appear nationwide in news media reports.

The attending physician or escort should advise the service member if NOK have been notified.

WALTER C. RODGERS, a senior international correspondent for CNN, has over thirty-nine years' experience as a broadcast journalist, covering many major events in the Middle East including several wars from Lebanon to Afghanistan, suicide bombings in Israel, and the assassination of Israeli Prime Minister Yitzhak Rabin. From 1974 to 1982, at the White House, he covered Presidents Gerald Ford, Jimmy Carter, and Ronald Reagan and numerous presidential summit conferences and national political conventions. During the Mikhail Gorbachev years, Rodgers was bureau chief for ABC News in Moscow, followed by five and a half years as bureau chief for CNN in Jerusalem. He has a passion for Atlantic salmon fishing, birding, sailing, and Shakespeare. He is married to Eleanor Pelton Rodgers.